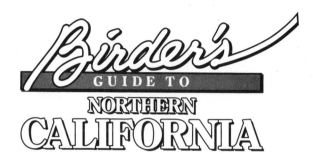

Birder's
GUIDE TO
NORTHERN
CALIFORNIA

Birder's GUIDE TO NORTHERN CALIFORNIA

LoLo and Jim Westrich

Gulf Publishing Company

Birder's Guide to Northern California

Library of Congress Cataloging-in-Publication Data

Westrich, Lolo.
  Birder's guide to northern California / Lolo and Jim Westrich;
illustrations by Lolo Westrich.
    p.   cm.
    Includes indexes.
    ISBN 0-87201-063-5
    1. Birds—California, Northern.   2. Natural history—California,
Northern—Guide-books.   3. California, Northern—Description and
travel—Guide-books.   I. Westrich, Jim.   II. Title.
QL684.C2W46   1991
598'.07234794—dc20   90-39851
                                                                CIP

Contents

Crescent City. Redwood National Park. Humboldt Lagoons State Park. Eureka. Humboldt Redwoods State Park. Standish Hickey State Recreation Area. Sinkyone Wilderness State Park. Northern California Coast Range Preserve. Mendocino. Hendy Woods State Park. Lake County.

Northern Sonoma County. Santa Rosa. Sonoma Coast State Beach. Bodega Head. Bodega Bay/Doran Park. Point Reyes. Bolinas Lagoon. Samuel P. Taylor State Park. Mount Tamalpais State Park. Muir Woods. Marin Headlands. China Camp State Park. Upper San Pablo Bay Area. Napa/Solano Counties.

Dedication

To our mothers, Rosena Westrich and Viola Vallier, who separately inspired us with their passion for nature, their sense of adventure, their appreciation for beauty, and their footloose gypsy ways.

"And what is there to life if a man cannot hear a lovely cry of a whipporwill or the arguments of the frogs around a pond at night? For all things share the same breath — the beasts, the trees, the man. The white man must treat the beasts of this land as his brothers. What is man without the beasts? If all the beasts were gone, man would die from a great loneliness of spirit, for whatever happens to the beast also happens to the man. All things are connected. Whatever befalls the earth befalls the sons of the earth."

— Chief Seattle, letter to President Franklin Pierce, 1855.

Acknowledgments

We couldn't have written *Birder's Guide to Northern California* without the help of many other Californians as enthralled with birds as we are and just as excited about the places to go to see them. That's why we called upon more than 400 park rangers, preserve managers, ornithologists, teachers, biologists, professional and amateur naturalists, Audubon Society members, state department employees, and backyard birders from all parts of the state to help us gather the material we needed.

In almost every case the response was immediate and positive. In fact, it was the enthusiasm and generosity of our fellow birders that kept our spirits from flagging sometimes when our task seemed formidable.

Special thanks are due Allen Fish of the Golden Gate Raptor Observatory and Dave Shuford of the Point Reyes Bird Observatory. Their expertise, generosity, and good counsel have contributed vitally to the success of this work.

We're thankful too for special help from Cheryl Anderson, Dr. Jack Arnold, Ira M. Bletz, Jackie and Robert L. Bruns, Betty Burridge, Dolora Burton, Ted Chandic, Bruce Deuel, Arthur L. Edwards, Gary Eifert, Raymond Ekstrom, Ted Ellico, Dick Erickson, Shawna Gannon, Tyler Gannon, Bob Gendron, Dr. John G. Hewston, Chuck Holmes, William C. Kent, Tom Leskiw, Gary Lester, Alberta Lewallan, Dave Marquart, Eva McCleland, John "Mac" McCormick, Larry Miller, Harold Reeve, John Schick, Shirley Schmelger, Lora Simington, Tootie Simington, Jim Steele, Steve Stocking, Dale Whitmore, Donald Yasuda, and David Yee.

Others who've given of their time and energy to add to the comprehensiveness of this book include Thomas Alan, Clayton Anderson, Paul Anderson, Robert E. Anderson, Steve J. Anderson, Karen Austin, Kathryn

Baem, Bonnie Balanda, Bruce Barrett, Dick Bauer, Brian Barton, Mr. and Mrs. Douglas Beard, Dennis Becker, Warren Beers, Steve Berenzen, E. Clark Bloom, William Bohart, Eileen Bowen, Carrie Brant, Barry Breckling, Robert Breen, Paul H. Brown, Carl Burger, Josie Calousek, Sharon Campbell, Jim Carpenter, James D. Carson, Joanne Castro, Thomas J. Charmley, Jan Chappell, William Chilson, Richard S. Cimino, Janice Clark, Richard W. Clinnick, Katie Colbert, Nicholas T. Coiro, Richard A. Coleman, Pat Cook, Perry R. Crowley, Annis Cunningham, Denise Dachnor, Joanne Dolan, Stacy Edge, Stephen Edinger, Bruce G. Elliott, Ron M. Elliott, Michael Ellis, Jules Evens, Kenneth Fetherston, Melanie Findling, Mary and Mickey Finn, Jay Galloway, Bernard Garrison, Georgia and Jay Garner, R. H. Gerstenberg, Kurt and Mary Glaeseman, Greg Gnesios, Jessica Lynne Gonzales, Jim Gordon, Helen Green, Charles E. Grennell, Tom Griggs, Marguerite Gross, Bill Grummer, Christina Hargis, Susan Harper, Lois Harter, Diana E. Hawkins, Ira Heinrich, Erica Hendricks, Victor A. Herrick, Sidney G. Hibma, Gerald E. Hillier, Linda Hoile, Erik Holst, Bambie Hopkins, John Jennings, Diana Jorgensen, James K. Kaderabek, Alan I. Kaplan, Dick Kaufmann, Curtis D. Kraft, Gary A. Kramer, Mike Krause, Isobel Krell, Bill Krumbein, J. Kuhn, Harry V. Latham, Hal P. Latta, Robin Leong, Fred Lew, George and Jean Lestch, Gary Lester, James L. LeWhite, Robert Lockett, Henry Lomeli, Garald K. Loomis, Mary Lowe, Eileen Marckx, Michael A. Martin, Sandra L. MacPherson, David McKay, Tim McKay, Len McKenzie, Joseph L. Medeiros, Patsy Mervis, Larry Miller, Mia Monroe, Enrique Morales, Michael J. Moran, Joe Moreland, David L. Mues, Don Munson, Edward C. Murczek, Shirley Murphy, David Neighbor, Don L. Neubacher, Tom Newman, Carl A. Nielson, Tom Nixon, Pamela Noyer, Robert O'Brien, Ginelle O'Connor, John Ofstedahl, Charlotte and Ralph Opp, Larry Perkins, Paula Penningt, Bill Peters, Donna Peterson, B. "Moose" and Sharon Peterson, Margaret Pearson Pinkham, Pamela Poe, Carlos Porrata Judy Powell, Julie Rechtin, Richard E. Redmond, Michael Reeves, Larry Reid, Paul Remeika, Don Richardson, Clifford G. Richer, Dave Riensche, Mike Rivers, Don Roberson, Lynn Roberts, Caroline Rodgers, Terry Roeder, Gary W. Rotta, Walter Saenger, Don Schmoldt, Marsha Schreiner, Shirley Schmelger, Dan Severson, Stephen D. Shane, Debra L. Shearwater, Alison Sheehey, Bob Short, Gary L. Shook, Mark Silbertein, Bruce Slocum, Robert Smart, Scott Smithson, Edward Sneider, Louise Spalding, Michael Stalder, Jon Mark Stewart, Mitchell Stewart, J. B. Stone, Noel

W. Stoughton, Gary Strachan, Emile Strauss, Chris Stromness, Karen Suiker, Alan K. Thomas, Jean E. Takekawa, William "Gil" Thomson, Britt Thorsnes, Roger Titus, Jim Todd, Terriann Tomlin, Geri Treloar, Dr. Lynne Trulio, Steven Underwood, Shirley Valencia, Mike Van Hook, Kent R. Van Vuren, Richard L. Vance, Claudia Vogel, Landon Waggoner, Sue Warren, Roger Weiss, John Weldon, Bill and Donna Whipple, Jerry White, Onnid Wintehman, Barbara Wilkinson, Kevin Williams, Marc Williams, Peter A. Willmann, Sue Wittorff, Brian Woodbridge, Sarah Wooston, Al Wrench, and Marty G. Yamagiwa.

We are grateful to the many helpful individuals who asked that their names not be mentioned, as well as anyone we may have inadvertently failed to list.

We're grateful to all of the following groups, organizations, businesses, and publications (some of the representatives of which are listed above) that have assisted us: the California Department of Fish and Game, the United States Department of the Interior Fish and Wildlife Service, the California Department of Transportation, California Department of Parks and Recreation, American Birds Magazine, Point Reyes Bird Observatory, the Sierra Nevada Field Campus of the San Francisco State University, the U.S. Army Corps of Engineers, The Eifert Gallery, Garner's Trinity Wilderness Campground, the Inn at Shallow Creek Farm, Shearwater Journeys, and U Wanna Kamp.

Of course, special thanks are due Julia M. Starr and the rest of the staff at Gulf Publishing Company for their advice, assistance, and enthusiasm as well as for the vote of confidence that launched this project.

We want to add a few words of appreciation to our children and our grandchildren for the understanding and moral support they gave us during a period when we often had to absent ourselves from them.

About the Authors

LoLo and Jim Westrich are native Californians who have been birding in their state for more than fifteen years. The Westriches' delight in and knowledge of northern California's many exceptional birding locations are evident in this painstakingly researched guide, along with their appreciation of natural history, wildlife biology, conservation, and preservation issues. This is their first collaboration, although LoLo's short stories and essays have appeared in many magazines and anthologies. She is also the author of *California Herbal Remedies,* a sourcebook of botanical history and lore.

Introduction

It's almost as important to know what kind of a book *Birder's Guide to Northern California* isn't as to know what kind it is. Otherwise, roving birders might tuck it into their travel bags without also tucking in another book that ought to keep it company wherever it goes, namely one or another of the following old standby "birders' bibles": *A Field Guide to Western Birds* by Roger Tory Peterson; *A Guide to Field Identification, Birds of North America* by Robbins, Bruun, Zim, and Singer; the National Geographic Society's *Field Guide to Birds of North America*; or *The Audubon Society Field Guide to North American Birds* by Miklos D. F. Udvardy. These books are guides to the identification of birds. *Birder's Guide to Northern California*, however, guides you to the places to go to find birds.

A book of this order necessarily covers a lot of ground and a lot of water — so much, of course, that there's some of it upon which we ourselves have never had a chance to set foot or sail! With maps and directions for getting to its featured places, the book describes in detail state parks, national forests, specific ranger districts within those forests, regional parks, national wildlife refuges, Nature Conservancy preserves, and other favorite birding locales.

Of course, there are many more aspects of birding in northern California than simply maps and descriptions of places. And so, *Birder's Guide to Northern California* has something to say on all sorts of bird-related subjects, matters like local bird lists and how and where to get them; endangered, threatened, sensitive, and "blue-listed" species of the state; useful tips from veteran California birders; something of the history of birding in California.

Thus brimming, *Birder's Guide to Northern California* is bound to be a boon to visitors and newcomers who want to learn as much as possible about birding in the northern part of this far western state. Yet because its scope is so broad, there's something on its pages for most long-time residents as well. After all, veteran California birders too are always dreaming of the places they've yet to explore, the rare birds they may chance to see there.

There's not a place in the continental United States that matches California's variety and diversity of wildlife. It's almost as if it's a separate land, an ecologically wondrous world apart, boasting plants and birds unseen elsewhere. Consider, for example: tropical beaches, waving palms, towering mountains, teeming tidepools, exotic islands, salt marshes, shady forests, shifting sands, steep sea cliffs, ancient conifers, lush riverlands, cattle ranchlands, mountain meadows, humid marshes, delta sloughs, fertile farmlands, prairie-like plains as flat as ironing boards. To the newcomer, the sights here are as fabulous now as they were to Thomas Nuttall when he came here in the nineteenth century — when California was still a wilderness beleaguered by bears.

The first of the American naturalists to set foot on this far western soil, the indomitable Nuttall saw much that he called "new to my view" including gooseberry flowers "as brilliant as those of a fuchsia" and "rare blooming aloe," and birds whose existence had never been recorded by anyone else, like the one that's now his namesake, the head-bobbing, drum-rolling, crest-raising little Nuttall's Woodpecker, which he found gleaning the undersides of the limbs of the ubiquitous oaks.

Another enthusiastic sojourner here in the 1800s, Professor William H. Brewer, was just one of many other early observers who had much to say about the avifauna of California. "There are many birds of great beauty," he wrote, ". . . owls are very plenty, and the cries of several kinds are often heard the same nights. Hawks of various sizes and kinds and very tame, live on the numerous squirrels and gophers. I see a great variety of birds with beautiful plumage, from humming birds up."

Today's observers are no less enthused about the birding opportunities offered here than those who came here in the 1800s. This was made plain to us by the answers we got when we asked hundreds of birders the following question: "In your opinion what's special about birding in the state of California?" The overwhelming response validated these words from Harold M. Reeve, author of the fine checklist and date guide, *Birds of Stanislaus County, California:* "California's selling point is its diversity of habitats and variety of bird species within one state. Where else can you bird the coast, redwood forest, dry oak woodlands, chaparral, grassland, riparian woodland, salt and freshwater marshes, montane forest, and desert habitats in a single 200-mile transect in one day?" These three words were repeated again and again: diversity of habitat, diversity of habitat.

It's not surprising that the flora, the fauna, and the avifauna of California differ from that of the rest of the continent. Although the state is immensely popular and constantly growing in population, there's a sense in which it's an isolated land nonetheless, a world cut off from other western states by topography and climate, by a concurrent multitude of species and a variety of habitats in which these species dwell. It's fitting, really, that this western edge of the continent was once mistakenly thought to be an island, that it was even identified with the writings of the sixteenth-century Spaniard, Garcia Rodriguez Ordonez de Montalvo, whose purple pen described an imaginary place "called California, very near the Terrestrial Paradise."

In writing this guide, we've adopted and modified the concept of the "Californias" developed by the State Office of Tourism and so widely used today by those whose business it is to depict this diverse land. Actually, the "Californias," which appear on maps as little mini-states within a state, are simply sectors of California, set apart for the sake of convenience and on the basis of such features as geological conditions, habitat, history, and general ambience.

These, then, are our "Californias": North Coast, North Bay, San Francisco Bay, Monterey Bay, North Country, Central Valley, and High Sierra.

As we've mapped it, there are 45 counties in northern California, and we've made certain to feature birding locales in every one of them. In our opinion every county in the state has its special beauty, its own enticements, its excellent birding opportunities.

Of the many birds known to breed in northern California, more than 80 familiar species nest in at least six of the seven specified northern California regions. A few of these are so common in their appropriate habitats, so immediately identifiable, and so well known to even beginning birders all across the country that to list them repeatedly in locale descriptions would be redundant. Hence, except in special cases, as for example when a certain species appears in particular abundance and/or is highly representative of the area under consideration, the following 22 birds will not be mentioned specifically: Mallard, Turkey Vulture, Red-tailed Hawk, American Kestrel,

Crescent City

Tulelake

Alturas

Eureka

NORTH COAST

Redding

NORTH COUNTRY

Susanville

Tehama

Loyalton

Oroville

Downeyville

Lakeport

Colusa

Santa Rosa

Placerville

South Lake Tahoe

Markleeville

NORTH BAY

Sacramento

HIGH SIERRA

Petaluma

Napa

CENTRAL VALLEY

Bridgeport

Stockton

San Francisco

Oakland

San Francisco Bay

SAN FRANCISCO BAY

Mariposa

San Jose

Merced

Santa Cruz

Madera

San Juan Bautista

Monterey

Salinas

MONTEREY BAY

The Regions of Northern California

American Coot, Killdeer, Rock Dove, Mourning Dove, Northern Flicker, American Crow, Brown Creeper, American Robin, European Starling, Western Meadowlark, Brewer's Blackbird, Brown-headed Cowbird, House Sparrow, Violet Green, Tree, Cliff, and Barn Swallows, and Yellow-rumped Warbler.

Other birds common in northern California but more apt to be included in area descriptions are distinctly western species less well known to out-of-staters; species boasting western subspecies of interest to birders from elsewhere; species such as bitterns, rails, owls, and certain warblers that are typically difficult to sight; much-favored birds like egrets and herons, which appeal to most birders; those which, though common, are not readily recognized by all birdwatchers.

Falling into these categories, and therefore to be included in many of the locale descriptions, are the following 61 common or fairly common nesting species: Pied-billed, Eared, and Western Grebes, Great Blue Heron, Black-crowned Night-Heron, Great and Snowy Egrets, Northern Pintail, Northern Shoveler, Ruddy Duck, Cinnamon Teal, Gadwall, Northern Harrier, California Quail, Virginia Rail, Black-necked Stilt, American Avocet, Least Sandpiper, Ring-billed and California Gulls, Barn and Great Horned Owls, Anna's Hummingbird, Belted Kingfisher, Acorn and Downy Wood-

Barn Swallow

peckers, Olive-sided Flycatcher, Black Phoebe, Western Wood-Pewee, Horned Lark, Common Raven, Steller's and Scrub Jays, Wrentit, Bushtit, Bewick's and Marsh Wrens, Western Bluebird, Water Pipit, Warbling Vireo, Black-headed Grosbeak, Dark-eyed Junco, Rufous-sided Towhee, Red-winged and Tricolored Blackbirds, Northern Oriole, Purple and House Finches, Pine Siskin, Lesser and American Goldfinches, Savannah, Song, White-crowned, Golden-crowned, and Chipping Sparrows, Common Yellowthroat, and Orange-crowned, Yellow, MacGillivray's, and Wilson's Warblers.

ADDITIONAL NOTES

We cannot, of course, claim to have touched upon every good birding spot in northern California. This is one of the reasons why we asked roughly 400 birders to name their favorite birding locales and to tell us the reasons for their choices. Interestingly enough, these reasons were as varied as the locales themselves. Consider this sampling: "A large variety of birds are known to have been seen here," said one informant of the state park she'd named. "Rare or uncommon birds have been sighted here," a ranger told us of another. Said a park host, "Although this location may not boast an exceptionally large number of species, it's a good place for close-up viewing, wildlife photography, and behavior observation." Of his choice, one preserve manager said, "It's outstanding for the amount of birdsong heard here, a genuine audio delight."

We've gone to great lengths to include in this guide as many good northern California birding locales as possible. If we've failed to mention any place that readers may feel deserves to be featured, this means that at least two of the following factors somehow prevailed: Even after extensive research and extensive travel on our part, this particular place and/or the birding opportunities it offers escaped our attention; not a single one of our hundreds of collaborators (including rangers, biologists, preserve managers, ornithologists, and birders from every county in northern California) named this locale as a good, fairly good, or favorite birding locale; the ranger or supervisor of this area actively discourages birding in this locale; access is difficult and birdwatching opportunities reportedly not outstanding.

We also have not attempted to list every bird ever seen at every location, but rather, have provided a representative selection of birds that might be expected at each site.

LoLo and Jim Westrich
Santa Rosa, California

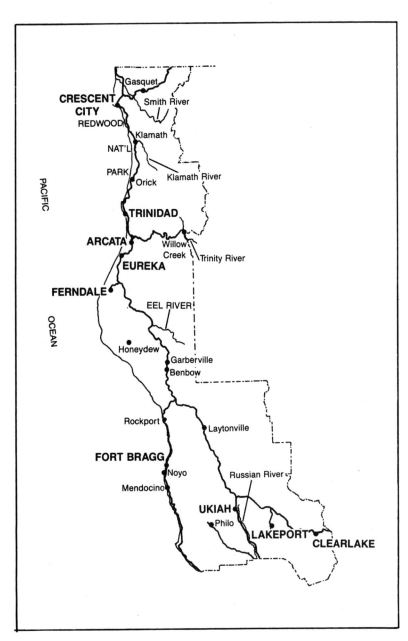

North Coast

Chapter 1
North Coast

 The North Coast of California is a land of rugged shores and towering redwoods; of rushing streams and mirror-calm lakes; of bays and bogs, lagoons and estuaries; of remote mountains and virgin forests. A land of broad-shouldered mills and quaint villages. A land of logger and fisherman, of farmer and rancher, of artisan and tourist. And a land of birds and birders.

From the burrowing storm-petrels of Castle Rock to the soaring Bald Eagles of Anderson Marsh, from the threatened Spotted Owl of Six Rivers to the chattering Belted Kingfisher of Jughandle Reserve, from the Tufted Puffins at Trinidad to the elusive Red Crossbill of Horse Mountain, this is a diverse and bountiful region for birders of every level from back-yarder to expert.

The North Coast region is the northwest coastal section of the state, extending approximately 230 statute miles north to south, and from 20 to 70 miles inland. The total area is 9,399 square miles, and represents 11% of the area covered by this book.

The geology is exclusively Coastal Range except at the very north-western corner, where the Klamath Range intrudes. Elevation increases quickly from sea level to peaks well over 6,000 feet. The area is drained by five major river systems — the Smith, Klamath, Mad, Eel, and Navarro, and to some extent by the Trinity to the east and the Russian to the south.

Sparsely populated by California standards, the inhabitants of this area are mostly centered around the county seats of Crescent City, Eureka, Ukiah, and Lakeport. Other cities of substantial size are Arcata and Fortuna in Humboldt County, Willits and Fort Bragg in Mendocino County, and Clearlake in Lake County.

The primary industries are fishing, lumber, and agriculture, the latter including dairy, cattle, sheep, and horse ranches, pear and walnut orchards, and an ever-increasing premium wine production. Tourism is important too, with attractions like the redwoods, the coast, the lakes and rivers, and quaint, delightful towns such as Mendocino, Ferndale, Old Town in Eureka, Trinidad, and Lakeport.

US 101, which traverses the area from north to south, is the area's lifeline, carrying the major portion of goods and traffic. SH 1 meanders up the shoreline until the terrain gets too rugged around the "Lost Coast," and it turns inland to rejoin 101.

BIRD LISTS FOR THE NORTH COAST REGION

There are several good lists available for the North Coast Region, among them the following:

Field Checklist of Northwest California Birds, by Stanley W. Harris
 Redwood Region Audubon Society
 Box 1054
 Eureka, CA 95521
 Price: 35 cents

Birds of Redwood National Park
 Available at the Visitor Centers or
 Redwood National Park Headquarters
 2nd & K Streets
 Crescent City, CA 95531
 Price: 56 cents

Birds of the Redwoods
 North Coast Redwood Interpretive Association
 Prairie Creek Redwood State Park
 Orick, CA 95555
 Suggested donation: 75 cents

Birds of Mendocino County, compiled by Greg Grantham
   College of the Redwoods
   Fortuna, CA 95540

Birds of the Clear Lake Basin, by Michael Bradeen
   Clear Lake State Park Interpretive Association
   Clear Lake State Park
   Kelseyville, CA 95451
   Price: 25 cents

If you wish to purchase your bird lists by mail, be sure to enclose a stamped, self-addressed envelope along with your request.

CRESCENT CITY

Lake Earl

Five miles north of the town of Crescent City, in the lush wooded land of Del Norte County lies the Lake Earl Wildlife Area — 5,000 acres of coastal plain irresistible to nature lovers of every sort. Here, besides the two connected, shallow, and nutrient-rich lakes that comprise its most commanding feature, are sandy dunes, bright-blooming tansy, glossy-leafed wild strawberry, and birds enough to satisfy the most demanding of ornithophiles.

When we visited here one late evening in mid-August we experienced some of the best birding of our lives. We stood on the shore just a few feet away from a dozen or so of the smallest phalaropes, the delicately lovely Red-necked, which were spinning on the water like so many wind-up toys. At our feet were a busy group of Least Sandpipers, their tiny legs moving faster than the eye can see. Among other birds we saw that day were Downy Woodpecker, Yellow Warbler, Marsh Wren, Black Phoebe, and a flock of Band-tailed Pigeons high up in the branches of a roadside conifer.

Still, our summer good fortune notwithstanding, fall and winter truly are best times to bird here at Lake Earl Wildlife Area. This is when you'll sight waterfowl flocks so large they blotch the sky. Expect Aleutian Goose (an endangered subspecies of the Canada Goose), Wood Duck, Green-winged Teal, Northern Shoveler, Gadwall, Common Goldeneye, Mew Gull, and multitudes of Canvasbacks.

Common here in the spring are 3 species of loon, Great Egret, 3 species of grebe, Great Blue Heron, Cinnamon Teal, Surf and White-winged Scoters, Bufflehead, Northern Harrier, Greater Yellowlegs, and Canada Goose.

Seen all year long are Double-crested Cormorant, Virginia Rail, Steller's Jay, Common Raven, Black-capped and Chestnut-backed Chickadees, Winter and Marsh Wrens, and Golden-crowned Kinglet.

Rare or uncommon species found here include Peregrine Falcon, Chestnut-sided Warbler, Grasshopper Sparrow, American Redstart, Northern Parula, Tufted Puffin, Pileated Woodpecker, Bald Eagle, and Tundra Swan.

From the scenic town of Crescent City in Del Norte County, take Lake Earl Drive northward. Turn left on old Mill Road. Proceed 1.5 miles to the wildlife area headquarters. From there you can take the Cadre Point Trail through conifer woods and meadows to the south end of the lake. Access can also be gained further north on Lake Earl Road at Lakeville and Buzzini Roads.

Crescent Harbor/Crescent City

This northernmost city on the California coast (population 3,500) lies at the very top of one of the most scenic strips of land in the country, that narrow belt of redwood forests that once stretched 450 miles down the Pacific coastline from the Oregon border to the Santa Lucia Mountains of southern Monterey County. There are, of course, other beautiful stands of redwood in Northern California (and even a few isolated narrow groves between Monterey and San Luis Obispo) but, for the most part nowadays, the prime redwood forests in the world are located in Del Norte and Humboldt counties and in Santa Cruz County south of San Francisco.

There's much to see in this lovely coastal city, as is roundly verified at the Redwood National Park headquarters at 2nd and K streets, and aptly extolled in all the free literature available at the Crescent City Cultural Center and Chamber of Commerce building on Front Street. The latter graces the beautiful Beachfront Park where visitors may lounge, picnic, stroll, or bird to their hearts' content.

Not far away is the famous old Crescent City lighthouse and museum at Battery Point, a must for most tourists, birders or otherwise.

There's good birding all along SH 1 from Crescent Beach to the harbor as well as in Beachfront Park. At the harbor itself, we like the breakwaters

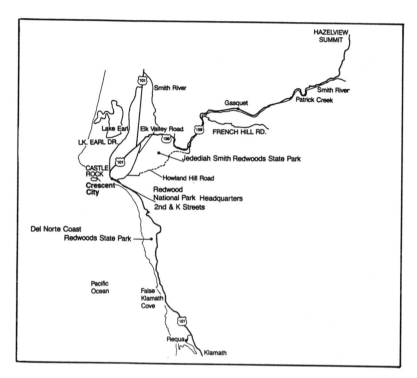

Crescent City

at Battery Point on the northwest side, and Anchor Way on the southeast.

A tourist/birder will certainly want to take the scenic tour on Pebble Beach Drive, which runs along the high coastal bluffs in the northern part of the city. Take 9th Street east, which ends at Pebble Beach, and turn right. Sea Lions, California Gray Whales (in the fall and winter migrating seasons), and all sorts of birds can be seen anywhere along this drive, especially at Point St. George, a favorite haunt of the rare Harlequin Duck.

Visible from this point is famous Castle Rock, privately owned by The Nature Conservancy and managed by the U. S. Fish and Wildlife Service. Castle Rock boasts the second-largest seabird rookery in California. This area can be scoped from the point, but since it's at least 0.5 mile from the mainland, it's best experienced by boat. You can board an excursion boat or rent an outboard at Crescent Harbor. Or you might consider an educational program that focuses on birding the Rock from the water. For information about seminars co-sponsored by Humboldt State University and Redwood National Park, contact the university's Office of Continuing Education in Arcata, (707) 826-3731, or the Park headquarters at 2nd and K Streets in Crescent City, (707) 464-6101.

Castle Rock birding is good all year, especially in spring and summer. Cassin's Auklet and the Rhinoceros Auklet nest here in the island's soil. Pigeon Guillemot, loons, grebes, cormorants, and Tufted Puffin are regularly seen, and this is one of the few places in California to see the Fork-tailed Storm-Petrel.

Summertime visitors who'd like some personalized tips from a local resident about birding in and around Crescent City may want to contact elementary school teacher Cheryl L. Anderson, whose love of birds and wildflowers is such that she graciously offers her services to nature lovers new to the area. "I'm free in the summer months," she tells us, "and available to show or direct birders to good locations." She may be reached at 707-464-2697. But, please don't call her during the school year.

Among the many species commonly seen on the harbor or its rocks and beaches are Red-throated, Pacific, and Common Loons, Horned, Eared and Western Grebes, Double-crested Cormorant, Great Blue Heron, Snowy Egret, Black-crowned Night-Heron, Tundra Swan, Least Sandpiper, Long-billed Dowitcher, and Heermann's, California, Ring-billed, Glaucous-winged, and Mew Gulls. Less commonly sighted are Pied-billed and Red-necked Grebes, American White Pelican, Blue-winged Teal , and Gadwall.

Commonly seen on land in and around Crescent City are Bewick's Wren, Golden-crowned Kinglet, Common Raven, Wrentit, Varied Thrush, Steller's Jay, Solitary Vireo, Rufous-sided Towhee, Fox Sparrow, and many other species.

Crescent Harbor is on US 101 at the southern entrance to Crescent City in Del Norte County.

Gasquet to Hazelview Summit, Along US 199

This is an extended trip up the beautiful Smith River canyon and then to the mountains at the eastern side of the County, and should be appreciated for its scenic and historic value, as well as birding opportunities. It's interesting to note that the first road into the county wound its way down this canyon from Oregon in 1858; until then all commerce came in by boat through Crescent Harbor, and it was some time later that the area was connected to the south by road.

The first stop is at French Hill Road, which branches off from US 199 just before the town of Gasquet. This area offers some open woodland birding, and is a good place to look for the Ruffed Grouse. After a mile or two of French Hill Road, come on back and bird the town of Gasquet. Lewis' Woodpecker, White-headed Woodpecker, and Common Poorwill have been seen here, along with the regular mix to be found in Douglas fir woods.

Continue up US 199 as it winds along the river and up the canyon toward Hazelview Summit. Stop along the way to check the river, the canyon areas, or the shores of Patrick Creek for Belted Kingfisher, American Dipper, and Canyon Wren.

At the summit, check the rest area on the left just before the highway goes through Collier Tunnel, near the Oregon border. The real inducement for this trip, however, lies higher up, as for example, the way to Sanger Peak. Just beyond the point where US 199 and the river part company, there's a road that takes off from the highway, continues along the Smith for a while, and then winds along Knopf Creek. Another road takes off just across from the rest area at the top, and meanders along the Del Norte/Siskiyou county line for a while.

Although chickadees (Mountain Chickadee at the higher altitudes, Chestnut-backed at the lower) are probably the most representative birds of the area, it's the Ruffed Grouse that bring so many serious birders to Gasquet.

Other birds seen here include American Dipper, Belted Kingfisher, Cassin's Finch, Fox Sparrow, Dusky Flycatcher, Green-tailed Towhee, Clark's Nutcracker, Townsend's Solitaire, Ruby-crowned Kinglet, and Common Poorwill. The White-headed Woodpecker is here too, and there's been a recorded sighting of a Williamson's Sapsucker.

Raptors include the Golden Eagle, Northern Goshawk, and Peregrine Falcon. And of course, the Spotted Owl may show up anywhere there's good old-growth timber.

US 199 runs northeast from Crescent City to the Oregon border, a distance of about 45 miles. Gasquet is about 15 miles from Crescent City.

Peregrine Falcon

REDWOOD NATIONAL PARK

This is a most unique national park, this pride of Del Norte and Humboldt Counties, for it's literally wrapped around three state parks: Jedediah Smith Redwoods, Del Norte Coast Redwoods, and Prairie Creek Redwoods.

There are many fine educational programs available to nature lovers interested in the Redwood National Park. Experiences like these are unforgettable, to which fact Cheryl Anderson of Crescent City gives testimony. When we asked her to name her most exciting birding experience in the state of California, she said, "It was on a Redwood National Park ornithology field study course around Crescent City. We took an evening hike into Howland Hill Outdoor School (run by the park) to call and observe the Barred Owl, the first one seen and documented west of the Rockies."

Seminar topics include Night Birds; Stream Ecology; Wildlife, Reptiles and Amphibians; Rock and Gold; Basic and Advanced Nature Photography; and Marine Ecology. Anyone interested in learning about the field seminars offered at Redwood National Park may write Humboldt State University, Office of Continuing Education, Arcata, CA 95521, or inquire at the information center. Registration fees range from $25 to $85. University credit is available.

Apart from the seminars, special naturalist-led programs include tidepool walks; walks through old growth redwoods such as those at Stout Grove; and the Trestle Loop walk, featuring second growth redwood forest, views of Mill Creek, a historic old railroad trestle, and birdwatching. For more information about such activities inquire at the visitor centers.

The Tall Trees Shuttle bus provides transportation through various sections of the park. Tickets and schedules are available at the Redwood Information Center, one mile south of Orick.

A good selection of field guides, maps, and books is available at the three information centers in Orick, Hiouchi, and Crescent City and publications pertaining to park subjects may be obtained by writing The Redwood Natural History Association at 1111 Second Street, Crescent City, CA 95531, or by calling (707) 464-9150. To arrange for wheelchair access call (707) 458-3310.

Campgrounds located in the three state parks that lie within the boundary of Redwood National Park all have sites with tables, fireplaces, and food cupboards. All have hot showers except for Gold Bluff Beach, which is equipped with solar showers. No hookups are available. For details on how to reserve your campsite, see state park reservation information in the appendix.

An information center, open from 8 a.m. to 6 p.m. daily, is located at each end of Redwood National Park, and in Crescent City on 2nd and K Streets. Northbound visitors may stop at Orick Redwood Information Center, which is located 40 miles north of the town of Eureka. Those going southbound will find the Hiouchi Redwood Information Center four miles east of US 101 on US 199.

Many birders come to Redwood National Park to sight the birds of the shore, the estuaries, the lakes, lagoons, and rivers, and the open ocean. From these categories, the following are commonly sighted at appropriate seasons within the confines of this park: Marbled Murrelet, Red-throated

Ross' Goose

and Pacific Loons, Double-crested Cormorant, Great Blue Heron, Wood Duck, Northern Shoveler, Surf and White-winged Scoters, Ring-necked Duck, American Wigeon, and Brown Pelican. Rare-to-casual species sighted here include the Red-necked Grebe, Short-tailed Shearwater, Snow Goose, Ross' Goose, Emperor Goose, Bald Eagle, Peregrine Falcon, Blue Grouse, and Ruffed Grouse.

Nesting species in Redwood National Park include Pied-billed Grebe, Great Blue and Green-backed Herons, Wood Duck, Black-shouldered Kite, California and Mountain Quail, Spotted Sandpiper, Common Murre, Marbled Murrelet, Rhinoceros Auklet, Western Screech-Owl, Purple Finch, Red-shouldered Hawk, and the endangered Peregrine Falcon.

Opportunities for behavior observation are sometimes excellent here. To Park Ranger Walter Saenger, there's no single more exciting sight in store for a birder than watching Brown Pelicans diving for fish.

Among the many resident mammals here are Black-tailed Deer, Raccoon, Coyote, River Otter, Marten, Gray Fox, Cougar, Roosevelt Elk, Black Bear, and a variety of rodents.

Redwood National Park extends along the coast in a fairly thin strip from Crescent City to Orick, and then extends inland in a somewhat wider band to the east and south from Orick. US 101 runs through the park for several miles between Orick and Crescent City. Another good access is Bald Hills Road just north of Orick, but it's very steep and trailers and motor homes are prohibited. There is a shuttle during the summer between the Information Center and the Tall Trees Trailhead.

Jedediah Smith Redwoods State Park

Because this park is visited by less fog and more sunshine than many of its neighbors, the play of light and shadow is more dramatic here. The sun breaks through the redwoods in golden bars and turns the fern-covered forest floor into a patchwork quilt of a hundred shades of greens and yellows, which flash in sharp contrast to the blue-grays of deepest shadow. Hundreds of California artists have tried to capture this drama on canvas, with varying degrees of success, but not a one has matched the feat of Mother Nature.

This park boasts all of these features: 46 memorial groves; many virgin redwoods, fine stands of hemlock, tan oak, fir, cedar, and madrone; undergrowth of redwood sorrel, rhododendron, huckleberry, and the wonderful leathery-leaved salal; summertime interpretive programs; inviting foot trails;108 campsites complete with tables, stoves, and cupboards; conveniently located restrooms; and hot showers.

Birds common to this area are Steller's Jay, Wilson's Warbler, Purple Finch, Savannah Sparrow, Dark-eyed Junco, Song Sparrow, Orange-crowned Warbler, Belted Kingfisher, Great Blue Heron, Downy Woodpecker, Western Wood-Pewee, Hairy Woodpecker, Common Raven, Chestnut-backed Chickadee, Black-shouldered Kite, California Quail, and Black Phoebe. And, of course, Barn Owl, Great Horned Owl, Western Screech-Owl, and Northern Pygmy-Owl are residents of these northern forests.

Other wildlife seen in the park includes Douglas Squirrel, Marten, Black-tailed Deer, Raccoon, Coyote, Gray Squirrel, and occasionally a bear or cougar.

Jedediah Smith Redwoods State Park lies at the confluence of the Smith River and Mill Creek on US 199, about 10 miles northeast of Crescent City.

An alternate, scenic route through the center of the park is Howland Hill Road, which follows the route of the old plank road to Oregon and offers outstanding views of old growth redwoods and the clear, turquoise waters of the Smith River. From US 101 at Crescent Harbor, take Elk Valley Road to Howland Hill. This road is not recommended for trailers and RVs.

Del Norte Coast Redwoods State Park

Besides its towering redwoods which grow nearly to the edge of the Pacific, this park is graced by handsome red alders that flash a kaleidoscope of color in Indian Summer. It's a handsome park with a restful ambience, inviting campsites, and a number of fine hiking trails. Look for birds along Mill Creek Trail, an easy 2.6 mile hike that follows its namesake, a shallow creek often visited by wildlife; Trestle Loop Trail, a moderate 1 mile hike through second growth redwoods; or Saddler Skyline Trail, a moderate 1.5 mile hike through Douglas fir and young redwoods.

Birds seen here include Barn Owl, Allen's Hummingbird, Scrub Jay, Common Raven, Winter Wren, Golden-crowned Kinglet, Varied Thrush, Northern Mockingbird, Warbling Vireo, California Quail, Swainson's Thrush, American Robin, Common Yellowthroat, Orange-crowned Warbler, and many others.

Nesting species in the vicinity are the same as in Redwood National Park.

US 101 runs the length of the park. The campground entrance is about 5 miles south of Crescent City Harbor.

Lagoon Creek

Developed as a cooperative project of Del Norte Wildlife Conservation Board and California Department of Fish and Game, this idyllic spot where river otters play, pond lilies bloom, passersby stop to picnic, and anglers fish is also the northern trailhead for the famous Coastal Trail.

Birds common here are Black Phoebe, Steller's Jay, Mountain Chickadee, Common Raven, Wrentit, Winter Wren, Band-tailed Pigeon, Allen's Hummingbird, Red-breasted Nuthatch, Marsh Wren, Song Sparrow, and various swallows.

Lagoon Creek is located on the west side of US 101 at False Klamath Cove, 4 miles north of the town of Klamath and about 0.25 mile north of the Trees of Mystery tourist attraction with its huge statue of Paul Bunyan.

Coastal Trail/Hidden Beach Section

This trail, which is well maintained and boasts a visitors' overlook complete with modern restrooms, is 4 miles long. The southern trailhead, the Klamath Overlook, which offers a spectacular view of the mouth of the Klamath River, is at the very end of County Road D-7, past Requa. The northern end is at the lovely Lagoon Creek, on US 101.

There are many other fine nature hikes in the Redwood National Park and other sections of the Coastal Trail, but the Hidden Beach walk is special not only for its breathtaking scenery but also for the opportunity to see Common Murres perched on a rock that is clearly visible from the northern portion.

Other birds seen along the trail include Red-throated Loon, Pied-billed Grebe, Double-crested Cormorant, California Quail, Western Gull, Chestnut-backed Chickadee, Golden-crowned Kinglet, Hermit Thrush, Wrentit, Rufous-sided Towhee, White-crowned Sparrow, Dark-eyed Junco, House Finch, and Pine Siskin. Nesting species are the same as in Redwood National Park.

Other animals of the Redwood National Park include Coyote, Black-tailed Deer, Web-footed Muskrat, Marten, Western Pond Turtle, Green Tree Frog, River Otter, and a wide variety of rodents.

To reach the trail, take US 101 to just north of Klamath, and turn west on County Road D-7 toward Requa. Stay on the main road up the hill until you reach the parking area at the end of the road, where the trail begins. It's about 4 miles down to Lagoon Creek on US 101, so unless you're up to hiking that far back up the hill, you should make prior arrangement for return to your car.

Alternately, you can begin your hike at Lagoon Creek, on the west side of 101, north of the town of Klamath. This is a steep walk, but it's no more than 10 minutes to the point where the murres can be seen, and probably a mile to the hidden beach. Binoculars are a necessity; a scope is a definite advantage.

Prairie Creek Redwoods State Park

This is the southernmost of the three state parks encompassed by the far-reaching Redwood National Park, and is known for its great stands of virgin redwoods, its handsome Roosevelt Elk, its verdant fern canyons, its enticing trails, its sometimes-impenetrable summertime fogs, and the 100-inch annual rainfall that lends it the ambience of a tropical rainforest.

Prairie Creek has a number of attractive features, including an easily traversed five-minute nature loop located near the visitor center and a hollowed-out tree, partially boarded up now, which actually served as a family residence back in the 1930s. Here too is a walkway named Revelation Trail, which, with rope and wood guide rails, tactile displays, and nearness to areas where sounds and scents are pronounced, is especially devised for the blind.

The park has 2 developed family campgrounds, the Elk Prairie with 75 sites, and Gold Bluffs Beach with 25. Each campsite is equipped with a table, a cupboard, and a stove. Piped water and restrooms with flush toilets are available. Primitive walk-in campsites, with available water and pit toilets nearby, are located at Butler Creek. For these, permits must be acquired.

As Ranger Michael Stadler points out, this is the right destination for anyone who wants to get a good look at Marbled Murrelets. They can be seen here most of the year, commonly in the summer, less often in the winter. This fascinating alcid, which is believed to nest in the old growth redwoods of this very area, is currently the subject of considerable scientific investigation. Until 1974, not a single one of its North American nest sites had ever been discovered. Even now, there's data on fewer than a dozen. It's known, however, that young Marbled Murrelets avoid direct sunlight. The nests face the north, chicks feed only at night, and fledglings must reach either ocean or lake on their very first flight from nest sites sometimes as far as 20 miles inland. Expect some noise from the Marbled Murrelet at dawn and dusk alike when it goes flying over Boyes Prairie. This is a highly vocal species.

Although this deep redwood country is not celebrated for a large variety of species, a watchful birder will never walk away unsatisfied. Birds such as the Chestnut-backed Chickadee, Winter Wren, Marsh Wren, Golden-crowned Kinglet, Varied Thrush, Common Loon, and Water Pipit are seen here all year long. In the summer expect to sight the Pacific Loon, Brandt's

Cormorant, Heermann's Gull, Caspian Tern, Common Murre, the endangered Brown Pelican, and many more.

Sometimes the drumming of Ruffed Grouse can be heard at the west end of Ossagon Trail. More often, from the old-growth redwoods of the Boyes Creek area, the call of that sensitive species, the Spotted Owl, resounds through the woods like the bark of a dog. Nesting birds are the same as in Redwood National Park.

Prairie Creek is known especially for its Roosevelt Elk, which can sometimes be seen from Cathedral Trees Trails or from Elk Prairie, a large expanse of meadowland bordering US 101. Other animals of the area are Black-tailed Deer, Coyote, Raccoon, Marten, Gray Fox, Gray Squirrel, and other rodents.

Prairie Creek Redwoods State Park is on US 101 about 6 miles north of the town of Orick, in Humboldt County. There's a long stretch of parking spaces on the west side of the highway, specifically installed so that passersby may observe the elk in the big meadow that adjoins the highway at the entrance to the park.

HUMBOLDT LAGOONS STATE PARK

Humboldt Lagoons State Park has an excellent visitor center, complete with a specimen museum, interesting books for sale, and enthusiastic and capable volunteers, like Louise Spalding and Annis Cunningham, who are ready and willing to answer most any question pertaining to the flora, the fauna, and the avifauna of this fascinating area. That birding is good here is not surprising for Humboldt County marks the southern limit for some species, the northern limit for others.

Stone Lagoon is a 521-acre estuary, fed from many small rivulets which keep well within their bounds in the summertime. Sometimes in the winter however, when heavy rains come on, the lagoon level rises and pours over the sand bar that walls it away from the sea. The sand erodes, a channel forms, and the lagoon level drops and becomes dependent upon tidal action until the time, usually just days or weeks away, when the sand fills the channel back up, and the lagoon becomes a separate entity once again.

It's beautiful here. The much less brambly land around the water is covered with wild yarrow — enough to thrill the heart of any herbalist — and with dock and thistle. A stroll along the water's edge is as pleasant for a birder as it is for the anglers who find that the combination of fresh

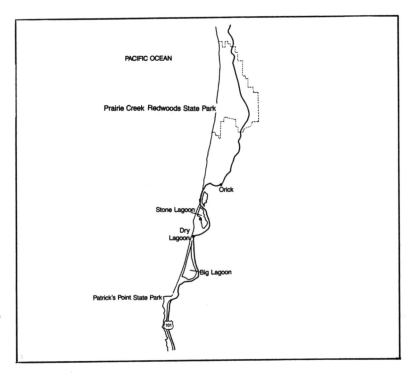

Humboldt Lagoons

and brackish water here makes for interesting fishing.

If you're planning to camp here at Stone Lagoon, which you can only do if you've brought along a boat, you can reach the sites by rowing an easy 0.75 mile to the west side of the lagoon. There are 6 campsites available, and one primitive toilet. Driftwood can be gathered for burning in the available fire rings. Otherwise bring your own campstove. And unless you want to boil water, carry your own in with you.

If you don't have a boat and you like the idea of environmental camping, you might prefer to spend the night at Dry Lagoon instead. To reach these sites you need only walk 300 yards from parking lot to campsite.

To register for sites at either Stone or Dry Lagoon, if you're headed south on US 101, stop at Prairie Creek Redwoods State Park, about 11 miles to the north. If you're heading north, check the bulletin board next to the Stone Lagoon boat launching area at Mile Post 115.4 for updated registration information.

Birding is best at Stone Lagoon in the winter, when many species are readily seen. Even in the middle of summer, however, you can expect Double-crested Cormorants, a multitude of gulls, the endangered Brown Pelican, and land birds such as the salt-tolerant Savannah Sparrow.

Dry Lagoon boasts a long list of interesting avian visitors and residents including American Bittern, Wilson's Phalarope, Eurasian Wigeon, Northern Mockingbird, and Heermann's Gull.

Humboldt Lagoons State Park is on US 101, about 35 miles north of Eureka, between Patrick's Point State Park and Prairie Creek Redwoods State Park. To reach the Stone Lagoon boat launching area, where you can do some interesting birding even if you're not a boater or a potential overnight camper, turn off of US l0l at Mile Post 115.4 and drive down to the parking area. To reach Dry Lagoon from US 101, turn into the Dry Lagoon day use area at Mile Post 114.5. The gate can be opened with a combination which is supplied at the time of registration.

Big Lagoon Beach and County Park

This park is bordered by the ocean, by the very scenic Big Lagoon, by a conifer forest, and a marshland, all of which are as inviting to the birds as the shady, wooded campsites are to travellers.

Seen here are Double-crested Cormorant, American Wigeon, Redhead, teal, and Canvasback. Land birds commonly sighted in the vicinity include Brown Creeper, Western Wood-Pewee, Red-breasted Nuthatch, Bewick's Wren, Golden-crowned Kinglet, Hermit Thrush, and Wrentit.

Big Lagoon Park is located just off US 101 about 8 miles north of the town of Trinidad. It adjoins Patrick's Point to the south and Humboldt Lagoons to the north.

Patrick's Point State Park

It's a breathtaking sight that meets your eyes when you stand at the top of the high and rugged cliffs at Patrick's Point and look down upon the gem-covered sands of Agate Beach.

Just 30 miles north of the town of Eureka, situated in coastal redwood country, this 625-acre park has countless attractions: shells and agates that tantalize the beachcomber; piles and piles of driftwood, with specimens of every shape and form conceivable; a large picnic area; miles of trails for eager hikers; spruce and hemlock forests as lovely to smell as they are to look upon; good fishing; carpets of wildflowers in the spring and summer; tidepools to study; wild animals to observe; family campsites and group campgrounds; a visitor center with bookstore; and a reconstructed Miwok Indian village currently in the making.

Birds common to Patricks Point State Park include Mew Gull, three species of cormorants, Common Murre, Pigeon Guillemot, Greater Scaup, Caspian Tern, White-winged Scoter, Black Oystercatcher, Ruddy Turnstone, Surfbird, Northern Oriole, Chestnut-backed Chickadee, Yellow Warbler, and Brown Pelican.

Some less common birds you may hope to see here include Tufted Puffin, Cassin's Auklet, Arctic Loon, Red-breasted Merganser, MacGillivray's Warbler, Red-throated Loon, and an interesting anomaly: a wintering albino Rufous-sided Towhee.

Bears and Raccoons are so common here that visitors are warned to keep their campsites bearproof by storing food with the umost care, and to remember that wily animals are not to be daunted by closed doors on campsite cupboards or latched tops of ice chests.

Patrick's Point State Park is just off US 101 in Humboldt County, 30 miles north of Eureka. Access is well marked by freeway signs.

Trinidad State Beach

Because this is the southernmost spot where the Tufted Puffin can predictably be seen, Trinidad State Beach attracts many tourist/birders from around the country, and, in fact, from all over the world. The islets off the shore here are inhabited by so many of these bright-beaked alcids that one is unofficially named "Puffin Rock." There could, as well, be one called "Leach's Storm-Petrel Rock" too, for these rocks have soil enough to accommodate this nocturnal, burrow-nesting bird, which is best seen from the mainland on overcast, moonless nights — by flashlight.

Other species seen at Trinidad State Beach are Black Oystercatcher, Brandt's Cormorant, Pigeon Guillemot, Western Gull, and Common Murre.

Even if it's birds only that bring you to the area, be sure to explore the town of Trinidad before you leave. You'll fine a fine array of restaurants, shops, and guest facilities extending practically all the way to Patrick's Point.

The town of Trinidad is off US 101 in Humboldt County, 19 miles north of Eureka; Trinidad State Beach is just north of the town. Best viewing point is at Elkhead, which can be reached from Stage Coach Road, a mile north of the beach.

To get to the nighttime viewing area for the Leach's Storm-Petrels, take Scenic Drive south from the town of Trinidad.

EUREKA

Willow Creek and Groves Prairie
(Six Rivers National Forest, Lower Trinity Ranger District)

Although enthusiastic about the birding opportunities throughout Six Rivers National Forest, Ranger Tom Leskiw, of the Lower Trinity Ranger District, favors Willow Creek with its nesting Bald Eagles, and Groves Prairie with its resident Spotted Owls.

Overall, the Six Rivers National Forest encompasses 1,120,000 acres and six major northwestern California rivers. The Lower Trinity Ranger District, where Groves Prairie and Willow Creek both lie, boasts all of the following: developed campgrounds (with potable water, picnic tables, toilet facilities, and fireplaces) at three locations; primitive campsites at four locations; three picnic areas equipped with tables and stoves; plenty of opportunities for hiking, birding, boating, swimming, and tubing.

194 species have been sighted in the Six Rivers National Forest, among them the rare Spotted Owl, who's very much at home in the dense overhead canopies that typify this area. Northern Flicker and Steller's Jay are abundant. Commonly seen are Hutton's Vireo, California Quail, Band-tailed Pigeon, Winter and Bewick's Wrens, Red-breasted Nuthatch, Common Nighthawk, and Acorn Woodpecker. Less commonly sighted are Golden Eagle, Osprey, and Sharp-shinned Hawk.

Also seen here are 20 species of amphibians, 18 species of reptiles, and 74 mammal species, including Mule Deer, Spotted Skunk, California Ground Squirrel, and Raccoon.

The Lower Trinity Ranger Station is located at Willow Creek, on US 299, about 51 miles east of Eureka. To get to Groves Prairie, go east on

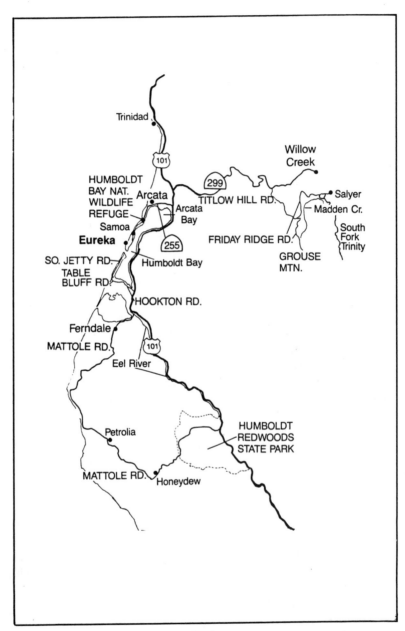

Eureka

299 to Hawkins Bar, take Route 4 (Forest Road 7N04) to the north and continue on to Groves Prairie.

Titlow Hill Road/Friday Ridge Road Loop

Twenty-five miles east of Arcata on SH 299, Titlow Hill Road takes off to the south. After 5 or 6 miles you'll come to a gravel road that leads up Horse Mountain, an area known for its excellent open pine forest birding, and a good place to explore if you have the time. Titlow Hill Road continues on to Titlow Hill itself, where Friday Ridge Road takes off to the left. This latter follows the ridge down to Madden Creek, which flows into the south fork of the Trinity River, and on back to SH 299, where the South Fork joins the river near Salyer.

Alternatively, you can stay on Titlow Hill Road to Grouse Mountain, and come back the same way.

Expect to see Mountain Chickadee, Red-breasted Nuthatch, Townsend's Solitaire, Dusky Flycatcher, Green-tailed Towhee, and raptors such as Golden Eagle, Great Horned Owl, and Spotted Owl. Goshawks have been seen in the area, and there is one recorded sighting of the Flammulated Owl. There are also Red-breasted Sapsucker, White-headed Woodpecker, Blue Grouse, Mountain Bluebird, and a chance to see Red Crossbill, Clark's Nutcracker, and Evening Grosbeak. A Calliope Hummingbird was reported at Titlow Hill, and Rock Wren, Spotted Sandpiper, Common Merganser, and American Dipper have all been seen at the mouth of Madden Creek.

Titlow Hill Road leads south from US 299 about 25 miles east of Arcata, and a mile or so east of Redwood Creek. At Titlow Hill turn left on Friday Ridge Road, which comes back into US 299 at Salyer.

Arcata Marsh and Wildlife Sanctuary

The real wonder of this 154-acre marsh and Sanctuary is that it wouldn't be here at all if not for the innovativeness, creativity, and concerted efforts of concerned groups that range from Humboldt State University to the Boy Scouts of America, from the City of Arcata Public Works Department to the Sierra Club. As incredible as it may seem, the Robert Gearheart Marsh was once pastureland; where the George Allen Marsh now lies was once an abandoned log deck; the grassy hill called Mount Trashmore was reclaimed from a sanitary landfill; and Franklin Klopp Lake, now used for sports fishing and shorebird observation, used to be a leachate basin for landfill.

According to Robert Lockett of the Redwood Region Audubon Society, the Arcata marsh is probably the best spot in the state to see Peregrine Falcons and Merlins during the fall and winter.

On a visit to the marsh in August of 1989, we counted 30 species in just twice that many minutes. Among these were 60 American Avocets, 6 Brown Pelicans, 15 Double-crested Cormorants resting on islands in the Franklin Klopp Lake; a Belted Kingfisher, countless Least Sandpipers, 15 Canada Geese, 8 Red-necked Phalaropes, 20 Snowy Egrets, 35 Marbled Godwits, 4 Great Blue Herons, and 4 Marsh Wrens in the Dan Hauser Marsh; a lone American Coot, innumerable Cinnamon Teals and Mallards in the Robert Gearheart Marsh; Savannah Sparrow, Black Phoebe, and approximately 100 Great Egrets (some perched in trees, festooning branches like enormous white flowers in full bloom) in the George Allen Marsh.

Lockett reports many sightings of uncommon birds and/or vagrants at the marsh: Oriental Greenfinch, Tufted Duck, Snowy Owl, Peregrine Falcon, Sharp-tailed Sandpiper, Little Gull, Franklin's Gull, Hudsonian Godwit, Dusky-capped Flycatcher, Sharp-tailed Sparrow, White-faced Ibis, Common Moorhen, White-winged Dove, and Yellow-headed Blackbird.

David McKay, director of the Northcoast Environmental Center at Arcata, is another frequent visitor at Arcata Marsh who touts the place for its visiting vagrants, notably Chestnut-sided Warbler and Common Grackle.

From US 101 in Arcata, take Samoa Blvd (SH 255) west to "I" Street and turn left. The road meanders through the marshes to the parking lot at the end, with pull-offs along the way.

Humboldt Bay/Humboldt Bay National Wildlife Refuge

This great bay is visited by large concentrations of migrating species, and attracts a good number of vagrants as well. The bay covers the area from Arcata to Table Bluff, which means that the visitor traveling north or south on US 101 traverses over 20 miles of scenic bayshore, and may sight a hundred or a thousand times that many birds along the way.

A wide diversity of species inhabit the 8,600 acres of wetlands at this fine refuge. Most notable of these are the handsome Brants, thousands and thousands of which stop off here on their migration route from their wintering grounds in Mexico. Many shorebirds are year-round residents, while in the fall and winter the area is well populated with ducks and Tundra Swans. In spring, it's the egrets and herons that are most conspicuous, for the area boasts the second largest colony in California. Their rookery lies in the cypress and blue gum trees at the edge of the preserve.

Good birding is possible all along the bay, including even that area which lies in the city limits of Eureka, a town with a population of 25,000. Known for its historic and beautifully restored "Old Town," Eureka offers fine accommodations and good restaurants to visiting birders.

Seen in and around Humboldt Bay are Common and Pacific Loons, Double-crested Cormorant, Great Blue Heron, Western Grebe, White-winged and Surf Scoters, Cinnamon Teal, Northern Shoveler, American Wigeon, Osprey, Black-shouldered Kite, Red-shouldered Hawk, Greater Yellowlegs, Belted Kingfisher, Whimbrel, Sanderling, several species of gull, and the Brant, for which the refuge serves as staging area.

Nesting species in the county include Blue-winged and Cinnamon Teal, Osprey, Turkey Vulture, Black-shouldered Kite, Red-shouldered Hawk, Blue Grouse, Virginia Rail, American Coot, Barn Owl, and Belted Kingfisher.

Seen here too are the thousands of Harbor Seals who bear their winsome pups right here in the refuge. Whale watching is excellent here also, especially from the vantage point of the nearby Table Bluff County Park.

The Humboldt Bay National Wildlife Refuge is open from sunrise to sundown all year long. For more information about the preserve, contact: Humboldt Bay National Wildlife Refuge, 539 G Street, Suite 167, Eureka, CA 95501, or call (707) 826-3415.

The City of Eureka is on US 101, 280 miles north of San Francisco. The best vantage points for Humboldt Bay are:

King Salmon Picnic Area (PG&E). Three miles south of Eureka, take the King Salmon Avenue exit. Turn right on King Salmon Avenue and go about half a mile. A path leads to a small rise that offers a commanding view of the bay.

North Spit. From US 101 in Eureka, take SH 255 to Samoa. Stop off at Samoa Cookhouse to replenish your calories with one of their world famous home-style meals, then continue to the end of the spit.

South Spit and Table Bluff Park. Go south on US 101 from Eureka, turn right (west) on Hookton Road, which runs into Table Bluff Road, which runs into South Jetty Road. There are several vantage points along this route, both for the bay and the marshlands. These spits also offer the best chances to spot vagrants.

Eel River Delta

The delta is more than five miles at its widest, and with its marshes, sloughs, willows, and plains, offers the very best of classic coastal birding. The area is known for many species, including a sizable flock of elegant Tundra Swans, and many wintering raptors. It's on the flyway for the migrators, who come through from mid-October to early December on their way south, and then again in February on the return trip north. Vagrants are often seen. Shorebirds abound, as do the passerines in the summertime.

There are several great vantage spots to view all this delta activity. On the north side, the Eel River Wildlife Area consists of 168 acres, mostly a narrow spit that extends down from Table Bluff between the ocean and McNulty Slough. It's a 2 mile walk south from the county park at Table Bluff, but is well worth the effort. Also on the north side, Crab Park, at the very end of Cannibal Drive, offers closest automobile access to the mouth of the river and has a boat launch where canoes and kayaks may be put in. There's also a road down from Cannibal Drive to Cock Robin Island.

As to the south, or Ferndale side we're indebted to Larry Eifert of Eifert Galleries for providing us with his fine little flyer, *Wildlife Guide to the Eel River Valley*, showing 9 different birding areas and giving short descriptions of each. Larry's 3,000-square-foot gallery is devoted almost exclusively to nature and wildlife subjects, featuring his own and about a dozen other artists' work. Stop by the gallery, say "hi" to Larry, and pick up a copy of the guide. If you like, Larry also conducts guided tours, and offers combination tours and art lessons.

Larry's guide includes, among others, stops at these places: Fernbridge, (just across the river) a sand bar in one direction and a cottonwood/willow grove in the other; Fulmor Pool at the end of Fulmor Road; the ends of Dillon Road and Camp Weott Road, on Morgan Slough; and Centerville Beach, where one can follow the dunes on a 5 mile hike up the south spit between sloughs and winter ponds on one side and the ocean on the other.

The third, and maybe the best, approach to the delta is from the middle, by boat. Private boats can be put in at several places on both sides of the delta: Crab Park or Cock Robin Island on the north side, or Morgan Slough on the south. Bruce Slocum of Camp Weott Guide Service (707-786-4187) takes individuals or groups on comprehensive tours at very modest prices.

Birding is good all year round. Tundra Swans arrive in mid-November, and stay until February or early March. One might see hundreds of these large, elegant birds on the marsh at any given time. The 1987 Christmas count listed 1,502 individuals.

A total of 256 species have been recorded. Northern Pintail, American Wigeon, teal, scaups, scoters, loons, grebes, cormorants, Brown Pelican, Northern Shoveler, Bufflehead, mergansers, and Ruddy Ducks are just some of the water birds that can be predictably seen, and in good numbers. Plovers, sandpipers, curlews, godwits and gulls abound. Bitterns and rails are in here if you can find them. Hawks, falcons, and owls patrol the marshes and fields.. Migrating landbirds by the thousands come through in the fall, and again in spring. Passerines inhabit the cottonwoods and willows. And there's always the good possibility of spotting a vagrant.

The Eel River Delta is south of Humboldt Bay, about 12 miles south of Eureka. To get to the Table Bluff/Eel River Wildlife Area, take Hookton Road west five miles from US 101. Get to Crab Park and Cock Robin Island by taking the Loleta exit from 101, and then Cannibal Road west from Loleta. For the south side of the delta, take the Fernbridge/Ferndale exit, cross the river, and you're there. Take Goble Lane to Dillon Road and Camp Weott Road. Stay on the main road to go to Ferndale. Centerville Road runs to the Centerville Beach area from the center of Ferndale.

Ferndale to Honeydew via Mattole Road

Mattole Road rises quickly out of Ferndale and works its way up Wildcat Ridge. The area is heavily wooded on the north facing slopes for the first few miles, but quickly breaks out into the open forests and grasslands of the Coastal Range.

About six or seven miles out, Bear River Ridge Road branches east and returns to US 101 at Rio Dell. The drive from Ferndale to Rio Dell takes about an hour and offers great opportunities for raptor watching. Mattole Road, however, continues to be spectacular. It stays right on the shoreline south of Cape Mendocino (one of the most secluded beaches in California) for 5 miles before again turning inland toward the little town of Petrolia, and then follows the Mattole River to Honeydew. From Honeydew it's 23 miles back to US 101, passing through Humboldt Redwoods State Park on the way.

This drive takes you through excellent habitat for riparian birds in the willows and cottonwoods along the Mattole River, for shorebirds and sea birds at the beach, and for warblers, woodpeckers, jays, sparrows, finches and flycatchers.

But this is primarily the land of the raptors, especially in the fall and winter. Along with the easily seen Red-tailed Hawk, expect Red-shouldered, Sharp-shinned, Cooper's, and Rough-legged Hawks, Black-shouldered Kite, Osprey at the beach, Northern Harrier skimming low, and an abundance of American Kestrels. Peregrine Falcons are seen here, as are Golden Eagle and Merlin, and there have been confirmed sightings, although rare, of Bald Eagle, Ferruginous Hawk, and Prairie Falcon. Mammals seen here include deer, coyote, lynx, and cougar.

To get to Ferndale, take the well-marked exit on US 101. In Ferndale, look for Mattole Road, also known as Wildcat Road, and/or SH 211.

To start from Honeydew, take the first exit north of Weott from US 101, go west on Bull Creek Flats Road through Humboldt Redwoods State Park and proceed to Honeydew.

HUMBOLDT REDWOODS STATE PARK/
AVENUE OF THE GIANTS

More than a hundred miles of hiking and riding trails wind through this beautiful park. Likewise winds a certain famous road, known as the Avenue of the Giants. This is SH 254 (old Highway 101), now by-passed by the freeway; 33 miles of splendor that follows the south fork of the Eel River through old growth redwoods, interesting little highway towns, and miles of typical redwood birding.

There are pull-offs all along the avenue, in the deep redwood groves, in the settlements, in meadows over which the meadowlarks wing their way, along the bluffs above the Eel, and in designated groves with restroom facilities, places to picnic, cool water to drink, sights to see.

The state park offers good fishing, hiking, and birding and has a visitor center, 247 family campsites in 3 separate campgrounds, 6 trail camps,

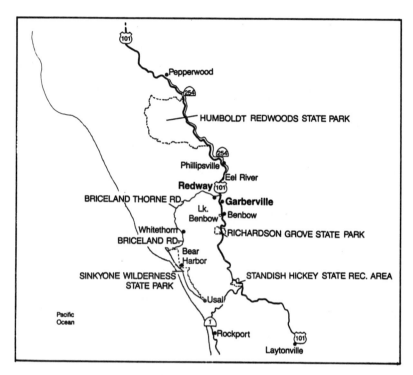

Humboldt Redwoods State Park

and 5 secluded environmental campsites. There's also a campground for equestrians, Cuneo Creek Horse Group Camp, set up to accommodate 50 riders and their horses, complete with tables, barbecues, corrals, and hitching posts.

The Common Raven is certainly the most visible bird here, and the one most easily identified. The Steller's Jay is conspicuous and the Pileated Woodpecker can be sighted regularly in old growth forest.

Less easily seen but present nonetheless are Cooper's Hawk, Golden Eagle, Osprey, Mountain Quail, Great Blue Heron, Bald Eagle, chickadees, nuthatches, Lazuli Bunting, California Quail, Evening Grosbeak, Chipping Sparrow, Common Nighthawk, Spotted Owl, Peregrine Falcon, Hooded Merganser, and Marbled Murrelet. A bird list is available at the visitor center.

Humboldt Redwoods State Park is on SH 254 (old US 101), 9 miles north of Garberville in Humboldt County. The park covers 33 miles from the town of Phillipsville up to Pepperwood. From US 101, watch for "Avenue of the Giants" signs.

Benbow Lake State Recreation Area

The focal points of this 1,200-acre recreational area are its 26-acre lake, created by a dam on the lovely Eel River, and the summertime water sports it affords — the good fishing, the boating, the lounging and sunning. But the park seems to derive its character and its rather touristy ambience from the lovely old Benbow Hotel which lies on a rise above it and appears to preside over it like a lord of the land.

Among the park's attractions are a Summer Arts Festival, a Shakespeare Festival, and an assortment of campfire programs. Facilities include a campfire center, picnic tables, fire rings, food lockers, a trail that leads to a historic old mill, 75 campsites, flush toilets, and cold showers.

Osprey, Bald Eagle, and Pileated Woodpecker can be seen here. Other birds include Winter Wren, Hermit Thrush, and Great Blue Heron.

Benbow Lake SRA is in Humboldt County, on US 101 at Benbow, 4 miles south of Garberville.

Richardson Grove State Park

Richardson Grove has more than just redwoods. Here too are tan oak, wax myrtle, Douglas fir, madrone, and maple. And in their shadows huckleberry thrives, and salal too, and wildflowers and ferns. It's a tangled land here, much of it steep and rugged, with elevations varying from 383 to 1,440 feet. One of its three main hiking paths, the Durphy Creek-Tan Oak Trail, is a challenge not meant for casual strollers.

This park has all of the following features: 170 family campsites in three separate park campgrounds, each equipped with picnic tables, food lockers, and fire rings, hot water and shower facilities, year-round camping areas for hikers and cyclists, an easy-to-walk self-guided nature trail, summertime campfire programs, Junior Ranger gatherings, a gift shop, a one-log dining room, and a visitor center located in the picturesque old Richardson Grove Lodge, which is open every summer, serving lunch and selling wares. Birding is best here in the spring and fall.

Most at home in this land of river and woods are Steller's Jay, Belted Kingfisher, Winter Wren, Hermit Thrush, Wrentit, and in the fall and winter, Great Blue Heron, Osprey, and the endangered Bald Eagle.

Newcomers to California's northwest coastal ranges need to be forewarned that the species dwelling right in the thick of a redwood forest are not easily sighted. Nevertheless, the birds one does see here make it well worth visiting Richardson Grove.

On US 101 just north of the Mendocino/Humboldt County line, Richardson Grove serves as a harbinger of the majesty in store for the tourist throughout Humboldt County. You cross into Humboldt County and immediately you're into this awesome grove.

There is no by-pass. The main highway runs directly through the heart of the grove. Entrances to the campgrounds and parking areas are on the north end of the park.

STANDISH HICKEY STATE RECREATION AREA

Although most of the old virgin trees are gone from this area, and the groves at Standish Hickey are largely second growth, the ambience of Redwood country could scarcely be more pronounced than it is here in this Mendocino County parkland, just a mile north from the town of Legget. In their hush and coolness, the groves seem pervaded with a sense of history.

Notably, there are trees here other than redwood. Of special interest are the stands of *mature* Douglas fir, a sight seldom viewed elsewhere due to the fact that this species is usually used commercially before it has a chance to reach maturity. Here too are tan oak, madrone, big-leaf maple, dogwood, and California laurel. The woods are full of shrubs and ferns and mosses.

This park has all of the following features: 162 family campsites in three separate park campgrounds, each equipped with tables, food cupboards, and fireplace, hot water and shower facilities, restroom access for wheelchairs, several fine hiking trails, ranging from easy to strenuous, campfire programs, Junior Ranger activities, summer nature hikes, swimming, and fishing.

This recreation area is named for Edward Hickey, whose family donated the first 40 acres to the state, and A.M. Standish, a descendant of the famous Captain Miles Standish, whose family donated, to the Save-the-Redwoods-League, the 512 acres that ultimately comprised the second development phase of the area.

Common in the park are Steller's Jay and Common Raven. The Pileated Woodpecker is here too, and along the river you'll find Great Blue Heron, Great Egret, and Osprey. In winter, the endangered Bald Eagle is sometimes sighted at the park.

Standish Hickey State Recreation Area is in Mendocino County, about a mile north of Leggett on US 101. The entrance is well marked.

SINKYONE WILDERNESS STATE PARK

This park is known for all of the following: A past rich enough to satisfy any history buff or archaeologist, beautiful vistas, unspoiled countryside, challenging hikes, opportunities for excellent photographs, dense forests, a herd of Roosevelt elk, other wildlife, whale watching during winter and early spring, wildflower meadows, two dozen primitive backcountry campsites, picnic tables and fire pits, and very exciting birding. This is unadulterated wilderness and distinctly no place for the faint at heart.

Birds typical of the Sinkyone Wilderness include Osprey, Pileated Woodpecker, cormorants, murres, Red-tailed Hawk, Brown Pelican, American Dipper, Bald Eagle, and Spotted Owl. Here too is a highly unlikely albino Cliff Swallow.

The albino swallow is only a curiosity, but the Bald Eagle and the Spotted Owl are truly legendary. The eagle, in fact, figured prominently in the folklore of the California Indians. According to the nineteenth century pioneering anthropologist, Stephen Powers, the eagle was one of the few animals known "into which the devil never does enter."

Currently the Spotted Owl is listed by the US Fish and Wildlife Service as a threatened species in California, Oregon, and Washington.

A bird list of Mendocino County birds, compiled by Greg Grantham of the College of the Redwoods, is available at a number of the county's state parks.

An abundance of wildlife resides here at Sinkyone and because of the remoteness of the park, good sightings are frequent. The park boasts a herd of Roosevelt Elk, Mountain Lion, Black Bear, foxes, Bobcat, Raccoon, skunks, and many rodents. Migrating whales can be easily sighted from the shore during winter and early spring.

This remote parkland is located in the very northwest corner of Mendocino County. To reach the northern portion of the park at Bear Harbor,

Spotted Owl

take Briceland-Thorne Road from the town of Redway, 2.5 miles west of Garberville on US 101. The park lies approximately 20 miles west of Garberville. The access roads are unpaved and very rugged for the last 9 miles. Six miles south of Whitethorn the unpaved two lane road becomes one lane only.

To reach the south section of the park at Usal Beach, take SH 1 three miles north of Rockport, turn west on County Road 431 and continue 6 more miles on this rough and unpaved road. The road is passable for passenger cars in the summer, but in winter 4-wheel-drive vehicles are advisable. No trailers or RVs.

NORTHERN CALIFORNIA COAST RANGE PRESERVE

Established in 1959, on land once beloved by the Kato Indians, this quiet 7,520-acre preserve was The Nature Conservancy's first acquisition. As an oldster in a long line of treasured preserves, it's held in special esteem by many Californians.

Birders wishing to visit the preserve would do best to notify the conservancy. Call (707) 984-6653, or write to The North Coast Range Preserve at 42101 Wilderness Lodge Road, Branscomb, CA 95417. Those who come unannounced should check with the overseer at the preserve headquarters before scouting about.

Anyone wishing to learn more about The Nature Conservancy would do well to puchase a copy of the highly readable book, *California Wild Lands, A Guide to the Nature Conservancy Preserves,* by Dwight Holing, published by Chronicle Books of San Francisco.

Supported by membership only, The Conservancy is a non-profit national conservation group which exists for the purpose of preserving biological diversity.

Species sighted here include Northern Goshawk, Western Screech-Owl, Wood Duck, Spotted Owl, a variety of warblers, and Pileated Woodpecker.

Mammals seen here include Coyote, Mountain Lion, Badger, Black Bear, Mule Deer, squirrels, hares, skunks, and a tiny rodent, a tree dweller, aptly called the Red Tree Vole.

The Northern California Coast Range Preserve is located in Mendocino County, 150 miles north of San Francisco, on US 101. From the town of Laytonville, turn west on the Branscomb Road, drive 13.9 miles to Branscomb and then 3 miles beyond. Turn north on Wilderness Lodge Road and go 3 more miles. The preserve headquarters is at the end of the road.

MENDOCINO

Lake Mendocino

Lake Mendocino is formed by a dam 3,500 feet long and 160 feet high on the east fork of the Russian River. There are 300 family campsites in campgrounds with picnic tables and firepits at each; a primitive 19-site

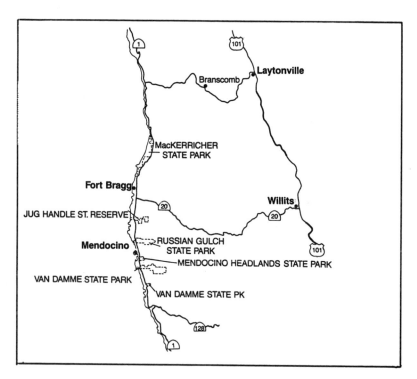

Mendocino

boat-in campground, 100 picnic sites; 9 group picnic shelters with barbecue pits; exercise courses, playgrounds, 14 miles of hiking trails; a horse staging area; swimming, and fishing for bass, crappie, and catfish.

For information write: Park Manager, Lake Mendocino, 1160 Lake Mendocino Drive, Ukiah, CA 95482, or call (707) 462-7582.

According to park ranger, Noel W. Stoughton, the most representative bird here is the California Quail. Other birds seen here include Pileated Woodpecker, Golden Eagle, House Finch, Scrub Jay, Acorn Woodpecker, Nuttall's Woodpecker, vireos, and Bald Eagle. Birding is best in spring and summer.

Lake Mendocino is a US Army Corps of Engineers facility located in Coyote Valley, in inland Mendocino County. Take US 101 to Lake Mendocino Drive, north of Ukiah and proceed east to the park office, the dam, an overlook, picnic access, Chekaka campground, and a boat ramp.

Alternatively, proceed north on US 101 approximately 4 miles and turn east on US 20. Marina Drive will take you to the Visitor Center, marina, Kyen campground, and a boat ramp.

Or continue east on US 20 past Marina Drive, across the east fork of the Russian River, and turn right. Bu-Shay campground and Mesa picnic area are on this road, as well as the head of the trail that extends through the wildlife area running along the entire eastern side of the lake.

MacKerricher State Park

MacKerricher State Park is located just 3 miles north of the town of Fort Bragg, set like a jewel on the much-photographed Mendocino Coast. This park has all of the following: forests of Bishop and shore pine, tan oak, salmonberry, salal and other thriving shrubs and trees; coastal dunes with coverlets of sand verbena; a trout-loaded lake named Cleone surrounded by cattails, sedges, and willows; inviting beaches; hiking trails; good fishing; abalone in season; 143 campsites with fire rings, tables, and food lockers; piped water, and restrooms.

In the winter, many of the park's visitors come here especially to bird, but there are interesting mammals to be seen here as well — most especially the Harbor Seals that live on the rocks just off the park's coast.

Birds seen here include Sanderling, Snowy Plover, Burrowing Owl, Red-winged Blackbird, Ruddy Duck, Great Blue Heron, Caspian Tern, Great and Snowy Egrets, Osprey, Canada Goose, Marbled Godwit, Dunlin, and an assortment of swallows.

MacKerricher State Park is on the Mendocino Coast just off US 101, 3 miles north of Fort Bragg. The entrance is well marked on the highway.

Jughandle State Reserve

Here there is an ecological staircase, a wonder to botanists, geologists, and nature lovers from all corners of the earth. The ecological staircase is a series of natural terraces wrought by centuries of geologic and climactic conditions. The "steps" of land, with their varying plant forms, stand as testimony to the steps that nature took to form them, the long evolutionary process that rendered each one distinct from the other, of a separate age, and different appearance. The youngest step of the staircase, bright with poppies and Indian paintbrush, is one hundred thousand years old, while the eldest and highest fifth step is more than five hundred thousand years old. The young terraces boast normal-sized trees, while the higher terraces are home to incredible dwarfs of the plant kingdom: pygmy pines and cypresses, midget manzanita and huckleberry.

A good representative bird of Jughandle State Reserve is the Belted Kingfisher. These industrious land excavators are perfectly at home here where steep canyon banks might be custom-made for their remarkable nesting holes sometimes dug as deep as 6 or 7 feet.

Jughandle boasts many shore and water birds, the most conspicuous of these being Killdeer, sandpipers, and a variety of gulls. Other birds seen in the vicinity include Osprey, Black-shouldered Kite, Barn Owl, Anna's Hummingbird, Acorn Woodpecker, Scrub Jay, and Bewick's Wrens.

Jughandle State Reserve is on SH 1 in Mendocino County, 5 miles north of the pictureque village of Mendocino.

Russian Gulch State Park

There are many unforgettable sights in this highly photogenic Mendocino County park: the magnificent bridge over Russian Gulch; scenic paths for bicyclists; a waterfall; a collapsed coastal tunnel called the Devil's Punch Bowl; second growth redwoods; many other beautiful trees such as big-leaf maples, Douglas fir, hemlock, tan oak, and California laurel; 30 creekside family campsites, each with table, stove, and food locker; and restrooms with hot showers and laundry tubs.

For further information write or call: Russian Gulch State Park, Mendocino District, P.O. Box 440, Mendocino, CA 95460, (707) 937-5804.

Birds seen in the vicinity are Osprey, Pileated Woodpecker, Steller's Jay, California Quail, Belted Kingfisher, Black-shouldered Kite, Red-shouldered Hawk, Orange-crowned Warbler, Anna's Hummingbird, White-breasted Nuthatch, Bewick's Wren, Hermit Thrush, Yellow-rumped Warbler, Varied Thrush, Hermit Warbler, Common Yellowthroat, and Rufous-sided Towhee.

Nesting species in this general area include Orange-crowned Warbler, Anna's Hummingbird, White-breasted Nuthatch, and Brown Creeper.

Russian Gulch State Park is on the coast, on SH 1 just north of the village of Mendocino. The entrance is clearly marked on the highway.

Mendocino Headlands State Park

The entire village of Mendocino is a designated Historic Preservation District, and well it should be. There's no place more picturesque in all of northern California. So similar is its ambience to that of a small coastal town in Maine that it's served more than once as the scene for the filming of the popular TV show, "Murder She Wrote."

Come to Mendocino for the "Mendocino experience." Check out the shops, the many fine restaurants, the museum. And, of course, all the while, keep an eye out for the birds.

Under the bridge near the Big River Beach parking lot, look in the rain-filled ponds for Common and Barrow's Goldeneyes. Or take Heeser Drive westward to the headlands for good sightings of cormorants, loons, grebes, Common Murre, and Pigeon Guillemot. The Double-crested Cormorant is commonly seen from the headlands and at the mouth of the picturesque Big River. On the grassy tableland, where the village lies, you'll see Lesser and American Goldfinches, Golden-crowned, White-crowned, and Savannah and Song Sparrows, House Finch, and other passerines. Expect too Surf Scoter, California Gull, Black Oystercatcher, and other birds of sea and shore. Raptors in the vicinity include Red-tailed Hawk, American Kestrel, and Osprey.

A checklist, *Birds of Mendocino County,* has been compiled by Greg Grantham of the College of the Redwoods.

From US 101 in Cloverdale, take SH 128 through Anderson Valley to the Coast Highway (SH 1) and go north about 10 miles.

Van Damme State Park

This lush Mendocino County Park, with its fern-walled canyons, jungle-like ambience, and its lazily-running Little River, is most notable for its rare pygmy forest with full-grown, cone-bearing pine and cypress trees that range in height from six inches to a bare five feet. Here too are fine hiking trails; a museum that has as its theme "Man and the Sea";73 campsites with stoves, picnic tables, and food lockers; piped water; hot showers; quietude.

Land birds of this vicinity include Gray Jay, Winter Wren, Northern Flicker, Common Raven, Red-breasted Nuthatch, Golden-crowned Kinglet, Wrentit, Ruby-crowned Kinglet, Hermit Thrush, and Townsend's

Warbler. From the sandy beach look for Double-crested Cormorant, scoters, loons, grebes, and a variety of gulls.

Van Damme State Park is on the Mendocino Coast where the Little River meets the Pacific. SH 1, the Coast Highway, goes through the park 3 miles south of the village of Mendocino.

HENDY WOODS STATE PARK

The majority of Hendy Woods State Park is situated on the north slope of picturesque Greenwood Ridge, overlooking the much-photographed Anderson Valley. Two redwood groves lie on flatlands along the Navarro River and the scenery is beautiful whichever way you look.

Besides its beauty, the park boasts the following features: several good trails, including an easy half-mile discovery path with access for wheelchairs; excellent fishing; seasonal kayaking and canoeing; two campgrounds (Azalea with 43 sites, and Wildcat with 49), barbecue stoves; food lockers; paved parking spaces; piped drinking water; restrooms with hot showers.

Most at home in this land of river and woods are Belted Kingfisher, Winter Wren, Steller's Jay, Hermit Thrush, and Wrentit. But the Golden Eagle and the endangered Peregrine Falcon are seen here too, and less often, the Spotted Owl.

Hendy Woods State Park is on the south bank of the Navarro River 4 miles northeast of Philo, in Mendocino County's Anderson Valley. From US 101 in Cloverdale, take SH 128 through Philo to Cottonwood Road and turn left. The park entrance is just across the river.

LAKE COUNTY

U Wanna Camp RV Park

This quiet little family park, 2 miles west of Lakeport, bears mention as an excellent birding locale of Lake County despite the fact that it's privately owned. Not a large park, it boasts 30 campsites, restful grounds, and a private fishing pond. The campground is the property of Mr. and Mrs. Doug Beard of Lake County. The number to call for reservations at U Wanna Camp is (707) 263-6745.

U Wanna Camp is an excellent place to get a close look at the elusive Green-backed Heron. On a half-hour stroll to the pond and back the bird

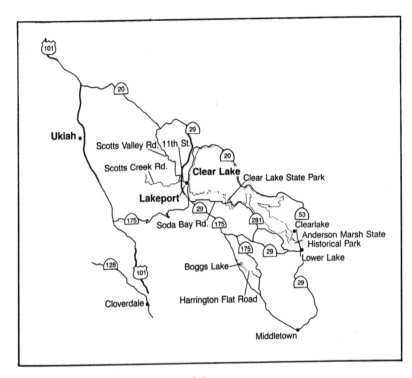

Lakeport

list can quickly grow to more than 20 species, including Western Bluebird, Black Phoebe, Purple Finch, and California Towhee. Many of these birds can be viewed uncommonly closely.

U Wanna Camp is located 2 miles west of Lakeport at 2699 Scotts Creek Road. From SH 29, take the 11th Street/Scotts Valley Road off-ramp, go west on Scotts Valley Road 0.5 mile to Scotts Creek Road and follow the signs to the campground.

Clear Lake State Park

Clear Lake State Park is located right on the shore of its showy namesake, the second-largest natural lake fully within the confines of California. It's a serene spot that offers excellent birding as well as boating, hiking.

organized nature walks, fireside programs, and a Junior Ranger program. A modern visitor center is replete with fine interpretive exhibits, and the grounds are graced with handsome old oaks, as beloved to Acorn Wood-peckers as to shade-seeking humankind.

The park is a nesting place for many varieties of waterfowl including Wood Duck, Mallard, and American Coot. Here too are American Goldfinch, Great Horned Owl, Bushtit, and many other birds, all of which are listed on a checklist available at the visitor center for 25 cents.

The 1988 Christmas bird count, which was centered 3.5 miles southeast of Mt. Konocti and included the park, had 124 species and 22,949 individu-als. The entire Clear Lake area, the gem of Lake County, offers excellent birding, especially in January and February, when the area is virtually teeming with bird life.

Clear Lake State Park is 0.5 miles west of Soda Bay on the south shore of Clear Lake. From SH 29 heading northwest, 7.5 miles from Lower Lake, take Soda Bay Road (SH 281) to the right, and proceed 10 miles to the park.

From Lakeport, follow the main street (which is SH 29 Business Route) south until it intersects with Soda Bay Road, and continue about 5 miles to the park.

Anderson Marsh State Historic Park
and McVicar Audubon Sanctuary/Cache Creek

From the historic old ranch house that stands near the entrance to the soaring Bald Eagle who regularly winters on the grounds, from the rock art of prehistoric Indians to a coyote with his muzzle pointing moonward, the attractions of Anderson Marsh State Historic Park are as diverse as the particular interests of the people who come here.

Five hundred and forty of the 870 acres that comprise this Clear Lake area park have been designated as a natural preserve. This is a wetland area, a marsh noted for its diversity of foliage and abundance of wildlife.

There are restrictions on motorboats in the marsh, but Ranger Tom Nixon reports that the very best way to see the avifauna is by canoe. Regrettably, rental boats aren't always readily available, so unless you're a canoe-owning birder this alternative may be out.

The Bald Eagle is a regular winter visitor here, for Anderson Marsh forms a vital link in an ecological chain that's very important to this great raptor. In fact Cache Creek, which serves as drainage to Clear Lake, offers excellent eagle watching elsewhere — in an area called Capay Valley — as well as here in Lake County. To reach this other superb Bald Eagle country take SH 16 south from SH 20 or west and north from I-505 in the Sacramento Valley. Cache Creek runs alongside SH 16 for approximately 5 miles in the very northwestern tip of Yolo County, where, in the words of Allen Fish, of the Golden Gate Raptor Observatory, " . . . there are at least a dozen places where you can literally sit and wait for the next Bald Eagle to come along."

But, back at Anderson Marsh and McVicar Audubon Sanctuary one can see many species besides the soaring eagles. Noteworthy too is the Great Blue Heron, which thrives in the marshland here, as do Great and Snowy Egrets and other herons. This is, in fact, one of northern California's major rookeries.

Other birds seen here are American White Pelican, Black-shouldered Kite, Red-shouldered Hawk, Great Horned Owl, Anna's Hummingbird, American Goldfinch, and a long list of others. Birding is best here in the winter. At a cost of 25 cents, a bird checklist, *A List of the Birds of the Clear Lake Basin,* is available at the historic old ranch house, which serves as a visitor center to the park.

This is a good place for sighting other wildlife including raccoon, opossum, mink, beaver, Gray Fox, and bats.

The park itself is open to the public at any time, but as of this writing, the parking lot is open only on Friday, Saturday, and Sunday from 10:00 a.m. to 4:00 p.m. There is space enough for four or five cars on the highway shoulder across from the entrance, or you can park down at Lower Lake and hike in one mile.

For the canoe owner, there is another parking area on the north side of Cache Creek off old US 53, from which it's an easy portage to Cache Creek, and from there to the marsh.

The Park headquarters is located in the old Anderson farmhouse on SH 53, a mile north of Lower Lake in southern Lake County.

Boggs Lake Preserve

It's the unique plantlife that brings most visitors to this lovely pool, which is unfed by streams or springs, replenished by rainfall only. They come to see rarities like the Hedge Hyssop with its yellow-tubed, white-petaled blooms, and the many-flowered navarretia with flowers of a blue that rivals that of the Western Bluebird often seen flying overhead.

Like the vernal pool itself, which never measures more than half a mile across, the preserve is small. It boasts only 141 acres all told, the majority of which The Nature Conservancy acquired in 1972. (An additional 40 acres was added in 1986.) Yet these 141 acres account for 142 different bird species, many of them easily observed from a long and sturdy boardwalk that extends from the shore, out over the reeds and cattails.

Birds seen here include Red-winged Blackbird, Marsh Wren, flycatchers, Great Blue Heron, Osprey, Bald Eagle, Hooded Merganser, Hairy Woodpecker, Purple Martin, Wood Duck, Common Poorwill, and Rufous-sided Towhee.

For further information about The Nature Conservancy in general or this preserve in particular, contact The Nature Conservancy, 785 Market St., 3rd Floor, San Francisco, CA 94103, (415) 777-0487.

From Middletown, in southern Lake County, take SH 175 northeast 10 miles to Cobb. Turn left on Bottle Rock Road and go northeast another 6.5 miles. Keep a sharp eye out on the right for Harrington Flat Road. Turn right and go 1 mile. The lake is on the left. Park on the left shoulder at the preserve entrance.

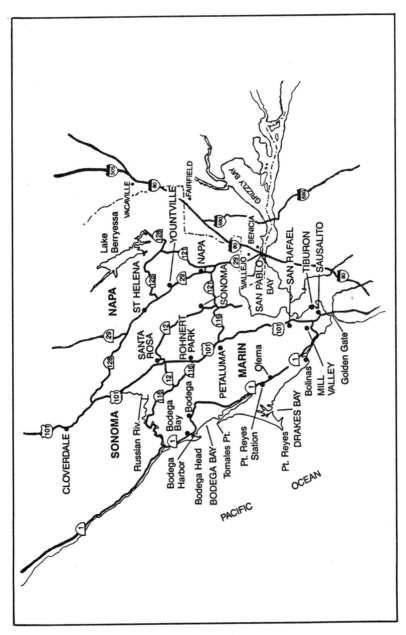

North Bay Region

Chapter 2
North Bay

 "I firmly believe, from all I have seen, that this is the chosen spot of all the earth, as far as nature is concerned." These words of Luther Burbank were spoken from the famed horticulturist's headquarters in Sonoma County early in this century, and athough this four-county area is today home to more than a million people, much of that natural ambience yet remains for the enjoyment of today's nature lover.

The North Bay region is bounded by the rugged coast of the Pacific on the west, from the Gualala River to the Golden Gate; by the marsh-lined shores of San Francisco, San Pablo, and Suisun Bays, and the labyrinthine waterways of the Sacramento River delta to the south and east; and by the coastal range of hills extending down from the north. It encompasses 3,855 square miles, which is 4.9% of the area covered by this book.

Along with what is arguably the number one birding spot in the state, the region offers major fishing and boating ports, surviving stands of pristine redwoods, the world's largest geyser field, a citrus belt in its northernmost reaches, gold mining, farms and ranches, teeming cities and suburbs, and sparsely settled coastal and mountain areas.

Agriculture is still the area's primary industry. The dairy and cattle and sheep ranches of the coastal areas thrive yet today, and there are still remnants of what was once the "Egg Basket of the World," but the apple, prune, walnut, and pear orchards of the inland valleys are giving way to suburbia, and to the premium vineyards of the ever-expanding wine industry.

Above all, this is wine country. California's wine industry was born here, and the great vineyards of Napa and Sonoma Counties have become recognized as second to none in the world.

The geology is coastal mountain range in Marin, Sonoma, and Napa Counties, with broad plains and valleys, while Solano County is bay and delta country, edging into the Great Central Valley. Habitat includes coastal bays, lagoons, estuaries; the fecund marshes of the bays and delta; open grasslands; needle-leafed and broad-leafed woods; chapparal ridges; fertile valleys, and rivers, creeks, and lakes.

The major north-south arterials are SH 1 up the coast, US101 from San Francisco through Marin and Sonoma Counties, SH 29 in the Napa Valley, and I-80 through Solano County. From east to west, SH 37 crosses the top of the bay, SH 12 traverses the entire region from Rio Vista to Bodega, and SH 116 goes from the Sonoma area northwest to the Russian River and the coast.

BIRD LISTS FOR THE NORTH BAY REGION

There are several good lists and books available for the North Bay Region, among them the following:

Field Checklist of the Birds of Marin County, Alta California
  Compiled by David Shuford
  Published by Point Reyes Bird Observatory
  4990 Shoreline Highway
  Stinson Beach, CA 94970

Birds of Sonoma County, California
  Gordon Bolander and Benjamin D. Parmeter
  Published by Redwood Region Ornithological Society
  199 Calistoga Road
  Santa Rosa, CA 95405
  (707) 539-4544

Best Birding in Napa and Solano Counties
  Published by Napa-Solano Audubon Society
  702 Via Palo Linda
  Suisun City, CA 94585

To obtain a copy of *Field Checklist of the Birds of Marin County, Alta California* please send 50 cents and a stamped, self-addressed envelope along with your request to the Point Reyes Bird Observatory at the above address.

Copies of *Birds of Sonoma County, California* ($4.95 plus tax, postage, and handling) and *Best Birding in Napa and Solano Counties* ($6.95 plus tax, postage, and handling) may be purchased from the Book Nest, 376 Greenwood Beach Road, Tiburon, CA 94920, (415) 388-2524.

NORTHERN SONOMA COUNTY

The Mouth of the Gualala River

In summertime, a sandbar separates the Gualala River from the sea, thereby forming a lagoon that's rich in birdlife, a small body of water that can be observed either from the quaint little town of Gualala in Mendocino County or from the regional park in neighboring Sonoma County.

On the Sonoma County side, Gualala Point Regional Park, which is open year-round, has all the following features: 18 family campsites; 7 walk-in or cyclists' sites; bicycle and foot paths; miles of beachfront covered with driftwood; a visitor center; whale watching in season; good fishing; and the good birding that typifies both sides of the lagoon.

Acorn Woodpeckers, Osprey, California Quail, and other land birds populate these lovely hinterlands, as well as many species of the sea and shore. In the winter look for Black-legged Kittiwake, Common Merganser, loons, and grebes. During the breeding season expect Heermann's Gull, Chestnut-backed Chickadee, Purple Finch, Brown Creeper, California Quail, and Acorn Woodpecker.

For further information about Gualala Point Regional Park call (707) 785-2377.

Gualala is on SH 1 (the Coastal Highway) approximately 45 rugged miles north of SH 116 and the Russian River mouth. Skaggs Springs Road is a good (but slow) country backroad that follows the Gualala from its headwaters almost to the coast. It runs into Dry Creek Road at Warm Springs Dam/Lake Sonoma, which in turn connects with US 101 at Healdsburg.

Acorn Woodpecker

Salt Point State Park

Salt Point State Park lies on a rugged coastline as typical of northern California as the velvet gray fog that sometimes enshrouds and blurs its jagged edges. This is a 6,000-acre park with features that include a marine reserve, a number of picturesque coves and promontories, stretches of open grassland, some of the best tidepooling and diving in the state, lush stands of madrone, tan oak, Bishop pine, Douglas fir, and groves of redwoods.

The park has a 30-unit campground in the upland area, an 80-site family camping area further from the shore, 20 walk-in sites, and 10 that are specified for hikers and cyclists. Campsites are equipped with picnic tables and stoves or fire pits. Drinking water, and bathroom facilities are available nearby.

Among the many birds seen here are the Osprey, Peregrine Falcon, Black-shouldered Kite, White-crowned and Golden-crowned Sparrows, American Goldfinches, House Finch, Common Raven, Double-crested Cormorant, Black Oystercatcher, Red-breasted Merganser, Black-bellied Plover, and Hutton's Vireo. Birding is good all year long.

From US 101, north of Santa Rosa, take River Road to the west. A pleasant drive takes you through the Russian River towns of Rio Nido, Guerneville, Monte Rio, and Duncans Mills to SH 1 at Jenner. Go north on this scenic coastal highway 20 miles to the park. The 19th-century Russian settlement at Fort Ross has been attractively restored, so you might want to stop there on your way.

Lake Sonoma/Warm Springs Dam

This popular man-made lake in the coastal foothills is one of the best places in Sonoma County to see the endangered Peregrine Falcon. It's a likely spot to view another splendid raptor too: the U.S. Army Corps of Engineers and the Pacific Gas and Electric Company have worked together to construct nesting sites custom-made for Ospreys. And, in the future, the park staff plans to participate in a program to aid the Bald Eagle.

Besides birds of prey, Lake Sonoma has all these attractions: 17,000 acres of parkland; a lake with 2,700 surface acres; free boat ramp and boat-in camping; fish hatchery; visitor center; educational programs and exhibits; 8,000-acre wildlife reserve; developed and primitive campsites; camping facilities for the handicapped; 40 miles of trails for backpackers, hikers, and horseback riders.

Birds common to Lake Sonoma include Western and Pied-billed Grebes, Double-crested Cormorant, Great Blue Heron, Wood Duck, Black-shouldered Kite, Osprey, California Quail, Wild Turkey, Great Horned Owl,

Belted Kingfisher, Black Phoebe, and Pileated Woodpecker.

Look for kingfishers, egrets, herons, and cormorants at the lake itself or near the fish hatchery where they can be found fishing. Watch for Osprey over the lake. Scan the shoreline of the Dry Creek arm of the lake for a view of Wild Turkeys.

Take the Dry Creek Road exit from Highway 101 in Healdsburg and go west 12 miles to the Visitor Center. Or continue on 101 past Geyserville to the Canyon Road exit, go west 2.2 miles to Dry Creek Road, and turn right.

SANTA ROSA

Howarth Santa Rosa Memorial Park

Popular with Santa Rosa residents and visitors alike, this 152-acre city park with its 25-acre lake, Ralphine, runs directly into a county recreational area, Spring Lake Park, which in turn runs into Annadel State Park. All three of these areas boast lakes; all three have a wide variety of trees and wildflowers; all three are populated by many species of birds.

The 1988 Christmas Bird Count for Santa Rosa had 133 species, many of which are represented in the park. Expect Bushtit, Steller's Jay, Ruby-crowned Kinglet, Black Phoebe, and Rufous-sided Towhee.

A bird list for the neighboring Spring Lake Regional Park can be obtained from Sonoma County Regional Parks, 2403 Professional Drive, Suite 100, Santa Rosa, CA 95403.

Howarth Park is located on Summerfield Road at Montgomery Drive. From SH 12 in east Santa Rosa, turn south on Mission Boulevard 1 block to Montgomery Drive, go right 1 block to Summerfield Road, turn left and go about 0.25 mile to the park entrance.

Spring Lake Regional Park

Spring Lake Regional Park itself is a haven for swimmers, hikers, joggers, bicyclists, and, most assuredly, for birders. It has two miles of shoreline; well-maintained trails that wind attractively around the lake; bicycle paths; good fishing; a sizable swimming hole fed by warm spring water; modern restrooms; 31 family campsites; 200 picnic setups with barbecues; 4 large group picnic areas; and more than 150 species of birds.

Campsites at Spring Lake are on a first-come, first-served basis. For information about this and other area parks, write Sonoma County Regional Parks, 2403 Professional Drive, Suite 100, Santa Rosa, CA 95401 or call (707) 527-2087.

Species seen here include American Bittern, Hooded Merganser, Virginia Rail, Wood Duck, Marsh Wren, Green-backed and Great Blue Herons, Black-crowned Night-Heron, loons, Northern Harrier, Pied-billed Grebe, Bewick's Wren, and Loggerhead Shrike.

Western Pond Turtles are common, as are King Snakes, Alligator Lizards, Bullfrogs, California Newts, and many other creatures.

Follow the directions to Annadel State Park, except take the first right turn after you get on Channel Drive, and go up the hill to the park entrance. Or park at Howarth Park and take a birding walk through both parks. It's about 4 miles, round trip, and beautiful.

Annadel State Park

Annadel Park boasts 35 miles of horseback riding and hiking trails, but no access whatever to touring automobiles. No murmur of traffic here, no honking horns to compete with the hammering of its many woodpeckers. This is a popular place. According to unit ranger Bill Krumbein, day use visitors number 170,000 annually, but the park is big enough and remote enough to absorb them all and still retain its back-country feeling.

Just 3 miles from the parking lot, by hiking trail, is Lake Ilsanjo, inhabited by bluegill and black bass that render Annadel as much a delight to anglers as it is to birders.

Elevation varies considerably at the park, from 300 to 1,800 feet, but except for Steve's "S" Trail, which is unquestionably a challenge, the rises are gentle and hiking is comparatively easy.

Spring and summer are reputedly best for birding the wooded areas of the park but any time is good for observing woodpeckers. Eight species are year-round residents in the woods of Annadel: Acorn, Lewis', Nuttall's, Hairy, Downy, and Pileated; Red-breasted Sapsucker, and Norther Flicker.

Other birds seen here include phoebes, flycatchers, Chestnut-backed Chickadee, nuthatches, Yellow-breasted Chat, Pied-billed Grebe, Wood Duck, Bald Eagle, Loggerhead Shrike, and the rare and controversial Spotted Owl.

A bird list, *Annadel State Park Birds*, is available from the Valley of

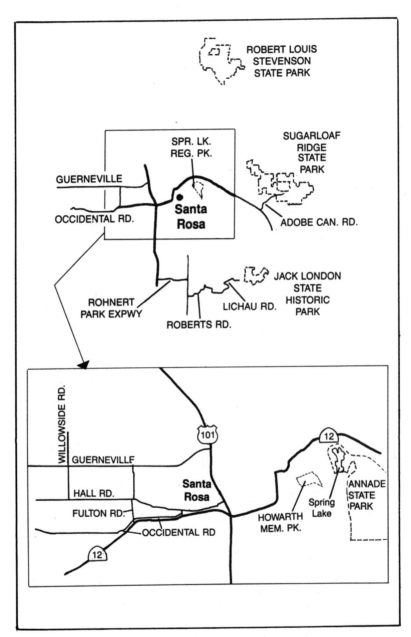

Santa Rosa

the Moon Natural History Association, 2400 London Ranch Road, Glen Ellen, CA 95442.

Black-tailed Deer are abundant in the park. Also seen are Raccoons, skunks, Bobcats, Muskrats, and foxes.

There are no overnight facilities at Annadel Park but campsites are available at the neighboring Spring Lake Park.

Take SH 12 to Mission Boulevard in eastern Santa Rosa, turn south one block to Montgomery Drive, and go east about 1.5 miles to Channel Drive. Turn right on Channel and follow it 2 miles to the parking lot. Coming from the east on SH 12, turn left on Los Alamos Road, which ends at Montgomery. Go right for 0.5 mile to Channel Drive, on your left.

Sugarloaf Ridge State Park

Just 14 miles from the city of Santa Rosa, in the midst of deer country, lies 2,500-acre Sugarloaf Ridge State Park. Set in Coastal hills and mountains, the park ranges in elevation from 600 feet at its entrance to 2,729 feet at the summit of Bald Mountain. From the summit on a clear day, you can see Napa and Sonoma valleys, San Francisco, Oakland, the Pacific Ocean, the Trinity Alps, and occasionally even the High Sierra. A strenuous hike, but a dandy.

Sugarloaf is at its loveliest in the spring when the meadow is bedecked with wildflowers such as cream cups, California poppy, penstemon, and Indian pinks.

The park, which is visited by approximately 50,000 people yearly, has 50 developed campsites, each equipped with tables and stoves.

This area is home to California Quail, Scrub Jay, Acorn Woodpecker, American Goldfinch, Purple Finch, an assortment of sparrows, and, among yet many other species, the magnificent Golden Eagle. A free bird list is available at the park headquarters.

Mammals that reside at Sugarloaf Ridge are Raccoons, Bobcats, rabbits, Gray Foxes, Black-tailed Deer, and Weasels.

From Highway 12 in Kenwood, take Adobe Canyon Road through the canyon to the park. The road is fairly steep, but well maintained.

Jack London State Historic Park

Jack London State Park, located in Glen Ellen on land once the haunt of the famous writer whose name it bears, is an area of many attractions: a museum of London memorabilia, historic old buildings, oak woods, and fine hiking tails. Few of its 90,000 yearly visitors come particularly for the purpose of birding, but apparently the birds don't know this, for much of this 800-acre park boasts birdlife well worth seeing.

Here you can see Red-shouldered Hawk, Dark-eyed Junco, Northern Mockingbird, Song Sparrow, Wrentit, Bewick's Wren, White-crowned and Golden-crowned Sparrows, Ruby-crowned Kinglet, Anna's Hummingbird, Warbling Vireo, Red-winged Blackbird, House Finch, and Pileated, Acorn, Downy, and Hairy Woodpeckers.

The road to Jack London Park takes off from the center of Glen Ellen, a fascinating little town just off SH 12 in the highly scenic Valley of the Moon, between Sonoma and Santa Rosa.

Fairfield Osborn Preserve

This preserve is located in the lush and verdant heart of the Sonoma Mountains on land donated to The Nature Conservancy and named for a past president of the New York Zoological Society, the late Fairfield Osborn. With its mixed habitats of grassland, chaparral, marshlands, and vernal pool, it's a beautiful place, and like so many Nature Conservancy preserves, it is quite unique. Its features include Copeland Creek with its unstable bed and lack of fish; 150 species of aquatic insects; and many rare and beautiful plants, including the seldom seen Lobb's buttercup, *Ranunculus lobbii.*

The preserve is the scene of an environmental education program, field trips for as many as 1,200 children annually, and hikes led by docents (by special arrangement).

Birds seen here include Wood Duck, Sora, Lazuli Bunting, Black-throated Gray Warbler, Red-breasted Sapsucker, Yellow Warbler, Loggerhead Shrike, Orange-Crowned Warbler, Dark-eyed Junco, and Wilson's Warbler. Birdwatching is most rewarding here in spring and summer. A bird list is available.

Take the Rohnert Park Expressway east from US 101, to Petaluma Hill Road. Go south, past Sonoma State University and turn left on Roberts Road. About a mile out, Lichau Road goes off to the right and the preserve (address: 6543 Lichau Road, Penngrove, CA 94951) is at the end of Lichau Road.

Laguna De Santa Rosa

In the halcyon days of the nineteenth century, 1,000 acres of riparian forests and nutrient-rich marshland stretched all the way from Rohnert Park north to the Russian River. Early visitors to this lush territory were astonished by the wildlife they found here, the birds and the beauty that abounded. Since then, however, the low-lying area between Sebastopol and Santa Rosa, a drainage system for 250 square miles, has been overgrazed and polluted, the marshland has dwindled away, and some of the species (the Yellow-billed Cuckoo, for example) have disappeared. It's a sad state of affairs and one that would certainly worsen in the next century if steps weren't taken now to modify the results of growth and development.

But happily, steps are being taken. Groups such as the California Department of Fish and Game, the U.S. Fish and Wildlife Service, Ducks Unlimited, County of Sonoma, the cities of Santa Rosa and Sebastopol, an assortment of civic, business, and environmental organizations — plus enthusiastic dedicated citizens — have banded together to protect the Laguna from further defilement. A "State of the Laguna" conference report states that there exists "an immediate and compelling rationale for using federal funds to acquire lands within the Laguna de Santa Rosa as a National Wildlife Refuge." This statement reveals one of the fondest dreams of the many northern Californians who come to the Laguna de Santa Rosa to revel in its flora and its avifauna. It's an earnest hope that this dream will soon be fullfilled. In the meantime, by all means, come here and bird. You won't be disappointed.

Because of its varied habitats, and its many resident birds, opportunities for good counts are here all year long. Land birds you can expect to see include the Acorn and Nutall's Woodpeckers, Northern Flicker, Dark-eyed Junco, House Finch, White-crowned and Golden-crowned Sparrows, Bushtit, American Goldfinch, Northern Mockingbird, and Rufous-sided Towhee. As to the wetland areas, these harbour thousands of migratory waterfowl and many shorebirds as well. The Laguna is a good area for raptors too. Keep an eye out for the Burrowing Owl, Northern Harrier, and unusual species such as Bald Eagle and Peregrine Falcon.

Rare or endangered plant species of the Laguna include white sedge, Burke's goldfields, Sebastopol meadowfoam, many-flowered navarretia, and Hoover's semaphore grass.

At this writing, according to the *State of the Laguna* Conference booklet,

Northern Flicker

the only public access is along the Santa Rosa Creek Flood Control Channel. Pick this up where it crosses Willowside Road, 0.5 mile south of Guerneville Road. There are good walking paths along the channel, but you'll have to work your way around the fence. It's about 1.5 miles to the Laguna. However, bridges cross the Laguna both on Guerneville Road and Occidental Road, and access can be had from those. Just be sure to respect private property.

SONOMA COAST STATE BEACH, INCLUDING BODEGA HEAD

From the precipitous headland of historic Duncan's Landing — nicknamed Death Rock — to the smooth and gentle sands of Wright's Beach and Salmon Creek, the Sonoma State Beaches comprise a shoreline of jolting contradictions, great beauty, and wondrous birding. The shores teem with sandpipers, plovers, godwits, and Willets; loons call on the bay and sea; Ospreys circle overhead. The hills and cliffs are dotted with goldfinches and White-crowned Sparrows and alive with the sounds of their singing. A Peregrine Falcon is often seen wheeling about in the clear blue sky.

Of course, each of these beaches holds its special charm, but it's Bodega Head, declared a favorite birding location again and again, that wins the most laurels. Incredibly scenic and highly photographable, it's considered the prime north bay location from which to scope for pelagic species from the land.

Duncan's Landing offers excellent birding too, especially in the winter. Look for cormorants, grebes, Northern Fulmar, and shearwaters as they fly by the point, and scan the rocks near the parking lot for Black Turnstone. Or, if you're not content with birding the coast by land, book an offshore trip to the famous Cordell Banks, an area 28 miles from Bodega Head where the upwelling food supply lures high concentrations of pelagic birds. Expect species such as Northern Fulmar, Black-footed Albatross, and Pink-footed Shearwater. Charter boats are available at the nearby town of Bodega Bay.

Approximately 2 million people visit the Sonoma Coast State Beaches yearly — some to tidepool, some to whale watch, some to bird, and some to camp at Wright's Beach and Bodega Dunes.

The Sonoma Coast State Beaches are located along the coast from the Russian River to Bodega Head. All are on or near SH 1, except Bodega

Head. For Bodega Head take Bay Flat Road 0.5 mile north of the town of Bodega Bay, to the bottom of the hill, and follow Westshore Road around the bay to the Head.

BODEGA BAY, INCLUDING DORAN PARK

To effectively describe this beautiful section of Sonoma County would be practically impossible, even if the name "Bodega Bay" meant the same thing to every avid birder who speaks of it glowingly. As it happens, however, this is not the case: some people are referring only to the land (and sea) that lies within the city limits of the quaint fishing town of Bodega Bay, some just to the harbor on which it's situated, some to a set of interfacing habitats within a few miles radius of the town and harbor, including not only the lean peninsula on which there rests a regional park called Doran Beach, but the verdant agricultural lands nearby. Suffice it to say that, however it's perceived, this is incredibly scenic country, literally bedecked with birds.

If it's pelagic species you yearn to see — birds as enticing as Northern Fulmar, Black-footed Albatross, Pink-footed Shearwater, and Ashy Storm-Petrel — try an unforgettable tour of the Cordell Banks aboard one of the charter boats available at the harbor.

But rest assured there's plenty of excitement here for the landlubber too. Consider, for example, all these unusual species sighted in and around Bodega Bay: Blackburnian Warbler, Buff-breasted Sandpiper, American Redstart, Lesser Golden-Plover, Palm Warbler, Northern Waterthrush, and the very lovely Snow Bunting.

Whichever popular local vantage point you choose, you're apt to be richly rewarded. Expect to sight Pigeon Guillemot, Common Murre, or Heermann's Gull from the western end of Doran Park. From the outer beach, scope for water birds, loons, scoters, grebes, and gulls. At the tidal pond at the park's entrance, keep an eye out for American Avocet, phalaropes, Pectoral Sandpiper, and Lesser Yellowlegs.

In the mudflats, look for Black-bellied Plover, Black and Ruddy Turnstones, Willet, Marbled Godwit, and the flashy Snowy Plover, which dedicated Sonoma County birder Betty Burridge sees as a special species of Bodega Bay.

All around the lagoon birding is excellent almost all year long, especially in fall when the migrating shorebirds come flying in. Rails, Sora, Common

Snipe, and Marsh Wren are all readily seen in the marshy areas.

This is a good place to watch for other animals too. Seals are often sighted in the harbor, sometimes right in the marina area. And Monarch butterflies gather in a cypress grove on SH 1, just north of town.

Doran Beach Regional Park is a year-round recreational area with 138 campsites, for which reservations are available on a first-come, first-served basis. There is also overnight camping at Wright's Beach and Bodega Dunes. Another recreational area, Westside Regional park, offers day use facilities.

SH 1 skirts the east side of the bay, but viewing from its vantage points is not spectacular. Two restaurants, Lucas Wharf and The Tides, are both located on working docks and offer excellent birding.

To reach Doran Park and the south end of the harbor, go south of the town about 0.5 mile on SH 1 and watch for the signs.

To get to the harbor proper, go north of the town about 0.5 mile and take Bay Flat Road to the bottom of the hill and bear right. It turns into Westshore Road, which skirts the north and west sides of the harbor and has several excellent places to pull off.

POINT REYES NATIONAL SEASHORE

When Sir Francis Drake beached the *Golden Hinde* on this land some 41 years before the Pilgrims arrived at Plymouth Rock, he set foot on one of the premier birding spots of the New World.

A geologically fascinating land mass that's moving north along the San Andreas fault as the rest of the continent moves west and south, Point Reyes consists of more than 100 square miles jutting prominently into the Pacific Ocean. It's this feature, along with pristine, varied, plentiful habitat, that makes Point Reyes so attractive to birds and birders.

During September and October, the great flocks of land birds come down through the fog and the darkness and look for the nearest land, and there, conveniently, is Point Reyes. Add to this the fact that the woodland habitats these birds are looking for are separate and distinct, one from the other, and you have not only great numbers of birds, but predictable, accessible places to find them.

Vagrants from all over (lost birds blown off course by storms, or possibly suffering from a kind of migration dyslexia, as the "mirror-image misorientation" theory submits) proliferate here, especially in the fall, and to a

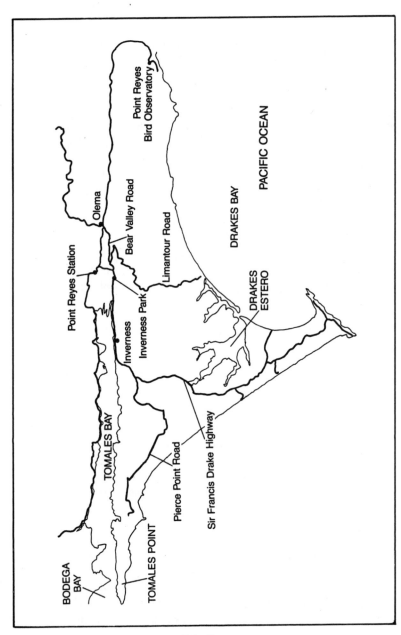

Point Reyes

lesser extent in spring. According to Dave Shuford, an authority on California birding associated with Point Reyes Bird Observatory, you can expect to see at least one or two eastern vagrants every day during the season. Some days there are 19 or 20 species of warblers — truly a phenomenal count for the West Coast.

And, of course, the second and entirely separate aspect of Point Reyes is its concentration of seabirds and shorebirds: winter visitors and year-round residents alike. It's superb too for wintering raptors, and during fall raptor migrations. With 430 recorded species, Point Reyes is considered the number one birding spot in California.

Bear Valley/Fivebrooks. A birder unfamiliar with the area will want to stop first at the Visitor Center and Park Headquarters in Bear Valley, not only to pick up information on the area, but also to check out the displays. Birding is good right here at the center: the picnic area, the creek, Earthquake Trail, and some short loop trails will produce a good count of the forest and grassland birds.

South of the Visitor Center about 4 miles is the Fivebrooks Trail. The park's meadowland and forest habitats are easily accessible, as well as a pond known for ducks, herons, coots, and rails.

Limantour Road/Estero. Slightly more than a mile north of the Visitor Center, Limantour Road takes off to the west. Check out the woodlands in the first half-mile, and pull off at the Sky Trail parking lot to look over Inverness Ridge. Keep your eye out for raptors, including Osprey, which nest on the ridge. The road then works its way down ridges and valleys to a parking lot at Limantour Beach, on Drake's Bay, which offers easy access to several excellent areas. A pond to the south promises bitterns and rails. Then there's a trail to the west that goes along Limantour Spit, with the shorebirds and seabirds on the side towards the bay, and herons, egrets, ducks, geese, grebes, loons, terns, and gulls around the saltwater marshes of the estero. Also from the parking lot, Muddy Hollow Trail goes between a couple of ponds to a bluff which gives yet another view of the estero, and a chance to check out the coastal scrub on the ridges.

Outer Point Reyes. Sir Francis Drake Boulevard runs north from the junction with Bear Valley Road, through the picturesque town of Inverness, and then swings west over the ridge and through several miles of grassland

Osprey

out to the point and the lighthouse. Pay particular attention to the clumps of trees along this drive — they offer the best chances of spotting vagrants. There's a visitor center at Drakes Beach, a trail along the beach to Drakes Estero, and another visitor center at the lighthouse. Side roads go to Chimney Rock, a point where you can scan the entire bay, with access to some fishing docks and a trail that goes to the rock; to The Great Beach (on the ocean side); to the oyster farm on Schooner Bay; to the Estero Trailhead, which offers views of both esteros from the bluffs above; and to Mount Vision Overlook, with its magnificent vista of the whole panorama of Point Reyes.

To curious individuals who'd like to learn more about this beautiful National Seashore, Park Interpreter Don L. Neubacher recommends the book, *Natural History of Point Reyes Peninsula*, by Jules Evens, which can be purchased at the visitor center. Available there also is a comprehensive bird list, *Field Checklist of Birds, Point Reyes National Seashore*.

The following is a partial list of the species regularly sighted here: Double-crested, Brandt's and Pelagic Cormorants, Northern Harrier, Black-shouldered Kite, Red-shouldered Hawk, Black Rail, Black Oystercatcher, Snowy Plover, Cassin's and Rhinoceros Auklets, Band-tailed Pigeon, Horned and Eared Grebes, Black-crowned Night-Heron, American Wigeon, Greater and Lesser Scaups, Bufflehead, Marbled Godwit, Black Turnstone, Glaucous-winged Gull, Common Murre, Great Horned Owl, Tricolored Blackbird, Purple Finch, and a variety of owls.

Birds rare to the area but sighted at Point Reyes include Golden Eagle, Spotted Owl, Poorwill, Ashy Storm-Petrel, Blue-winged Teal, Clapper Rail, Northern Pygmy-Owl, American Redstart, MacGillivray's, Black-and-white, and Tennessee Warblers, and Sage Sparrow.

Among other species casual or accidental to Point Reyes are Least Bittern, Tufted Duck, Northern Goshawk, Solitary Sandpiper, Semipalmated Sandpiper, Long-tailed Jaeger, South Polar Skua, Common Tern, Black Tern, Northern Waterthrush, Hooded Warbler, Northern Parula, Cape May Warbler, Ovenbird, and Virginia's Warbler.

A good source of comprehensive species lists for Point Reyes and other bay area locations, and one that we highly recommend, is Jean Richmond's excellent book, *Birding Northern California*, published by the Mt. Diablo Audubon Society.

The Point Reyes Lighthouse area is one of the best places in the state to watch for whales. The high granite cliffs of the Point Reyes Headlands at the end of Sir Francis Drake Highway are home to Sea Lions. There are Tule Elk here too, and Fallow Deer imported from the Mediterranean. Point Reyes is also an excellent place for tidepooling.

Take Sir Francis Drake Boulevard where it exits from US 101 in Larkspur and follow it through some very pretty Marin County countryside to the town of Olema, where it joins SH 1. Go north a couple of blocks to Bear Valley Road, which goes to the park headquarters and visitor center.

Coming from the south, you can get SH 1 at the first Mill Valley exit from US 101, and follow it up and over Mount Tamalpais and along the coast to Olema.

From the north, take D Street in Petaluma (off Petaluma Blvd. South),

which turns into Petaluma-Point Reyes Road. Again, some delightful countryside, and you might want to stop at the Cheese Factory for a wine and
cheese lunch. At Point Reyes Station, take SH 1 south to Bear Valley Road.

Tomales Bay/Northern Point Reyes

Tomales Bay is a major staging area for migrating birds, a winter home
for many species, and year-round residence for throngs of others, but it's
not always easy to get close-up views here. The bay extends 16 miles
south from Bodega Bay, between the mainland and the Point Reyes peninsula, but depending on the tides, a good portion of that is mud flats. Lots
of birds, but not an abundance of good vantage points from which to see
them. However, there are several pulloff points from SH 1 along the east
side of the bay, and Shield's Marsh near the Inverness Motel, Tomales
Bay State Park on the west side, and Tomales Point.

To bird from Tomales Point requires a 3 mile hike, one way, from the
end of Pierce Point Road. All along the hills and grasslands on the way
the birding is good, and from the point itself truly spectacular. On the
ocean side is Bird Rock, which is good for sighting Brown and American
White Pelicans, and nesting Black Oystercatchers, cormorants, etc. This
is also the northernmost breeding spot for the Ashy Storm-Petrel, but it's
not likely you'll see one since they only come in to their burrows at night.

According to Allen Fish, Director of the Golden Gate Raptor Observatory, this area is superb for wintering raptors, and also good for fall
migrators.

Tomales Bay State Park. Tomales Bay State Park is a popular recreational
area located on land that was once the home of the Miwok Indians. Where
the natives built their houses, preserved their berries, and raised their
families, latter-day Californians come to clam, picnic, boat, hike, and
swim. So too come birders — most of them hoping to lay eyes upon the
park's frequently-sighted, resident Spotted Owls.

Unfortunately, the last time we visited this park one warm midday in
late June, we didn't spot a single one of these rare and fascinating raptors.
However, on a lovely loop walk along Heart's Desire Beach we did count
fifteen species of birds in just twice that many minutes. Among these were
American White Pelican, Dark-eyed Junco, Lazuli Bunting, Purple Finch,

Yellow Warbler, and Acorn Woodpecker.

Tomales Bay State Park is located on Pierce Point Road on the way to Tomales Point.

Abbott's Lagoon and Pierce Point Road. Further along on Pierce Point Road you'll come to a parking lot for Abbott's Lagoon, which is just an excellent birding location in itself. A hike is also required here — this time a 3 mile round-trip.

Abbott's is a double lagoon, and the trail goes between the two lobes. There should be a lot of raptor activity over the grasslands on the way to the bluff, and keep an eye out for Burrowing Owl, Horned Lark, Loggerhead Shrike, and gulls, ducks, and a variety of sparrows.

The lagoons themselves will provide a good showing of winter ducks, water birds, gulls, herons, terns, and shorebirds. Continue on to the ocean beach for more gulls and terns, loons, cormorants, ducks, and alcids.

Back up on Pierce Point Road, the trails to Kehoe Beach and McClure's Beach should also be explored. Clumps of trees along here (as anywhere on the peninsula,) offer good opportunities to spot the vagrants that Point Reyes is famous for. Also, the marshy area near Kehoe Beach is reportedly a good place for seeing rails and snipe.

SH 1 parallels the bay from Walker Creek (3 miles from the mouth of the bay) to Point Reyes Station. Catch SH 1 either at Valley Ford out of Sebastopol, or at Tomales out of Petaluma. Stops at either of these towns are fun, as is Marshall, further down the line. Follow SH 1 south, birding the bay along the way, through Point Reyes Station to Sir Francis Drake Blvd. Turn right, and follow the boulevard along the west side of the bay, through the town of Inverness, and up over the hill to where Pierce Point Road heads north.

White House Pool

A cooperative project of Marin County, the Wildlife Conservation Board, and the Department of Fish and Game, this sylvan little park is memorable for its footbridge, winding paths, berry bramble, and wooden benches where one can stop and rest a while and listen to the birdsong. It's strictly a day use park. But it's located close to a number of better known birding spots, including Bolinas Lagoon, Tomales Bay, and Point Reyes National

Seashore, and is an excellent birding locale in its own right.

Seen here are Great Blue Heron, Green-backed Heron, Belted Kingfisher, Black Phoebe, Wrentit, Song Sparrow, and sometimes, unusual and unexpected species. A Brown Shrike, a rarity in northern California, has been seen here at White House Pool.

From SH 1 just south of Point Reyes Station, turn west on Sir Francis Drake Boulevard for 0.5 mile, and watch for the parking lot entrance on your right.

Point Reyes Bird Observatory

You'll never find a better way to get close looks at land birds than at Point Reyes Bird Observatory. Here ornithologists, interns, and volunteers run a year-round netting and banding operation in conjunction with their land bird population studies.

Visitors are encouraged at the observatory any time. The center is open 7 days a week, year-round. Netting and banding take place 6 hours a day, beginning 15 minutes after sunrise, every day from April through Thanksgiving; and on Wednesday, Saturday, and Sunday during the winter.

Since activity generally slows down as the day progresses, early morning is the best time to observe the banding. Warblers, finches, sparrows, flycatchers, and swallows are often netted, and occasionally raptors as well.

Point Reyes Bird Observatory is a member-supported, non-profit organization, dedicated to research, conservation, and education. In addition to the Landbird Station, there are projects going on in San Francisco Bay and the Farallon Islands, and a "Natural Excursions" program offers birding trips all over the world.

The visitor center is 3 miles north of Bolinas, on Mesa Road. From SH 1, just north of Bolinas Lagoon, take the Olema-Bolinas Road toward Bolinas, and go 1 mile to Mesa Road. The address is 4990 Shoreline Highway, Stinson Beach, CA 94970. Phone (415) 868-1221 for the office, or 868-0655 for the visitor center.

BOLINAS LAGOON AND AUDUBON CANYON RANCH

A haven of mud flats, tidal waters, cord grass and pickleweed, willow and eucalyptus, conifers and chaparral, the Bolinas bay area is one of the prime birding spots of northern California.

Good vantage points are easily accessible. The lagoon is triangular and SH 1 runs the full length of the eastern side, a good 4 miles, between the water and the hills. Pull-offs along the highway offer great views of shorebirds, and an abundance of water birds, especially in the winter. Willow clumps at the north end are a favorite haunt of warblers, vireos, kinglets, and sparrows. A path through the eucalyptus grove on the north side leads through a marsh to the lagoon, with great birding all the way. Short hikes up the hills to the east offer birds of chaparral and woodland habitat.

The area is also the home of Audubon Canyon Ranch, a non-profit corporation sponsored by Golden Gate, Sequoia, and Marin Audubon Societies, which has been designated a Registered National Natural Landmark by the Department of the Interior and the National Park Service. The Ranch is open to the public free of charge on weekends and holidays from early March through the Fourth of July, when a visit here is truly unforgettable. Along with all the birding opportunities of the mixed woods and canyon, the ranch has a major heron and egret rookery, with a unique overlook area that enables the birder to watch the nesting activities from above.

Another unique feature of this area is the colony of Osprey nearby; this is one of the major concentrations of this bird in California, and certainly the southernmost. The primary nesting area is at Kent Lake, just over the first ridge to the east, off the Bolinas-Fairfax Road. The lake is fairly difficult to get to, however, and the best viewing is at the lagoon itself, the primary feeding ground for the colony. It's not unusual to see 5 or 10 birds there at the same time during the spring and early summer. There's also a nesting area on an old duck blind in Tomales Bay, 15 miles to the north.

Birds you can expect to see here at Bolinas Lagoon, Audubon Canyon Ranch, and the vicinity include great numbers of water birds and shorebirds, rails, Osprey, cormorants, Band-tailed Pigeon, Peregrine Falcon, Merlin, herons, egrets, Canada Goose, Wrentit, Lazuli Bunting, Purple Finch, White-crowned and Fox Sparrows, Steller's and Scrub Jays, American Crow, and Downy and Nuttall's Woodpeckers. In the spring and summer expect to see a large variety of warblers. In September and October look for the many unusual vagrants for which this area is widely known.

Other attractions of Bolinas Bay are Harbor Seals and Monarch butterflies. The seals are readily visible at a protected pupping area in the lagoon.

The Monarch butterflies can be found clustered in the Eucalyptus trees at the Audubon Monarch Butterfly Grove near the intersection of Terrace and Ocean Avenues.

To reach Bolinas Bay from San Francisco, take US 101 to SH 1 (the first Mill Valley exit) and go over Mount Tamalpais and through Stinson Beach to the lagoon. Or take Sir Francis Drake Boulevard westbound from US 101 in Larkspur to its junction with SH 1 in Olema, and turn south. From the north, find "D" Street, off of Petaluma Boulevard South in Petaluma, which turns into the Petaluma-Point Reyes Road; pick up SH 1 at Point Reyes Station, and proceed south about 10 miles.

SAMUEL P. TAYLOR STATE PARK

This 2,800-acre park, one of the first areas in the United States to feature outdoor camping as a form of recreation, has all of the following attractions: lush, cool woodlands; ferny redwood groves; a riot of spring wildflowers; good seasonal fishing in Old Paper Mill Creek; 63 campsites nestled in the redwood groves; restrooms with hot showers; a special camping area for backpackers and cyclists; an equestrian campsite complete with corral, hitching racks, and water troughs for the horses; interesting wildlife and a fair share of birds, including Spotted Owl, Lesser Goldfinch, Steller's Jay, and Varied Thrush.

From US 101 in Larkspur, take Sir Francis Drake Boulevard to the west through 12 miles of Marin County countryside to the park headquarters. From SH 1, catch Sir Francis Drake Boulevard in Olema, and go 4 miles to the east.

MOUNT TAMALPAIS STATE PARK

If it weren't for the view of San Francisco from the top of Mt. Tamalpais, a visitor here might feel far removed from civilization and all its trappings, but the fact is, the city is clearly visible, a beautiful sight to see. Equally lovely are other views from the top of the mountain. On a clear day you can see the Great Central Valley, the Sierra Nevada, and the Cascade Ranges.

Tamalpais has all this and more to offer: 42 miles of footpaths that are part of a 200-mile network of trails; redwood groves in deep, shady canyons; vast grasslands; a wide variety of trees including Douglas firs, California laurel, redwood, and tanbark oak; walk-in campsites for tenters; a group camping area that can accommodate 100 people; 10 rustic cabins on a coastal bluff overlooking the Pacific Ocean.

Reservations for the cabins must be made by mail. Write to the Reservations Office, Department of Parks and Recreation, P.O. Box 2390, Sacramento, CA 92138-5705. To reserve walk-in campsites call 1-800-444-PARK.

Because of its various habitats, Tamalpais is visited by many of the 415 species found in Marin County. Expect to see Red-breasted Sapsucker, White-crowned Sparrow, Band-tailed Pigeon, Great Horned Owl, Vaux's Swift, California Quail, Cooper's, and Red-shouldered Hawks, Acorn Woodpecker, and a variety of swallows and flycatchers. This is a great place for sighting the Blue-gray Gnatcatcher.

From US 101, take SH 1 at the Mill Valley exit. After 3 miles, turn right on Panoramic Highway, and go 5 miles to the park headquarters. Coming south on SH 1, you can pick up Panoramic Highway in Stinson Beach.

MUIR WOODS NATIONAL MONUMENT

The words of its namesake, the famous naturalist John Muir, speak for this beautiful Marin County woods better than we can: "This is the best tree lover's monument that could be found in all the forests of all the world."

The park boasts 560 acres of peerless beauty; a 1,000-year-old tree; other specimens ranging in age between 500 and 800 years; a variety of ferns, mushrooms, and fungi; fields of primitive horsetail, once a useful herb of the California Indians; trails that connect with those in neighboring Mt. Tamalpais State Park; some paved paths accessible to wheelchairs; 6 miles of walking trails; a visitor center and gift shop.

The number of bird species dwelling right in the thick of a redwood forest is comparatively small. The reason is simple: redwood sap repels insects, which means, of course, that this habitat doesn't invite the presence of large concentrations of insect-eating species. Furthermore, the birds who do dwell here are not easily sighted. It's hard to see birds in tall trees and dark shadows.

Predictably enough, the most conspicuous species here is the Steller's Jay. Also frequently seen are Song Sparrow, and Pacific Slope Flycatcher. Fairly common are California Quail, Band-tailed Pigeon, Dark-eyed Junco,

White-crowned Sparrow, and Great Horned and Spotted Owls.

Muir Woods National Monument is located 12 miles north of the Golden Gate Bridge. Take SH 1 at the first Mill Valley exit from US 101, go 3 miles to Panoramic Highway, go right 1 mile to Muir Woods Road, and left another mile to the Visitor Center.

MARIN HEADLANDS

Hawk Hill

You're faced with a choice of tantalizing destinations once you've turned onto the road that's marked "Marin Headlands." A part of the Golden Gate National Recreation Area, this is beautiful country whichever way you turn, but if you're here to see raptors you'll want to follow the road up to the heights of Marin Headlands. You'll want to seek that point where the views of bay and sea and bridge and city are peerless, where many thousands of camera-toting tourists come yearly to capture the Golden Gate on film.

If you are here betweeen late August and January, you can count raptors until your heart's content. Allen Fish, director of the Golden Gate Raptor Observatory, states, "One of the interesting things about the raptor migration here is that it covers a very long period. It starts in August and extends well into December. We have many Red-tailed Hawks, and often Rough-legged Hawks and Peregrine Falcons that are still migrating right up through mid-December."

As Fish explains it, the high concentration of raptors here is largely due to geographic conditions. "Bald Eagles, Osprey, and Peregrine Falcons are semi-aquatic in their interests," he states, "but otherwise hawks are primarily land-based birds and, for the most part, will veer away from water, especially in migration when they're trying to economize (their energy) as much as possible. So what you have to imagine is that every hawk who winds up somewhere in Sonoma County with a predilection to move south on its migration could very easily get funneled into the Marin peninsula."

Fish offers yet another reason for the presence of raptors over the headlands: "air movements here — updrafts and thermals — provide another inspiraton for hawks to stay along the land mass."

Fish is assisted in his work by approximately 150 dedicated volunteers. One of these, retired school teacher Carter Faust, whose record-keeping prowess is indispensable, leads a weekly bird walk called "Wednesday for the Birds." Faust can be reached by calling (415) 453-2899.

Late August through mid-December is the best time for birding Hawk Hill.

Nineteen species of diurnal raptors are regularly seen in the course of a season, and a 20th species, the Mississippi Kite, was added to the count in 1976. Birds of prey aren't the only migrating birds to be sighted from this vantage point, however. Among other species seen are Band-tailed Pigeons, Blue-gray Gnatcatchers, Lewis' Woodpeckers, and White-throated, Vaux's, and Black Swifts.

For a more thorough list of other species seen here at the Marin Headlands see "Fort Cronkhite/Rodeo Lagoon."

Going south on US 101, take the last exit before the Golden Gate Bridge. Heading north from San Francisco, take the Sausalito exit, then take the first left back under the freeway. It's a winding 4 miles to the top, but excellent roads and majestic scenery all the way.

Fort Cronkhite/Rodeo Lagoon

According to Allen Fish, director of the Golden Gate Raptor Observatory, bay area residents have been birding this area for years. "Interestingly enough," he says, "From the 1890's to the 1930's the Golden Gate Audubon Society ran semi-annual excursions out here. You have to imagine men in knickers and the women in their beautiful dresses. They would take a ferry to Fort Baker near Sausalito, and then they would walk across the hills out to Point Bonita and bird the whole way . . ."

Of the bay area nature lovers who carry on the tradition of birding these headlands, many attend a weekly bird walk, a group event that's come to be known as "Wednesday for the Birds." Two of the group's recent bird lists (summer and winter) serve as ample testimony to the fact that birding is still excellent here all year round. Fifty-nine species were sighted on January 25, 1989, on a three-hour bird walk. These included Red-throated Loon, 5 species of grebe, Brown and American White Pelicans, Double-crested, Brandt's, and Pelagic Cormorants, Fox, Song, Golden-crowned, and White-crowned Sparrows, House Finch, American Bittern, Great Blue Heron, Bufflehead, Common Goldeneye, Red-breasted Merganser, and Wrentit. In three-and-a-half hours, on July 12th of the same year, 61 species were counted, including Brown Pelican, Brandt's and Pelagic

Cormorants, Great Blue Heron, Mallard, Ruddy Duck, Turkey Vulture, Red-tailed Hawk, California Quail, Common Yellowthroat, Black-headed Grosbeak, Lazuli Bunting, Purple Finch, and American Goldfinch. Unusual sightings include Indigo Bunting, Rose-breasted Grosbeak, Yellow-headed Blackbird, and Harlequin Duck.

Anyone wishing to inquire about the Wednesday morning bird walks at the Marin Headlands may call the group leader, Carter Faust, at (415) 453-2899.

Going south on US 101, take the last exit before the Golden Gate Bridge. From San Francisco, take the Sausalito exit, then the first left back under the freeway, and head up the hill. After a mile, the road to Fort Cronkhite is well marked on the right.

CHINA CAMP STATE PARK

Best known for its interesting past and its fascinating old Chinese village, which dates back to Goldrush days, China Camp has more to offer visitors than a thought-provoking glimpse into yesterday.

The following are just a few of the park's notable features: 1,640 scenic and unspoiled acres in a part of Marin County where undeveloped land is a rarity indeed; excellent trails along the San Pablo Ridge where hikers can scan not only the San Pablo Bay but the East Bay Hills, Angel Island, Mt. Diablo, the San Francisco Peninsula and Mt. Tamalpais; biking, fishing, swimming, wading, and windsurfing; many more bright and fog-free days (an average of 200 per year) than most bay area locales; opportunities for good landscape photography; primitive campsites with picnic tables, fire rings, and food lockers; attractive day use areas with lawn, picnic tables, barbecues, and running water; a small museum, open on weekends; a charming old-fashioned concession stand, open on weekends and run by Frank Quan, the single resident of this remarkable village, who just happens to be a descendent of one of the village's original settlers.

Anyone wishing to reserve the large group day use facility at the park should do so in advance by calling the Marin District Office at (415) 456-1286.

Birds seen here include Pileated Woodpeckers, Osprey, Great and Snowy Egrets, Great Blue Heron, Black-necked Stilt, and many other shore and water birds including, occasionally, the elusive, seldom-seen California Clapper Rail, *Rallus longirostris obsoletus*, listed as an endangered species federally as well as in California.

Take the San Pedro Road exit from US 101 at the Marin County Civic Center, which has the distinction of being the last building designed by Frank Lloyd Wright. From the civic center it's about 5 miles east to the park headquarters.

UPPER SAN PABLO BAY AREA

Petaluma Marsh

This marsh (which is not the "official" Petaluma Marsh on the west side of the river) is located on city-owned property in the confines of the town of Petaluma. This is an excellent place to observe many species in short order. In just two hours, for instance, on a hot midday in July and birding only a small section of the two-mile loop road that circles the marshland, we listed 31 different species. These included grebes, sandpipers, Green-backed Heron, American Avocet, Black-necked Stilt, Marsh Wren, Killdeer, Canada Goose, Western Meadowlark, Willet, Snowy Egret, Song Sparrow, Rufous-sided and California Towhees, Northern Harrier, and Black-shouldered Kite.

Take Lakeville Highway (SH 116) east from US 101 to the traffic light at South McDowell Boulevard. Turn right, go to Cader Lane, turn right again, and the gate is right there.

San Pablo Bay National Wildlife Refuge, Tubbs Island

The best way to observe the wonders of this bayland refuge is from the vantage point of its waterways, but since not all birders are boaters, it's good to know that a walk down the levee toward lower Tubbs Island runs a close second when it comes to observing the birds at San Pablo Bay National Wildlife Refuge.

This popular birding spot offers excellent shorebird and water bird sightings, great opportunities for wildlife observation and photography, and beautiful views of the bay. The shoreline is ever-changing, moving forward and receding, first covering, then exposing the vast mud flats and marshes beloved to so many species.

Boating is permitted in the open water of San Pablo Bay. The public

Pied-billed Grebe (immature)

launching ramp is on the west bank of the Petaluma River, beneath the SH 37 bridge.

For more information about this refuge write: San Francisco Bay National Wildlife Refuge, Post Office Box 524, Newark, CA 94560-0524.

Although fall and winter are unquestionably the best time to come birding here, it should be noted that many species are common to San Pablo and San Francisco Bay National Wildlife Refuges year-round. Among these are Pied-billed Grebe, American White Pelican, Great Blue Heron, Great and Snowy Egrets, Black-crowned Night-Heron, Black-shouldered Kite, Northern Harrier, Ring-necked Pheasant, Barn Owl and many others, including the endangered California Clapper Rail.

A bird checklist, *Birds of San Francisco Bay and San Pablo Bay National Wildlife Refuges*, which lists 228 species and 56 accidentals, is available at the San Francisco Bay National Wildlife Refuge visitor center.

From the traffic light at the intersection of SH 37 and SH 121, go east on 37 about one city block, cross Friday Creek, and the parking area is right there. Be prepared — it's a 3 mile hike to the bay.

White Slough, Solano County

Birders coming from or going to Tubbs Island or San Pablo National Wildlife Area frequently stop by this prime Vallejo birding spot, especially in the fall or winter when the 820 acres of wetland are teeming with bird life. Be careful if you choose to bird this locale from the heavily-travelled Marine World Parkway rather than seeking out other access points. Park well off the shoulder. Other good vantage points are located as follows: behind Standard Brands and K Mart parking lots, reached via Redwood Street; behind the Orchard Supply parking lot, at SH 29 and 37; the Self Service Furniture parking lot, reached via Sonoma Boulevard; at the end of Sereno Drive and Sonoma Boulevard.

The last time we stopped by here, we sighted 15 species in one sweeping glance. These included 24 Willets, countless Marbled Godwits, 15 American White Pelicans, 12 Caspian Terns, 35 Forster's Terns, countless Long-billed Dowitchers, 12 grebes, 25 American Coots, 12 Common Moorhens, a female Ruddy Duck with young, an American Avocet, 12 Black-necked Stilts, 24 Double-crested Cormorants.

Other species found here are Tundra Swan, Golden Eagle, Black Rail, Clapper Rail, Black-shouldered Kite, and Least Tern. Forster's Tern and Black-necked Stilt nest in the area.

White Slough is located in the town of Vallejo, just to the west of the intersection of SH 37 and 29. It extends along both sides of SH 37.

American Canyon Road

Northeast of White Slough on American Canyon Road is a rock quarry that provides year-round habitat for Golden Eagles. The eagles nest here, but can be seen best in fall and winter.

The rock quarry and its driveway are private property. Do not enter without permission and do not block the gate.

This is considered essentially a one-species site, but there are, of course, other birds to be seen along American Canyon Road. Ferruginous Hawks are here in the winter, and the surrounding hills are visited by Western Meadowlark, California Quail, American and Lesser Goldfinches, House Finch, and other species at home in the grassy Napa County hills.

From I-80 north of Vallejo, take the American Canyon Road exit and go west 1.7 miles. From SH 29, go east on American Canyon Road 1.2 miles. The quarry entrance is on the north side of the road.

Benicia State Recreation Area

Notable for its mud flats, bay shore, slough, grassland, and saltwater and freshwater marsh habitats, this prime parkland is located on the Carquinez Strait. It's here, at Dillon Point, that the waters of the San Francisco Bay complex are at their narrowest. To stand by the point where the wedded flow of the San Joaquin and Sacramento Rivers comes rushing through on the way to the sea, is to stand in awe.

The California Black Rail, no bigger than a sparrow, and listed by the Department of Fish and Game as a threatened bird in California, is a confirmed breeder and year-round resident here. Other species commonly sighted are Pied-billed and Western Grebes, Brown Pelican, Great Blue Heron, Great and Snowy Egrets, Canvasback, Surf Scoter, Common Goldeneye, Ruddy Duck, Black-shouldered Kite, Ring-necked Pheasant, Willet, Marbled Godwit, Least Sandpiper, Red-winged Blackbird, House Finch, Lesser and American Goldfinches, and Song, Golden-crowned, and White-crowned Sparrows.

Also seen here, though not so commonly, are Horned and Eared Grebes, American White Pelican, American Bittern, Canada Goose, Green-winged Teal, Northern Pintail, Cinnamon Teal, Gadwall, and American Wigeon.

Confirmed breeders at the park include Mallard, Northern Harrier, Red-tailed Hawk, Sora, Black, Clapper, and Virginia Rails, Killdeer, Mourning Dove, Great Horned Owl, Western Kingbird, Barn Swallow, and Song Sparrow. Look for Red-winged Blackbirds in the cattail marshes, Marsh Wrens along the marsh-mud flat trail, and ducks, gulls, terns, grebes, American Avocets and sandpipers on the mudflats. Expect a high population of Anna's and Allen's Hummingbirds as well. It's not unusual to sight 30 to 60 while walking along the trail of this remarkable wetland park.

Also seen at Benicia State Recreation Area are Raccoons, Striped Skunks, Norway Rats, California Voles, shrews, Muskrats, Botta Pocket Gophers, Salt-marsh Harvest Mice, and California Ground Squirrels.

Take the Columbus Parkway exit from I-780, 2 miles east of the junction with I-80. Turn on Rose Drive towards the marsh and continue to the main gate.

INLAND NAPA AND SOLANO COUNTIES

Skyline Wilderness Park

Skyline Wilderness features a creekside group picnic area that can accommodate 200 people; fishing for catfish and bass; 15 miles of hiking and riding trails; an archery range; superlative views of the Napa Valley with its beautiful vineyards; excellent opportunities for bird and wildlife photography.

In spring, this park is a riot of wildflowers including Fremont's camas, Indian warrior, mariposa lily, baby blue eyes, and many other species. Spring is also the season when the birding is best, for it's then that the Violet-Green Swallows and the Hutton's Vireos are nesting and the park abounds with warblers.

Other birds seen here include Lesser and American Goldfinches, Wild Turkey, Scrub Jay, California Quail, Pileated Woodpecker, Great Egret, Purple Finch, Black Phoebe, Nuttall's Woodpecker, Anna's Hummingbird, Black-headed Grosbeak, and Acorn Woodpecker.

A Black Bear has been sighted here and also, a Bobcat. Other mammals seen in or near the park include foxes, skunks, squirrels, and a variety of rodents.

Take SH 121 or SH 221 to the intersection of Soscol and Imola Avenues at the south end of the city of Napa. When you reach Napa State Hospital on the right-hand side, go east on Imola one mile.

Napa River Ecological Reserve

Visitors birding this Napa County reserve can walk a path on the west side of the river or take the loop trail that begins at the footbridge near the confluence of Napa River and Conn Creek. Whichever path you take, your bird count will likely be sizable, especially if you come in spring when up to 60 species are nesting here. Conspicuous among these breeding birds are Yellow-breasted Chats, as many as ten pairs of which may rear their young at the reserve during any given year.

Other birds seen here include Western Bluebird, Lesser and American Goldfinches, House Finch, White-crowned and Golden-crowned Sparrows, and Ruby-crowned Kinglet.

While in the area, you might want to visit some of the fine wineries Napa Valley is known for. Combining wine-tasting with bird-watching has resulted in some rare and colorful sightings, but this probably depends more on the wine than the birds. While you're in Yountville, you might check out the shops in Vintage 1890. Dinner at the French Laundry is always a delight, but you might have to wait months for reservations.

This reserve, which is operated by the Department of Fish and Game, lies north of the Napa River bridge on the Yountville Cross Road.

Bothe-Napa Valley State Park

This park's location in the heart of the beautiful Napa Valley renders it attractive to visitors who happen to be either history buffs or wine bibbers as well as birders. From tree-lined roadways to fine old wineries, the area's attractions are many, and the park has a swimming pool, visitor center, gift shop, specimen exhibits, 5 fine hiking trails, and 50 family campsites, 10 of which are for tent camping only, with one reserved for hikers and cyclists. Each of these is equipped with a table, cupboard, and barbecue stove. A group campsite located on a wooded hillside just above the picnic area accommodates up to 30 people. Restrooms have laundry basins, drinking fountains, wastewater drains, and hot showers. A sanitation station is near the park entrance.

Species of special interest sighted here are Spotted Owl, Pileated, Acorn, Downy, Nuttall's and Hairy Woodpeckers, Northern Flicker, Black-throated Gray, Wilson's, and Orange-crowned Warblers, Solitary, Warbling, and Hutton's Vireos, Dark-eyed Junco, and Plain Titmouse.

Hike 2 miles up Ritchey Canyon to look for the Spotted Owl; look for nesting woodpeckers along the first mile of your hike; seek Solitary Vireos in the lower canyon, Warbling Vireos in the upper, Hutton's Vireos in the oak woods.

Also seen here — and, notably, not just in the park's fine specimen museum — are Gray Foxes, Black-tailed Deer, a variety of rodents, and even an occasional Bobcat.

Located approximately halfway between the towns of St. Helena and Calistoga, the park may be entered at the junction of Highway 29 and Larkmead Lane.

Robert Louis Stevenson State Park

Just as Stevenson memorialized this lush area of northern California, the area has done him honor with this 3,000-acre state park that lies on the upper slopes of the beautiful Mt. St. Helena. Here tourists come to see the superlative scenery that so completely stole the heart of this romantic genius, a feat best accomplished via an enticing trail that leads to the summit of 4,343-foot Mt. St. Helena. Here you'll find a breathtaking panoramic view and a good place to scan the skies for raptors.

The Peregrine Falcon is a year-round resident at the park. Other birds are Purple Martin, Mountain Quail, Common Poorwill, Dusky Flycatcher, Canyon Wren, Prairie Falcon, White-throated Swift, and the soft grey Townsend's Solitaire whose song alone is lure enough to bring any birder to Robert Louis Stevenson State Park.

Peregrine Falcons can be seen all year, Townsend's Solitaires in the fall and winter, and Dusky Flycatchers in the breeding season. Purple Martins are known to have nested here too.

To reach Robert Louis Stevenson State Park follow Highway 29 approximately 7 miles north from the town of Calistoga.

Lake Hennessy

We prefer to bird the south side of this man-made Napa County lake where the woods abound with woodpeckers, raptors dot the skies overhead, Caspian Terns fish, Black Phoebes catch flies at the water's edge, and Northern Orioles and Bushtits nest on the surrounding hills. Other sites around the lake are excellent as well, however — like the junction of Pope Valley Road and Chiles Road where, if you're lucky, you may sight a Lewis' Woodpecker on a telephone pole, a Tundra Swan in the marsh, and Lark Sparrow and Western Bluebird in the grasslands.

Pileated Woodpecker, Rufous-crowned Sparrow and Rock Wren have been sighted on the north side of the lake.

Also seen at Lake Hennessey are Bald Eagle, Osprey, Say's Phoebe, Great Blue Heron, Snowy Egret, Northern Pygmy-Owl, several species of grebe, and merganser, and Common Goldeneye.

Bustling with activity in the springtime, a heron rookery is located across from the boat ramp parking lot on the south side of the lake.

To reach the south end of the lake take SH 128 from Silverado Trail. For north end birding, drive further north on Silverado Trail and turn right on Howell Mt. Road to its junction with Conn Valley Road. Follow Conn Valley Road to the lake.

Lake Berryessa

Visitors to this popular recreation area can windsurf, water ski, swim or fish for the King salmon, trout, bass, crappie, bluegill and catfish with which the California Department of Fish and Game amply stock this gleaming jewel of a Napa County lake.

The Lake Berryessa area also boasts boat launches, marinas, stores, restaurants, a visitor center, exhibits, and plenty of places to walk, jog, and bike. For more information about this area call the Bureau of Reclamation, Lake Berryessa Recreation Office, at (707) 966-2111.

Seen here are Great Blue Heron, Osprey, Black-shouldered Kite, Golden and Bald Eagles, Band-tailed Pigeon, Acorn Woodpecker, Lesser Goldfinch, House Finch, and White-crowned and Golden-crowned Sparrows. A bird list is available at the visitor center.

From SH 29 in Rutherford, take SH 128 east about 14 miles. Go left on Berryessa-Knoxville Road, which skirts the entire western side of the lake and offers several access points. Or you can stay on 128, which goes to the dam on the south side.

From the Central Valley, pick up SH 128 off of I-505 near Winters, and head west.

Lake Solano County Park

This popular Solano County parkland is known for all these features: three swimming lagoons of various depths; playground equipment; group picnic area; concession stand; archery range; fishing in season; good hiking trails; modern restrooms with showers; picnic tables; barbeques; boat ramp; rental boats; and 50 campsites located in an appealing natural setting.

All of the following species are seen in the vicinity of Lake Solano County Park: Osprey, Great Blue Heron, Wood Duck, Common Goldeneye, Lesser Goldfinch, House Finch, Great Egret, American Goldfinch, and many others.

Check out the upper end of the lake for Wood Duck, Hooded Merganser, Ring-necked Duck, Green-backed Heron, and Common Moorhen. Walk the east bank and keep an eye out for Red-shouldered Hawk, Nuttall's and Downy Woodpeckers, Osprey, Brown Creeper, White-breasted Nuthatch, Western Bluebird, Blue-gray Gnatcatcher, and with luck, even a Phainopepla.

From I-505 near Winters, take Russell Boulevard (SH 128) west about 5 miles to the park. From I-80 between Fairfield and Vacaville, take Pleasants Valley Road north about 13 miles.

Grizzly Island/Suisun Marsh

Suisin Marsh, 84,000 acres of bays and sloughs, and a meeting ground of river water and ocean tides, is the largest contiguous estuarine marsh in the United States. At its very heart lies the 14,300-acre Grizzly Island, a prime wildlife habitat alluring to birders, anglers, hikers, hunters, and wild plant enthusiasts alike.

To the birder, the most exciting times to visit Grizzly Island are in the fall and winter when enormous flocks of migrating birds convene here to eat, drink, and renew themselves. In autumn the migrating Northern Pintail ducks begin to arrive, and by the end of September the marsh is swarming with them as well as with the Tule Goose (*Anser albifrons gambelli*), a rare subspecies of the White-fronted Goose, for whom this is one of only three important wintering areas of the world's entire population of 7,000 individuals. August and September mark the arrival of great flocks of American White Pelicans. In the winter the wetlands are alive with as many as 250,000 ducks, vibrantly colorful in their courting garb.

The following species can be sighted here: California Clapper Rail, Black Rail, Peregrine Falcon, Golden Eagle, American Bittern, Black-shouldered Kite, Brown Pelican, Double-crested Cormorant, White-faced Ibis, Northern Harrier, Ferruginous Hawk, Sandhill Crane, Osprey, Loggerhead Shrike, and Belted Kingfisher.

Birding opportunities are excellent all year long in this lush wetland habitat. In the middle of the day, in hot midsummer, we counted 41 species in 3 hours. These included: Cinnamon Teal, Belted Kingfisher, American Avocet, Killdeer, Black Phoebe, Northern Harrier, family after family of introduced Ring-necked Pheasants, a flock of 75 American White Pelicans, a pair of handsome Great Horned Owls, and the easily seen Suisun Song Sparrow (*Melospiza melodia maxillaris*).

More than 230 species of birds have been sighted in Suisun Marsh, including, of course, the many herons that have their rookery here.

A birdlist may be obtained at Wildlife Area headquarters.

Also seen here are Tule Elk, River Otter, the Suisun Shrew (who lives exclusively in the tidal wetlands), the endangered Salt-Marsh Harvest Mouse, an abundance of rabbits, and many other rodents.

From Highway 12 in the eastern part of Fairfield, take Grizzly Island Road south. It's about 8 miles to area headquarters.

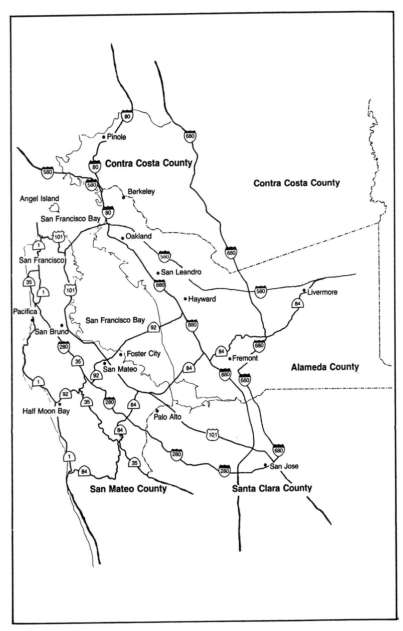

San Francisco Bay Area

Chapter 3
San Francisco Bay

 Even though it's one of the largest metropolitan areas in the nation, the Bay Area has reserved an abundance of public parklands for its birds, beasts, and people: great urban parks such as Golden Gate in San Francisco and Lake Merritt in Oakland; a superb regional park system in the East Bay; a multitude of fine city, county, and state parks throughout the area; the Golden Gate National Recreation Area, and a huge State Fish and Game Refuge on the peninsula. Add to these the natural habitats of bays and marshes and estuaries, of hills and streams and woods, of remote beaches and protected islands, and you truly have a treasure of birding opportunities, all within easy access.

The San Francisco Bay region covers the southern part of the greater Bay Area, from the Golden Gate to Point Ano Nuevo, and from the Carquinez Straits through the Santa Clara Valley. The five-county area encompasses 3,561 square miles, which comprises 4.5% of the area covered by this book.

The geology is Coastal Range hills, with the bay and Santa Clara Valley separating the two major ridge systems — the Santa Cruz Mountains on the west and the Mount Diablo range on the east. There are no major river systems, but the entire area is drained by a series of creeks running directly into the estuaries, sloughs, the bay, and the ocean.

The highway systems are oriented generally in a north-south direction: SH 1 along the coast, US 101 along the west side of the bay, and a complex of Interstates: I-280, "the most beautiful freeway in the world," along the spine of the peninsula, I-880 on the east shore, and I-680 east of the first range of hills. I-80 goes from San Francisco to the East Bay and then north, and I-580 traverses the area from east to west.

FARALLON NATIONAL WILDLIFE REFUGE

Although these islands are world renowned for their great seabird rookeries and comprise one of the nation's prime birding locales, it's a rare birder who's ever set foot upon them. Because human disturbance poses such a great threat to nesting seabirds, only authorized research personnel tread the islands' shores. Birders are content (and even excited) to do their observing from the decks of whale watching or pelagic tour boats.

Those individuals who have been fortunate enough to land on the islands are prone to reflect on the experience years afterward as if it happened the day before. So it is with our daughter, Dolora Westrich, who sailed to the islands aboard a Farallon Patrol boat with a group of research biologists in 1985. Not a naturalist, not even a dedicated birdwatcher, Dolora's eyes still dance when she tells what it felt like to view such a multitude of nesting birds. "It's an incredible place," she says. "If you're not a birdwatcher, you *feel* like a birdwatcher. Or maybe I should put it this way: you *are* a birdwatcher — at least for a day."

More than 2 million birds of the following species are known to breed in the rookeries of these remarkable islands: Leach's and Ashy Storm-Petrels, Double-crested, Brandt's, and Pelagic Cormorants, Black Oystercatcher, Western Gull, Common Murre, Pigeon Guillemot, Cassin's Auklet, Rhinoceros Auklet, and Tufted Puffin.

Among the 328 species sighted on these islands are Surf Scoter, Black Turnstone, Wandering Tattler, Willet, Herring Gull, Yellow Warbler, Brown Pelican, Sooty Shearwater, and Glaucous-winged Gull.

Steller's Sea Lions, some of which weigh in at as much as 2,200 pounds, are sometimes sighted "hauled out" on the rocky shores of the Farallon Islands. These can be viewed from excursion boats, as can migrating whales, dolphins, and porpoises.

As to its vital statistics, this 211-acre refuge consists of a group of rocky islands in the Pacific Ocean, approximately 30 miles west of the city of San Francisco.

For detailed information about this refuge and its available bird checklist contact: Project Leader, San Francisco Bay National Wildlife Refuge Complex, P.O. Box 524, Newark, CA 94560; call (415) 792-0222.

Whale watching tours and excursions to view the Farallon Islands depart from local marinas and are scheduled by conservation groups and environmental education organizations. For further information about these exciting trips contact The Ocean Alliance, at Fort Mason Center, Building E, San Francisco, CA 94123. The number to call is (415) 474-3385.

SAN FRANCISCO

Angel Island State Park

Any visitor to the San Francisco area is sure to delight in a trip to this spectacular 740-acre mountainous island with its photographic vistas, fascinating history, lovely wildflowers and trees, circling trails, and the world of wildlife that flourishes here. It may seem trite to call this park an island paradise, but that's precisely what it is.

Appealing to birders, botanists, anglers, and general tourists for all the respective reasons, the park has a fascinating past that endears it to history buffs as well. Its military history stretches back to the American Civil War. It was a point of debarkation for immigrants from the Pacific, and a prisoner-of-war camp during WWII. And long before then, for thousands of years, it was a home to native Californians who fished and hunted here, who lived out their lives in nature's plenty.

Birders can expect to find Chestnut-backed Chickadee and Common Raven among the trees of Ayala Cove, White-throated Swift and Anna's Hummingbird in coastal scrub areas, and Scrub Jay and a variety of sparrows in the chaparral. While you're reveling in the views of San Francisco, Sausalito, and Tiburon from the several excellent vantage points, take the time to scope for seabirds; and check out the beaches at Quarry Point and China Cove for shorebirds and more waterbirds.

Public ferryboats run to Angel Island from San Francisco and Tiburon every day from June 1st through Labor Day. The Tiburon Ferry runs every Saturday and Sunday all year as well. Red and White Fleet Ferryboats depart from San Francisco Saturday and Sunday from May through October with daily service June 1st through Labor Day. From November through May you must have your own boat in order to come or go on a weekday.

For further information regarding fares and ferry schedules call the Angel Island State Park Ferry, Tiburon, at (415) 435-2131 or the Red and White Fleet, San Francisco, 1-800-445-8880.

Those coming to Angel Island in their own boats must moor or anchor offshore after sunset. There are 30 mooring buoys in Ayala Cove and 20 at Quarry Beach. Bring a dinghy and be sure to make overnight storage arrangements with the ranger on duty.

The Presidio of San Francisco

Just a moment's ride from Golden Gate Bridge lies one of the most serene and park-like settings in northern California: the famous San Francisco Presidio, a military establishment known for a long and colorful history, scenic vistas, magnificent foliage, picturesque old brick homes, and barracks laid out as neatly as houses on a monopoly board. There are no sentry stations, but be sure to stop at the Military Police Station and ask for a map of the area before you set out on your birding tour.

On our last visit to the Presidio, from the vantage point of the path below Inspiration Point, we saw Yellow Warbler, Purple Finch, chickadees, Northern Flicker, American Kestrel, California Quail, Bushtit, American Robin, vireos, Song Sparrow, and Brown Creeper — not to mention the ubiquitous Mourning Dove. Also seen at the Presidio, from Inspiration Point or elsewhere on the grounds are Anna's and Allen's Hummingbirds, Hooded Oriole, Pine Siskin, Dark-eyed Junco, White-crowned and Golden-crowned Sparrows, and sometimes even that loveliest of songsters, the White-throated Sparrow.

Cooper's Hawk and American Kestrel breed here regularly, while Great Horned Owl and Western Screech-Owl appear to be fulltime residents.

The real treasure of the Presidio, however, is the Red Crossbill, whose presence here has been reported in every season. This bird is best seen along the edges of the Presidio Golf Course, in the woods between Lincoln Boulevard and Baker Beach, or down the hill from the Arguello Street overlook.

If you visit the Presidio in fall be sure to scan the sky for migrating hawks. Many of those species sighted from Hawk Hill, just across the Golden Gate, can be seen from here as well.

If it's water birds you're after, you won't be disappointed. From the baylands around Fort Point you may see such species as Red-breasted Merganser, loons, grebes, Surf Scoter, and possibly even an Oldsquaw in the winter.

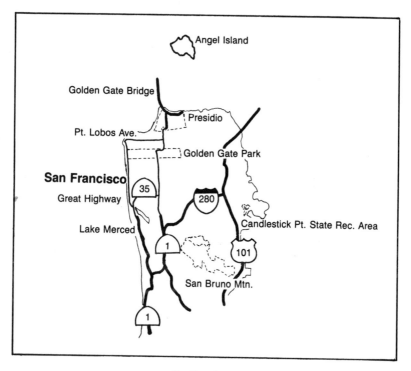

San Francisco

Fort Point and the Crissy Field landing strip are good places for close-up sightings of loons and cormorants.

The main entrance to the Presidio is Lombard Street, which is also US 101 through San Francisco. Heading west on Lombard, just go straight where 101 veers right toward the Golden Gate.

Coming from the north, turn right just after the toll plaza and go 2 blocks to Lincoln Boulevard, which runs all the way through the Presidio. From the south, there's access from Presidio Avenue, Arguello Boulevard, and Park Presidio Boulevard, as well as 25th Avenue, to Lincoln.

Land's End

Many birders look upon a visit to Land's End with its jagged cliffs, pounding sea, wind-sculpted cypress trees, and enticing paths as one segment of an excursion that also includes Lincoln Park, Cliff House, and Sutro Baths. Enjoyed separately or as part of a parcel of birding pleasures, it's a must for any nature lover sojourning in San Francisco. Birding is good here all year long.

The Brown Creeper is particularly common here in the trees that line the cliff's edge. Black Oystercatcher and Brandt's Cormorant nest on the rocks off shore and the Brown Pelicans are abundant in June. Willets, turnstones, and Sanderlings turn up in July.

There's a parking lot at the end of Merrie Way, which is off Point Lobos Avenue just east of where it makes the big curve at the Cliff House. There's another at the end of El Camino del Mar, on the north side of the Palace of the Legion of Honor. Get there by way of 35th Avenue from the south, or by following Lincoln Boulevard on around after it leaves the Presidio.

Cliff House and Sutro Baths

Located near the famous old Sutro Baths and across the street from a picturesque and much-photographed old windmill, the Cliff House is not only a great vantage point for pelican watching but a famous San Francisco landmark irresistible to tourists of every variety. It's a popular place, so if you want the experience of eyeing the avian world of the so-called "Seal Rocks" that lie offshore here (which is best accomplished from the observation decks behind the restaurants) then arrive in the early morning before the crowds of sightseers are on the scene.

After scoping the rocks in this area, be sure to scout about the few scant pools that are all that remains of the Sutro Baths, a splendid holiday mecca where, in another era, the leisure class lounged and tourists thronged. It's birds who throng here nowadays: Brown Pelican, Mallard, Ring-necked Duck, Lesser Scaup, Barrow's Goldeneye, American Wigeon, Brandt's Cormorant, Black Oystercatcher, Heermann's Gull, Surfbird, Sanderling, Willet, and other shorebirds, especially at high tide.

From a huge cement slab that lies north of the ponds at Sutro Baths you can scope the sea in fall and winter for Common Loon, White-winged Scoter, Western Grebe, Pacific Loon, and others. When riptides churn up a choppy line at the point where bay meets sea, expect to see Elegant and Forster's Terns and Bonaparte's Gulls.

Also seen here are California Sea Lions, Harbor Seals, and sometimes in the springtime, Harbor Porpoise. Whale watching too is popular along this strip of the coast.

Mallard

You can reach these remnants of the old Sutro Baths by following a short trail that lies just below the Coffee Shop at Cliff House, which is located at the very northern end of the Great Highway that runs along Ocean Beach the entire length of San Francisco. From downtown take Geary Boulevard, which turns into Point Lobos Avenue, which becomes the Great Highway right at the Cliff House.

Candlestick Point State Recreation Area

The facts about this 170-acre recreation area come as a surprise to bay area newcomers. It's located in the city limits of San Francisco right next to the famous ballpark that shares its name, yet this unique area affords more exciting wintertime birding than is found in many secluded wilderness places. Winter is distinctly the time to come, however, for the summer bird count here is not outstanding.

According to ranger Sharon Campbell, there's no bird more typical of this locale than the common Willet. Unusual sightings in the vicinity include Barrow's Goldeneye, Horned Lark, Merlin, Oldsquaw, Peregrine Falcon, and even the highly unlikely Rock Wren.

More common here are American Coot, Bufflehead, Common Loon, cormorants, Ruddy Duck, California Gull, scaups, Surf Scoter, Western Grebe, and Brown Pelican.

Access to this San Francisco Recreation Area is easy. Take US 101 south to the Candlestick Park exit. Follow the Hunters Point Expressway all around the stadium, and there you are!

Golden Gate Park

San Francisco's Golden Gate Park is one of the great urban parks of the world. Beautiful at every turn, it boasts all these features: more than a dozen lovely lakes and ponds; exotic species of trees and shrubs; fine places to picnic; a picturesque log cabin; a fuschia garden; a rhododendron dell; the Strybing Arboretum; a music concourse; a Japanese tea garden; the California Academy of Sciences; the DeYoung Museum, with outstanding art exhibits; snack bars; boat rental facilities; acres of lawn on which to lounge; miles of lovely paths to stroll at leisure.

Our favorite place to bird in Golden Gate Park is the lovely little Mallard Lake which lies nestled in trees and shrubs right by the road on South Drive between 25th Avenue and Sunset Boulevard. Besides the ever-present Mallard for which it's named, we've sighted Lesser Scaup, Common Goldeneye, Black Phoebe, Red-breasted Sapsucker, Brewer's Blackbird, and many other species in this vicinity.

Another much-favored place to bird is Middle Lake, one of three bodies of water in a chain of lakes located between 41st Avenue and Lincoln Way and 43rd Avenue and Fulton Street. Birds sighted or heard in this area include Sora, Virginia Rail, Downy Woodpecker, Anna's Hummingbird, California Towhee, Common Yellowthroat, and a long list of migrants.

Look for migrants around the Pioneer Log Cabin near the very popular Stow Lake, where Ring-necked Ducks can be seen in the wintertime. Find Wood Ducks at Elk Glen Lake near the 25th Avenue entrance on South Drive. Bird all through the park if you have the time. You're not apt to be disappointed, for birding is good here all year long.

Golden Gate Park is accessible from the south and north on 19th Avenue and Park Presidio Boulevard, and from the east on Fell Street.

Lake Merced

In addition to avian delights, and pleasant scenery, this park boasts all the following features: the Harding Golf Course, restrooms, a restaurant and bar, good walking trails, a footbridge, picnic facilities, fishing, and lots of open space for lolling, sailing frisbees, or playing ball.

When we birded Lake Merced in the late summer of 1989 we saw Great and Snowy Egrets, Common Moorhen, American Coot, Canada Goose, Double-crested Cormorant, Red-winged Blackbird, Mallard, grebes, Purple Finch, American Kestrel, Marsh Wren, Song Sparrow, Brewer's Blackbird, hummingbirds, Scrub Jay, and Northern Flicker. The birding might have been more exciting had we come a few weeks later, for in fall many migrants are reported in this area. And in winter and spring as many as 70 Black-crowned Night-Herons can be seen roosting in the willows at the lake's edge.

Our favorite places to bird in the park are at the parking lot near the golf course on Harding Drive, and from the vantage point of the footbridge over the narrows between the two halves of the northern lake.

The parking lot for the northern lake and the footbridge is at the south end of Sunset Boulevard. Harding Drive, with parking for the picnic areas as well as the golf course, is on the isthmus separating the two lakes. It's reached from Skyline Boulevard, which skirts the west side of the lakes, just north of where the Great Highway comes in.

San Bruno Mountain State and County Park

For a clear picture of this 2,064-acre parkland we quote one of the Northern California birders who knows it best, a San Francisco High School Biology teacher, John "Mac" McCormick, who has kept birding records for San Bruno Mountain State and County Park since 1984.

"San Bruno is a mountainous ridge running in a NW-SE direction, which almost completely divides the city of San Francisco from the rest of the peninsula," Mac explains. "The highest elevation on the ridge exceeds 1,300 feet. The vegetation includes coastal scrub, open grassland, oak and buckeye canyons, and groves of eucalyptus and cypress trees."

A park brochure refers to San Bruno Mountain as "a unique open-space island surrounded by adjacent urbanization." It's also an "island" for 14 species of rare or endangered plants and 2 species of endangered butterflies, as well as the birds that lure so many birders. It offers all these features too: magnificent vistas; family picnic sites around an open meadow; picnic tables, barbecue pits, drinking water, and restroom; a trail with access for the disabled; a day camp nestled in the watershed of Colma Creek; and 12 miles of superlative hiking, jogging, and riding trails.

San Bruno Mountain is especially good for land birds, but as Mac states, visitors needn't limit themselves to just one type of birding. "The eastern slope of San Bruno Mountain plunges into San Francisco Bay," he explains, "and at this point the causeway for SH 101 has created an estuary with excellent mud flats which at low tide abound with shorebirds.

Birds seen in the mountain's saddle area include: Anna's Hummingbird, Chestnut-backed Chickadee, Bushtit, Wrentit, Winter Wren, Bewick's Wren, Hermit Thrush, Golden-crowned Kinglet, Warbling Vireo, Purple Finch, House Finch, Pine Siskin, American Goldfinch, Rufous-sided Towhee, Dark-eyed Junco, Northern Harrier, Scrub Jay, Northern Mockingbird, Cedar Waxwing, Northern Oriole, and White-crowned, Fox, and Song Sparrows.

More unusual species sighted here include American Redstart, Rose-breasted Grosbeak, Green-tailed Towhee, Gray Flycatcher, Lawrence's Goldfinch, White-throated Sparrow, Cattle Egret, Sage Thrasher, Evening Grosbeak, Hammond's Flycatcher, Hermit Warbler, Broad-winged Hawk, adult Bald Eagle, and Hooded Warbler.

Unusual sightings observed on the mountain in areas other than the saddle include Ferruginous Hawk, Golden Eagle, Purple Martin, Sage Thrasher, Mountain Bluebird, Sage Sparrow, adult Bald Eagle, Broad-winged Hawk, Hooded Warbler, and White-faced Ibis.

Where the eastern slope of San Bruno Mountain plunges into San Francisco Bay, expect to see Red-throated Loon, Pied-billed Grebe, Double-crested Cormorant, Great Blue Heron, Great Egret, Red-breasted Merganser, Semipalmated Plover, American Avocet, Spotted Sandpiper, Long-billed Dowitcher, and Common Snipe.

Butterflies seen at San Bruno Mountain State and County Park include the San Bruno Elfin, the Calliope Silverspot, and the beautiful Mission Blue.

For further information about this prime birding location, write San Bruno Mountain State and County Park, 555 Guadalupe Canyon Parkway, Brisbane, CA 94005, or call (415) 992-6770 or 587-7511.

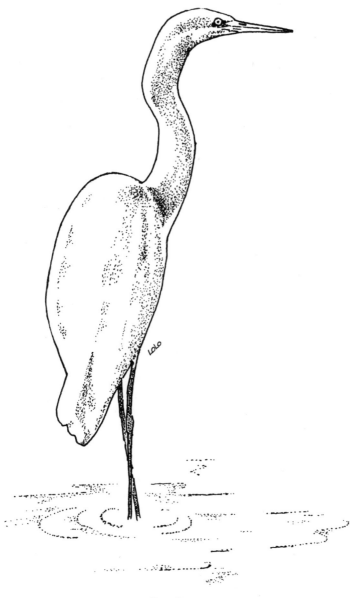

Great Egret

San Bruno Mountain can be reached by taking US 101 to Old Bayshore Boulevard, continuing south on Old Bayshore to Guadalupe Canyon Parkway, and then turning west on Guadalupe Canyon Parkway to the park entrance.

The lagoon at the eastern foot of the hill can be viewed directly from Old Bayshore, a little south of Guadalupe Canyon Parkway.

SAN MATEO COUNTY

Junipero Serra County Park

This bay area park, which we're recommending for drop-by birding, is known especially for these features: a variety of trees, including Monterey cypress, arroyo willow, California bay laurel, coast live oak, and madrone; an abundance of wildflowers and herbs such as Douglas iris, hound's tongue, miner's lettuce, California buttercup, amole, and owl clover; good hiking trails, including a self-guiding interpretive loop; several excellent overlooks, affording spectacular views; a visitor center; family and group picnic areas.

Birds most common here are year-round residents. These include California Quail, Scrub Jay, and California Towhee. Also sighted are Acorn Woodpecker, Rufous-sided Towhee, Bewick's Wren, and Lesser and American Goldinches. According to park ranger Mike Rivers, the Quail Loop Trail offers the best birding in the park.

To get here from southbound on I-280 in San Bruno, take the Crystal Springs Road exit and turn right 0.5 mile to the park entrance. Northbound on I-280, take the San Bruno exit, go under the freeway, and get back onto the freeway heading south. Immediately take the Crystal Springs road exit and follow directions above.

San Pedro Valley County Park

Seventeen-year-old Scott Smithson of Pacifica, who's been birding since he was five, touts this park for the rarities seen here through the years: Hooded Warbler, Red-eyed Vireo, Blue Grosbeak, Tennessee Warbler, Rose-breasted Grosbeak, and Palm Warbler. Scott knows the park well and considers its best birding spots to be the Old Trout Farm Trail, which passes through some fine riparian areas along Brooks Creek; the Brooks

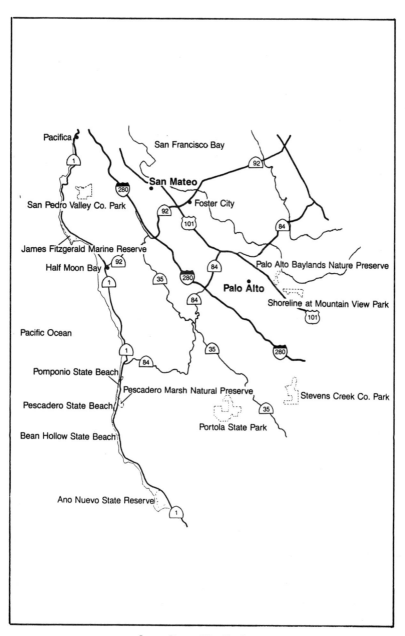

Lower Bay and Pacific Coast

Falls Overlook Trail, which runs up the hillside into an area graced with scattered pines and eucalyptus; and Linda Mar Beach, which boasts good gull and shorebird concentrations.

The park boasts many fine trails, all of them leading to one good birding locale or another; modern restroom facilities; a fine new museum with excellent exhibits; checklists and assorted descriptive literature. For further information call the Park headquarters at (415) 355-6489.

As to good birding locales outside the park's confines but located nearby, Scott speaks of these too. "A Red-footed Booby was once spotted off local Pedro Point, just south of the main beach," he notes. "And Sanchez Adobe turned up a Black-and-White Warbler once. Incredible possibilities there if it were birded more often. It's a Pygmy Nuthatch and warbler haven in those pines!"

Common year-round residents seen at San Pedro Valley County Park include California Quail, Anna's Hummingbird, Downy Woodpecker, Steller's and Scrub Jays, Chestnut-backed Chickadee, Wrentit, Bewick's Wren, Purple Finch, Pine Siskin, Song Sparrow, White-crowned Sparrow, and California Towhee.

Additional vagrants sighted here include Common Goldeneye, Solitary Vireo (eastern form), Lesser Nighthawk, Tennessee Warbler, Yellow-headed Blackbird, and Marsh Wren.

Mammals to be seen are Mule Deer, Brush Rabbit, Bobcat, Gray Fox, and Striped Skunk.

Take SH 1 to Pacifica, which is 10 miles south of San Francisco. Turn eastward on Linda Mar Boulevard. At its end, turn right on Oddstad Boulevard, where signs will lead you directly into the Park.

Sweeney Ridge Skyline Preserve

In recent years, raptor migration at Sweeney Ridge has been of keen interest to Golden Gate Raptor Observatory director Allen Fish. He and his team of avid hawk watchers have made the area the focus of hours of observation, hard work, and reams of documentation.

Apart from spring raptor sightings, Sweeney Ridge has both beauty and historicity to offer. It was here, in 1769, that members of the Gaspar de Portola expedition stood gazing down upon San Francisco Bay, a sight no Europeans had ever seen before.

Red-tailed Hawk (immature)

The following is a list of raptors sighted in 95.5 hours of hawk watching from Sweeney Ridge in the spring of l988: 143 Turkey Vultures, 4 Osprey, 2 Bald Eagles, 31 Northern Harriers, 58 Sharp-shinned Hawks, 49 Cooper's Hawks, 2 Red-shouldered Hawks, 1 Broad-winged Hawk, 504 Red-tailed Hawks, 1 Golden Eagle, 24 American Kestrel, 1 Prairie Falcon, and 47 unidentified birds. Other species common to the area are finches, quail, and a variety of sparrows.

Here are three entrances to the preserve:

1. From I-280, take Sneath Lane west. The entrance is at the end of the

road, with roadside parking for 6 or 8 cars.

2. Take Skyline Boulevard to Skyline College; park in Student Parking Lot 3; walk south 200 feet on the road to the maintenance facility, then west to the entrance gate.

3. From SH 1 in Pacifica, take Fassler Avenue to the east and follow it all the way up the hill. The entrance is at the end of Fassler. There's street parking in front of the houses there, but not much. There's a school about 0.5 mile back down Fassler where you can park and walk back.

Foster City

It's no wonder that so many birders visit the bird-bedecked network of small islands and lagoons that comprise Foster City. Whether on a field trip with the Audubon Society, the California Academy of Sciences, or here as a loner, you won't be disappointed. Expect Hooded Merganser, Barrow's Goldeneye, Red Knot, Eurasian Wigeon, Peregrine Falcon and such rarities as these reported by resident birder, Nicholas T. Coiro: Smew (Winter of 1981-January 1984), Tropical Kingbird, Tufted Duck, Sabine's Gull, Virginia's Warbler, and Sage Thrasher.

Good places to bird in the vicinity are Central Lake at Leo Ryan Park, the Marina Lagoon (also called Seal Slough), the bayshore, and the Foster City side of Belmont Slough. Look for Double-crested Cormorant, Forster's Tern, Brown Pelican, loons, grebes, and mergansers at Central Lake; Northern Pintail, Black-bellied Plover, Greater Yellowlegs, Spotted Sandpiper, Northern Shoveler, and wigeons at the Marina Lagoon; and Peregrine Falcon, Red-tailed Hawk, Black-shouldered Kite, and other raptors over the marsh and grasslands near the mouth of the lagoon near the intersection of Detroit Drive and Anchor Road.

From US 101, take either the SH 92 exit, or the East Hillsdale Boulevard exit, go east across Marina Lagoon, and start birding. Leo Ryan Park is on East Hillsdale. For very specific, detailed instructions, we recommend the book, *San Francisco Peninsula Birdwatching*, published by the Sequoia Audubon Society.

James V. Fitzgerald Marine Reserve

This remarkable park has features alluring to a variety of nature lovers. Twenty-five species of invertebrates and plants were unknown to science until discovered here, and the area marks a range limit for dozens of invertebrates and marine plants, from seaweeds and sponges to mollusks and starfish. There are also deep cypress woods, a cliffside path overlooking the sea, and excellent birding.

For the purpose of protecting this complex living community, which scientists have been studying for 70 years, the Fitzgerald Marine Reserve was established in 1969. With the exception of abalone, rockfish, lingcod, eel, croaker, halibut, cabezon, and kelp greenling, which may be taken by anyone holding a current California Sport Fishing license, all marine life is protected here.

Common birds here are Virginia Rail, Western Gull, Common Murre, Anna's Hummingbird, Downy Woodpecker, Scrub Jay, Chestnut-backed Chickadee, Bushtit, Wrentit, Marsh Wren, House Finch, California Towhee, and Song Sparrow.

Seen in the fall or winter are Golden-crowned Kinglets, Hermit Thrush, Townsend's Warbler, Wilson's Warbler, Savannah Sparrow, Dark-eyed Junco, and Golden-crowned and Fox Sparrows.

Pine Siskin, American Goldfinch, Rufous-sided Towhee, Plain Titmouse, Bewick's Wren, and Northern Mockingbird are less common but should be found.

Unusual birds sighted in the vicinity include Tropical Kingbird, Virginia's Warbler, Dickcissel, and Nashville and Black-throated Blue Warblers.

From US 1, turn west on Cypress Avenue, just south of Moss Beach. You can park alongside the road at the corner of Airport Boulevard, and walk in from there.

Pillar Point/Princeton Harbor

From teeming tide pools to quaint gift shops, fine eating places to fishing boats, Pillar Point has something to offer to scientists, beachcombers, anglers, hungry tourists, boaters and birders alike. To the latter, it's often experienced as a part of a field trip that includes a tour of the nearby James V. Fitzgerald Marine Reserve, a good birding spot in its own right.

Baird's Sandpipers have been reported here at Pillar Point in August and September. Marsh Wren, Sora, Virginia Rail, and Common Yellowthroat are year-round residents. Lincoln's Sparrow winters here.

There are several good places to bird here, one favorite being a small marshy area on West Point Avenue. Easy-access birding on the harbor is rewarding. So too is a vacant lot at the corner of Prospect and Capistrano, just across the street from Old Princeton Landing. Here runs tree-lined Denniston Creek through the lot, leading to the harbor where Brown Pelicans are readily seen. Look for Song Sparrow, House Finch, Scrub Jay, and Anna's Hummingbird.

Common year-round residents here at Pillar Point, as at the Fitzgerald Marine Reserve, include Virginia Rail, Anna's Hummingbird, Marsh Wren, House Finch, California Towhee, and Song Sparrow.

Common in fall or winter are Golden-crowned Kinglet, Hermit Thrush, Townsend's Warbler, Wilson's Warbler, Savannah Sparrow, Dark-eyed Junco, and Golden-crowned and Fox Sparrows. Less common but sometimes sighted in the general area are Pine Siskin, American Goldfinch, Rufous-sided Towhee, Nashville Warbler, Plain Titmouse, Bewick's Wren, and Northern Mockingbird.

Tropical Kingbird, Virginia's Warbler, Dickcissel, and the Black-throated Blue Warbler are some unusual species sighted here. A bird list of species sighted at the Fitzgerald Marine Reserve doubles for Pillar Point as well.

The town of Princeton is off SH 1, 12 miles south of Pacifica and 5 miles north of Half Moon Bay. From SH 1, turn west (into the town) on Capistrano Road and wind around the north side of the bay to Prospect. Bird this area, including the creek and the marsh behind the restaurant, then get back on Prospect, make a little jog onto Harvard and follow it to the junction with West Point Road. Make a left turn and go on out to the point.

Half Moon Bay Grasslands

This grassland area is good for Black-shouldered Kite, Rough-legged Hawk, Northern Harrier, and a wide variety of land birds including Savannah Sparrow, White-crowned Sparrow, Lesser Goldfinch, and House Finch. There is also a long list of shorebirds and water birds to be seen where the grassland meets the coastline, just a proverbial stone's throw away.

About a mile south of Half Moon Bay, you can bird anywhere along SH 1. There's also a nice loop drive of 8 miles that affords elevated views of the grasslands, and good land bird habitats along Arroyo Leon and Purisima Creek. From SH 1, take Higgins-Purisima Road to the Purisima Creek Redwoods Open Space Preserve, and return on Purisima Creek Road.

PALO ALTO BAYLANDS RESERVE

Park naturalist and long-time Palo Alto city employee Ted Chandick says, "People love this park." The reasons are obvious, for the reserve boasts all these attractions: easy access from the bayshore freeways, a heavily-populated duck pond, wooden benches overlooking a wetland rich in avifauna, 120 acres of marshland, an 800-foot-long boardwalk that reaches out over the cordgrass zones, a modern visitor center, ecology workshops and interpretive programs, exhibits, junior museum, nature walks, excellent opportunities for bird behavior observation.

The key bird at Baylands is unquestionably the California Clapper Rail. Although it can be sighted any time of the year, the best opportunity for viewing this endangered subspecies is in the winter, when the tides are at their highest during the daytime hours. This special bird lives only in the cordgrass zones of marshes. These areas are hard to get to, but there is a boardwalk that goes right out into the cordgrass zone and gives people an opportunity to see this interesting rail.

Another Baylands species that birders often come especially to sight is the elusive, seldom seen, sparrow-sized California Black Rail, which has been declared a threatened species by the resources agency of the California Department of Fish and Game. This bird can be seen only when there's an extremely high tide, preferably accompanied by wind and rain, and the marsh is flooded, a condition that occurs most often November through February.

Besides these two rails, Sharp-tailed Sparrow has been seen here as well — a rarity indeed.

There are many other interesting species to be seen at Baylands. Year-round residents include the Cinnamon Teal, Gadwall, Ring-necked Pheasant, Lesser Goldfinch, Wrentit, Chestnut-backed Chickadee, Northern Mockingbird, California Quail, Black-necked Stilt, American Avocet, and Savannah Sparrow. Common most of the year are Black-shouldered Kite, Snowy Egret, Black-crowned Night-Heron, Northern Shoveler, Willet, Least Sandpiper, and Band-tailed Pigeon. Many rarer species are sighted here as well.

A checklist of the Birds of Palo Alto and adjacent areas is available at the Baylands Visitor Center.

To reach this park from US 101 in Palo Alto, take the Embarcadero exit and go east to the end of the road.

SHORELINE AT MOUNTAIN VIEW

The city of Mountain View planned and negotiated for 15 long years to create this unique shoreline park with its slough, its forebay, its meadowlands, its shoreline lake, and its growing population of bay area birds. In a park publication entitled *An Achievement in Public/Private Partnership*, the story of these achievements is depicted in words and photographs. The gist of it is that this beautifully designed and developed park is the finest example of landfill end use in the United States. By using refuse as a resource, bane has become boon, blight has been transformed into beauty.

This 644-acre regional recreational area has turfed areas for picnicking; a championship golf course; a fully equipped clubhouse; sailing and surfing on the lake; a network of paths and roadways for joggers, strollers, bicyclists, and birders; and trails to the west that link up with Palo Alto Baylands.

A bird list, *Checklist of the Birds of Shoreline at Mountain View*, and a wonderful, illustrated guide, *Birds of Shoreline*, as well as maps and descriptive brochures are available at the park headquarters.

For high concentrations of certain species , the best time is from October through February when literally thousands of migratory birds stop off. For number of species rather than number of individuals, spring and fall are excellent, too.

Common or fairly common, all or most of the year, are Great Blue Heron, Great and Snowy Egrets, Green-winged Teal, Northern Pintail, Cinnamon Teal, Northern Shoveler, Surf Scoter, Bufflehead, Black-shouldered Kite, Black-necked Stilt, American Avocet, Marbled Godwit, Willet, Western Sandpiper, Dunlin, Short-billed Dowitcher, Forster's Tern, and Long-billed Dowitcher.

Rare species sighted here include the endangered California Least Tern, American White Pelican, yellowlegs, and Burrowing Owl.

To get here, take US 101 in Mountain View. Take the Stierlin Road exit and go north about a mile, to the end of Stierlin Road.

PORTOLA STATE PARK

Characterized by winding creeks, mixed evergreen woodlands, towering second growth redwoods, jungle-green ferns, miles of fine trails, an understory of huckleberry, and plenty of solitude, this is a favorite spot for hundreds of San Mateo County nature lovers and a fair share of out-of-staters as well.

This park, which we recommend for some truly exciting drop-by birding, boasts 52 developed campsites with picnic tables and fireplaces, restrooms with hot showers, a group campground designed to serve 100 campers, a group day use picnic area, summertime evening campfire programs, daily guided nature walks in season, and a superlative self-guided nature trail.

Reservations are advised for spring, summer, and fall weekends. At other times it should be no problem to find a vacancy, but reservations are necessary for large group picnics.

For more information about this lovely haunt of the showy Pileated Woodpecker, write or call Portola State Park, Star Route 2, La Honda, CA 94020, (415) 948-9098. Or contact the Santa Cruz Mountain Natural History Association, 101 North Big Trees Park Road, Felton, CA 95018, (408) 335-3174..

No bird list is available, but a trail map and brochure may be purchased at the Park headquarters for 50 cents.

Birds seen in this vicinity include Band-tailed Pigeon, Anna's Hummingbird, Steller's Jay, White-breasted Nuthatch, Winter Wren, Ruby-crowned Kinglet, Golden-crowned Sparrow, Red Crossbill, Song Sparrow, Rufous-sided Towhee, Fox Sparrow, Scrub Jay, and Pileated, Acorn, Hairy, and Nuttall's Woodpeckers.

The park's real hot spot for birding is the lovely and sylvan Iverson Trail which winds along Pescadero Creek. The Pileated Woodpecker (often sighted right in the confines of the park campgrounds), is often seen by hikers on the trail, especially in the area near Tiptoe Falls.

From I-280 take the Page Mill Road exit and go west 12 miles to Portola State Park Road. (Page Mill changes to Alpine Road at Skyline Blvd.) Or just go down Skyline, (SH 35) and turn west on Alpine.

STEVENS CREEK COUNTY PARK

Set in a creek-cut canyon in the steep foothills of the Santa Cruz Mountains, Stevens Creek County Park has all of the following features: shady, streamside paths; scenic vistas from the canyon's rim; full picnic facilities; boating; good fishing; horseback riding; a visitor center where maps of the park are available; a colorful past that renders it appealing to history buffs; plenty of wilderness to explore; good opportunities for nature study; mild climate; easy access; a fine variety of birds, including the nesting American Dipper. Among the many other species seen here at Stevens Creek are Sharp-shinned Hawk, Wrentit, Song Sparrow, Rufous-sided and California Towhees, California Quail, Anna's Hummingbird, Hermit Thrush, Bewick's Wren, Bushtit, Golden-crowned Sparrow, Scrub Jay, Acorn Woodpecker, White-crowned Sparrow, Plain Titmouse, Winter Wren, House Finch, American Goldfinch, Purple Finch, Nuttall's Woodpecker, Lazuli Bunting, Northern Mockingbird, and perhaps the most interesting species of all, the Northern Pygmy-Owl. Spring is definitely the best time to bird at Stevens Creek.

To get here, take Stevens Creek Boulevard west from I-280 in San Jose. Go 4 miles to Foothill Boulevard, turn left and go another mile to the Park. Foothill Boulevard turns into Stevens Canyon Road and continues through the park.

COASTAL SAN MATEO COUNTY

Pomponio State Beach

Although craggy bluffs form its backdrop, you don't have to put on your hiking shoes, pack a lunch, or scale a cliff to reach this lovely, clean-swept beach with its salt marsh and pond, and the good, easy, close-up birding it offers to the passerby. Just turn off the highway where a sign reads "Pomponio State Beach," park in the parking lot, climb out of your car, and there you are.

This fine state beach is reputed for fascinating beachcombing; excellent fishing; beautiful wildflowers; great places to walk. Facilities here include a parking lot, picnic tables, and barbecue grills.

Among the species seen here or in the general area of Pomponio State Beach are Herring Gull, Marsh Wren, a variety of sandpipers, Western Gull, Black-shouldered Kite, Bewick's Wren, Song Sparrow, California Towhee, Savannah Sparrow, California Quail, cormorants, Heermann's Gull, and the very abundant Red-winged Blackbird. Common Ravens nest here.

Since Pescadero Marsh is so near, its checklist (*A Bird Checklist for Pescadero Marsh Natural Preserve*) may be useful to those who choose to drop by at Pomponio State Beach.

Pomponio Beach is on SH 1, 12 miles south of Half Moon Bay. There is a day use fee of $3.00 per car.

Pescadero State Beach and Preserve

On the western side of SH 1, the beautiful Pescadero State Beach includes 2 miles of clean-swept sandy beach, rolling dunes, rocky outcroppings, and 380 species of plants, over all of which Brown Pelicans fly with the grace of ballet dancers. The Preserve, however, which protects one of the most significant coastal marshes in California and provides a vital stopping-off point for thousands of migrating birds, is located on the opposite side of the highway.

More than 230 species of birds have been recorded within the Pescadero marshlands and 66 species are known to nest in the area. A bird list, *A Bird Checklist for Pescadero Marsh Natural Preserve*, is available from the California Department of Parks and Recreation, San Mateo Coast District.

For more information about this and other San Mateo Coast State Beaches write or call the Pescadero Marsh Interpretive Association, P.O. Box 370, Pescadero, CA 94060, (415)-879-0832, or contact the San Mateo Coast District Office at (415) 726-6230.

This is a regular fall stop for Pectoral Sandpipers, many other rare sandpipers, and virtually any waterfowl, and a breeding ground for marsh birds. Offshore sightings include shearwaters, skua, jaegars, and various alcids. Even a vagrant White-faced Ibis has been sighted in the vicinity.

Common or fairly common here for all or most of the year are Pied-billed Grebe, Double-crested Cormorant, Great Blue Heron, Cinnamon Teal, Northern Shoveler, Northern Harrier, Virginia Rail, Willet, Marbled Godwit, Black Turnstone, Glaucous-winged Gull, Caspian Tern, Anna's Hummingbird, Downy Woodpecker, Black Phoebe, Scrub Jay, Chestnut-backed Chickadee, Bushtit, Bewick's and Marsh Wrens, Hermit Thrush, and Wrentit.

Pescadero State Beach and Preserve straddle SH 1, 15 miles south of Half Moon Bay.

Bean Hollow State Beach/Bean Hollow Road

Although Bean Hollow beach is best known for the crescent shape of its shoreline, the sandstone of which it's comprised (an unusual rocky material known as the Pigeon Point Formation), its Harbor Seal rookery, and its appeal to tidepool buffs, it has plenty to offer to birders as well. A short distance southward is Bean Hollow Road, where lies the lovely Lake Lucerne and a small marsh much favored by herons.

Access to the road is easy. A pull-off area just past the bridge offers a good place to park and an excellent vantage point for sighting a number of species without even having to step away from your vehicle.

Birds that can be immediately seen, in one sweeping glance, in the marsh or lake, or the surrounding hills of Bean Hollow Road, include Great Blue Heron, Long-billed Dowitcher, Willet, Greater Yellowlegs, Belted Kingfisher, Common Yellowthroat, and Savannah and White-crowned Sparrows.

Bean Hollow State Beach is on SH 1, 17 miles south of Half Moon Bay. The parking lot has a day use fee of $3.00. For the easiest viewing of the lake and marsh, you can park just beyond the bridge on Bean Hollow Road, which takes off from the highway just south of the state beach lot.

Ano Nuevo State Reserve

On the 1988 Christmas Count the Ano Nuevo area ranked 14th in the entire United States, with a count of 180 species and 26,158 individuals. A bird list compiled by reserve ranger Gary Strachan shows a year-round count of 281 species.

The reserve is best known for its abundance of marine mammals, especially the fascinating Elephant Seal. The males of this species, enormous animals weighing as much as three tons each, begin to arrive in early December. Shortly thereafter, the females appear on the scene, and give birth a few days later — to the young they conceived here the year before. Within a month they're ready to conceive again. During the Elephant Seal breeding season, which lasts from December through March and is generally considered the most exciting time to visit the reserve, the area south of Cascade Creek is open only for guided tours which involve about a 3 mile trek and take approximately 2.5 hours. For reservations for these memorable walks, call Ticketron.

The picturesque and much-photographed old Dickerman Barn, which is a designated site of the National Register of Historic Places, serves as the preserve visitor center, and is replete with specimen exhibits, books, literature, and gifts. Whatever the weather, whatever the season, this fine reserve is open from 8 a.m. until sunset every day.

Common here for all or most of the year are Western and Eared Grebes, Brandt's and Pelagic Cormorants, Northern Harrier, California Quail, Black-bellied Plover, Marbled Godwit, Sanderling, Common Murre, Pigeon Guillemot, Anna's Hummingbird, six species of swallow, Song Sparrow, Purple Finch, and Red-winged Blackbird.

Confirmed breeders in the reserve are Pied-billed Grebe, Pelagic Cormorant, Great Blue Heron, Mallard, Green-backed Heron, Black-shouldered Kite, Northern Harrier, Sharp-shinned Hawk, American Kestrel, Red-shouldered Hawk, California Quail, Snowy Plover, Killdeer, Pigeon Guillemot, Rhinoceros Auklet, Band-tailed Pigeon, Mourning Dove, and Barn Owl.

The reserve is famed for the Elephant Seals, Steller's Sea Lions, which begin breeding in August, Harbor Seals, whose pupping season is in April and May, and an occasional Fur Seal, as well as California Gray Whales during migration.

Summer is the least advantageous time for either birding or mammal watching at Ano Nuevo.

For further information about this exceptional locale, call (415) 879-0227.

Ano Nuevo Reserve is on SH 1, 20 miles north of Santa Cruz, and 30 miles south of Half Moon Bay.

SAN JOSE

San Jose Water Works

At first blush, these water company premises don't seem extraordinary. After all, they're reached via the bustling South Almaden Expressway; they're set in a well-populated residential area; they have their parking lot, their offices, their holding grounds. There's nothing in first-sight appearances to hint that here lie ponds beloved to waterfowl and shorebirds, that here is egress to a fine riparian habitat, an enticing sylvan setting, an irresistible pathway that winds along Guadalupe Creek, a sense of wonder, a good bird count.

Bird the ponds just behind the waterworks from the paved trail on their north side. Then follow that path on down to Guadalupe Creek, under

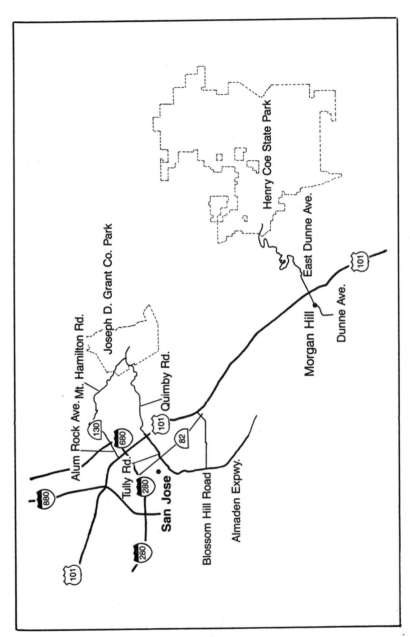

San Jose

Blossom Hill road, and walk alongside the stream to see what you can find on its banks. A leisurely 2 mile stroll is delightful and the bird counts generally rewarding.

Among the species sighted here are White-crowned and Golden-crowned Sparrows, Greater Yellowlegs, Spotted Sandpiper, Forster's Tern (in summer), Gadwall, Bufflehead, Northern Shoveler (in winter), Great Egret, Green-backed Heron, Common Moorhen, Red-winged Blackbird, and Pied-billed Grebe.

In San Jose, go south on Almaden Expressway to the first traffic light south of Blossom Hill Road, and turn left into the parking lot.

Joseph D. Grant Park

Located in the beautiful Mt. Hamilton Range, this handsome regional park, the largest in the Santa Clara County system, has all these attractions: open grasslands, imposing oaks, shady picnic grounds, 40 miles of hiking trails, horseback riding, fishing, overnight camping, and excellent birding. Species seen here include Great Blue Heron, grebes, California Quail, Nuttall's Woodpecker, Acorn Woodpecker, Northern Mockingbird, Scrub Jay, Anna's Hummingbird, Black Phoebe, Steller's Jay, Rufous-sided Towhee, Savannah Sparrow, California Towhee, Downy Woodpecker, Plain Titmouse, Bewick's Wren, and Hairy Woodpecker. Less common are Lawrence's Goldfinch, Common Snipe, and Western Kingbird, while special species of the area are Yellow-billed Magpie and Chestnut-backed Chickadee.

For further information call the Park Administration at (415) 358-3751.

From US 101 or I-680 in San Jose, take Alum Rock Road (SH 130) to the east. Two miles east of I-680, take Mt. Hamilton Road to the right. It's another 9 miles to the visitor center. Or, from further south on US 101, you can take the Tully Road exit. Tully turns into Quimby Road, which goes right into the park.

Henry W. Coe State Park

Of this park's 67,000 acres, 22,000 are pristine wilderness. This, coupled with the park's marvelously varied habitats, including oak savannah, grasslands, chaparral, pine forest, ridges, canyons, and creeks, spells an abundance of birdlife.

A backpacker's paradise, the area boasts all of the following: a park museum; 20 campsites, half of which are suitable for small motorhomes or trailers, the rest for tents; primitive hike-in campsites; mountain bike roads; horse-use camps; and enticing hiking and equestrian trails.

Hikers should not begin their treks without plenty of water and food and a map which can be obtained, as can a checklist of birds, at the park museum. Terrain is rugged. Wear good shoes, don't feed the animals, purify your backcountry water, and give the right of way to horses on the trail.

Common all or most of the year, and almost sure to be seen, are California Quail, Acorn Woodpecker, Steller's and Scrub Jays, Plain Titmouse, Ruby-crowned Kinglet (winter only), Anna's Hummingbird, House Finch, California Towhee, and Dark-eyed Junco.

Here all year, but either less common or more localized, are Great Blue Heron, Golden Eagle, Great Horned Owl, and Belted Kingfisher. Rare birds sighted here include Clark's Nutcracker, Pileated Woodpecker, and Prairie Falcon.

From US 101 in Morgan Hill, take Dunne Avenue due east 13 miles, to the park.

SAN FRANCISCO BAY NATIONAL WILDLIFE REFUGE

This refuge offers a wide expanse of wetlands, excellent hiking trails, a self-guided, educational tour along the Tidelands Trail, modern restrooms, excellent lookout points, platforms, overlooks, and bridges, an Environmental Education Center, naturalist-led interpretive programs, films, guided walks, and an unforgettable abundance of birdlife.

Along the Newark Slough Trail you can expect to see a variety of terns and gulls, Great Blue Heron, Snowy and Great Egrets, Black-crowned Night-Heron and, with luck, even California Clapper Rail. For more good birding take the trail just west of the boat launch, walk northward to the observation platform, and from that vantage point check out the ponds and mudflats for species such as American Avocet, Snowy Plover, and Lesser Yellowlegs.

Common here all year long are Pied-billed Grebe, Chestnut-backed Chickadee, Savannah Sparrow, Western Meadowlark, Great Blue Heron, Black-crowned Night-Heron, Great Egret, Northern Harrier, Ring-necked Pheasant, Black-shouldered Kite, and California Clapper Rail.

Regular winter or spring visitors are Northern Pintail, Cinnamon Teal, American Wigeon, Canvasback, Bufflehead, and Ruddy Duck.

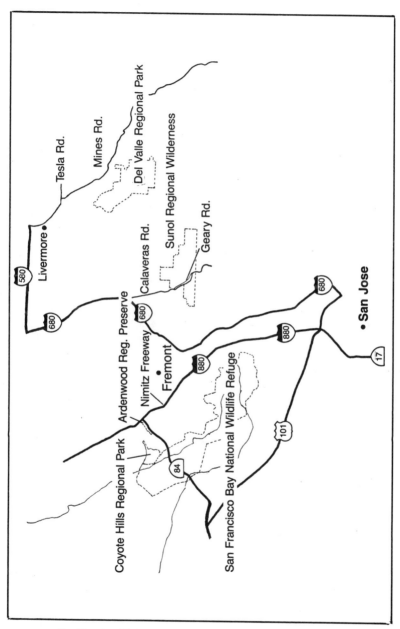

San Francisco National Wildlife Refuge and Central Alameda Co.

Here for at least half of the year are American White Pelican, Gadwall, Semipalmated Plover, Greater Yellowlegs, Red Knot, Short-billed and Long-billed Dowitchers, Caspian Tern, American and Lesser Goldfinches, and House Finch.

The wetlands abound in such creatures as brine shrimp in the salt ponds, and the snails that graze the mudflats, while on land, often seen from the Tidelands Trail, are rabbits, Ground Squirrels, Gopher Snakes, and many other small animals.

SH 84 (Dumbarton Highway) intersects the refuge. Take the Thorton Road exit, 2 miles west of I-80, and follow the signs to the refuge.

Coyote Hills Regional Park

Here are just a few of the experiences and sights that await the eager visitor at Coyote Hills Regional Park: historic Indian shell mounds left by the land's first inhabitants; group programs by the park naturalists; wonderful trails that wind around grassy hills, freshwater marshes, willow runs, and fallow fields; and a boardwalk out over the marsh from which to view an avian wonderland.

Look to the marsh for Tundra Swan, Greater White-fronted Goose, Snow Goose, Canvasback, Redhead, Greater Scaup, Surf Scoter, Common Goldeneye, Red-breasted Merganser, Ruddy Duck, and Common Moorhen.

In the vegetation along the waterways, where the willows and sycamore grow, expect to find Marsh Wren, Wrentit, Rufous-sided Towhee, and Lark Sparrow. Migrants seen in spring or fall include Solitary Vireo, Western Tanager, and MacGillivray's, Nashville, and Black-throated Gray Warblers.

In the conifer grove you may sight Cedar Waxwing, Loggerhead Shrike, Dark-eyed Junco, and Purple Finch. Other species seen here are Green-winged Teal, Great Horned Owl, Black-shouldered Kite, Burrowing Owl, Common Yellowthroat, Blue-Winged Teal, Blue-gray Gnatcatcher, Western Bluebird, Bewick's Wren, and Scrub Jay.

A bird list is available at the Coyote Hills Visitor Center, which is open from 9 a.m. until 4:30 p.m. every day except Christmas and New Year's day.

Coyote Hills is at the west end of Patterson Ranch Road/Commerce Drive in Fremont. Take the Thornton Avenue exit from SH 84, drive north on Paseo Padre Parkway, then turn left on Patterson Ranch Road.

Ardenwood Historic Farm

Nostalgia buffs, children, animal lovers, picnickers, and ordinary sight-seers, are just a few of the visitors drawn to this historic park. Here, where a glimpse into the past is everyday fare, draft horses are at work, lace makers are busy at their craft, artisans are making barrels, and hay wagons jostle through the barnyard. Here too there are plenty of birds to be seen, so many, in fact, that interest in regular Ardenwood bird walks is distinctly on the rise.

The following is a list of birds seen at Ardenwood between 7:00 a.m. and 9:00 a.m, on a clear and sunny morning in mid-February — in other words, on an ordinary day: Red-tailed Hawk, Rock Dove, Mourning Dove, Anna's Hummingbird, Northern Flicker, Downy Woodpecker, Nuttall's Woodpecker, Scrub Jay, Chestnut-backed Chickadee, Bushtit, Brown Creeper, Bewick's Wren, Northern Mockingbird, American Robin, Varied Thrush, Ruby-crowned Kinglet, European Starling, Yellow-rumped Warbler, Red-winged Blackbird, Brewer's Blackbird, House Finch, American Goldfinch, Rufous-sided Towhee, Dark-eyed Junco, and White-crowned and Golden-crowned Sparrows.

Admission to the park is $5.00 for adults, $2.50 for young people between the ages 4-18. Call (415) 791-4196 for tour information. The park is open from 10:00 a.m. to 4:00 p.m., Thursday through Sunday, April through November, and in December for a special Christmas program.

Ardenwood Historic Farm is located at 34600 Ardenwood Blvd., Fremont, CA 94555. From I-880 in Fremont, take SH 84 (Dumbarton Freeway) west and take the first exit, which is Ardenwood/Newark. Keep right on Ardenwood to the park entrance.

CENTRAL ALAMEDA COUNTY

Sunol Regional Wilderness

Of the East Bay parks, Sunol Regional Wilderness ranks particularly high with nature lovers of every variety. It offers all of the following attractions: interesting rock formations, including a huge basalt outcrop at

Indian Joe Cave rocks; the lovely Alameda Creek, surrounded by alder and sycamore and willow; hiking trails into the Ohlone Wilderness; a backpack area; rock climbing; overnight tent camping; 2 group campsites; picnic sites and barbecue pits; some of the most exciting birding in the San Francisco Bay Area.

Camping sites are available by reservation. Call (415) 531-9043. Backpackers wishing to camp in designated backpack areas must obtain a permit by advance reservation. Call (415) 862-2244 for details. Anyone wanting to camp on the Ohlone Wilderness Trail may do so by advance reservation only.

East Bay Regional Parks feature junior ranger programs, botanic garden walks, living history programs, nature films and slide shows, stargazing, snake talks, morning bird walks, and many other educational opportunities. For information regarding such activities write East Bay Regional Park District, ll500 Skyline Blvd., Oakland, CA 94619, or call (415) 531-9300.

With its rolling, oak-dotted hills and an abundance of ground squirrels, the Sunol Regional Wilderness is an excellent place for the Golden Eagle. Also seen here are California Quail, Nuttall's Woodpecker, California Towhee, Bushtit, Acorn Woodpecker, Northern Mockingbird, House Finch, and American Dipper.

To reach this area from the intersection of I-680 and Highway 84, take Calaveras Road southeast about 5 miles to Geary Road. The parking lot is at the end of Geary Road.

Del Valle Park

This 4,000-acre park boasts a visitor center, 2 swimming beaches, landscaped picnic grounds, a 5-mile-long lake, nature programs, access for the disabled, good fishing, windsurfing, a campground with 150 sites, 21 of which have water and sewage hookups, and toilet and shower facilities.

A special bird here is the handsome and chattery Yellow-billed Magpie. This brazen corvid is one of several species that nest only in California, and the only species that has never been sighted outside the state.

The following is a list of birds observed between 7:00 and 9:30 a.m., in June, 1988, on a six mile strip of road leading into Del Valle and within the park itself: Turkey Vulture, Sharp-shinned Hawk, American Kestrel, Red-shouldered and Red-tailed Hawks, California Quail, Killdeer, Caspian Tern, Forster's Tern, Mourning Dove, White-throated Swift, Anna's Hummingbird, Northern Flicker, Black Phoebe, Steller's Jay, Scrub Jay, Yellow-billed Magpie, American Crow, Chestnut-backed Chickadee, Plain Titmouse, Bushtit, Western Bluebird, American Robin, Yellow Warbler, Black-headed Grosbeak, Rufous-sided Towhee, Dark-eyed Junco, Red-winged Blackbird, Western Meadowlark, Brewer's Blackbird, Northern Oriole, American Goldfinch, House Finch, Lewis', Acorn, Nuttall's, and Hairy Woodpeckers, and Tree, Violet-green, Northern Rough-winged, Cliff and Barn Swallows.

From I-580 in Livermore, take the North Livermore exit; go south 3.4 miles to Tesla Road, then 0.5 mile to Mines Road. Turn right on Mines and go 4 miles to Del Valle Road.

Mines Road

The Mines Road trip takes the birder through some fairly isolated country in the eastern hills of Alameda County, southeast of Livermore.

Mines Road starts off gently enough, along Arroyo Creek with its riparian habitat and fine stands of cottonwoods and sycamore, and proceeds 5 miles through oak-studded flatlands and pastures. It then begins to ascend the canyon, through open grasslands, chaparral, and scrub oak woodlands, with some conifers higher up. It's a narrow and winding road as it gets up into the canyon (one lane in places) but it's very lightly travelled and has some spots to pull off.

Art Edwards of Livermore has been birding this area for years and reckons it one of the best locations in the state for regular sightings of uncommon interior landbirds. He has kept wonderfully detailed records, not only of the species sighted but also of the best places to look for them, which he makes available to other birders, and he in turn requests reports of any unusual sightings in the general area. His number is (415) 447-3720.

As documented by Art's work, Mines Road offers some unusual sightings, and these are the reasons birders find the area so appealing. These include Calliope Hummingbird, Williamson's Sapsucker, Cassin's Kingbird, Townsend's Solitaire, Northern Parula, American Redstart, White-throated Sparrow, Dark-eyed Junco (slate-colored race), Cassin's Finch, Gray Flycatcher, Phainopepla, Greater Roadrunner, and Lesser Goldfinch. Also listed as uncommon, but not as rare as the above, are Wood Duck, Bald Eagle, Prairie Falcon, Wild Turkey, Northern Pygmy-Owl, Poorwill, Lewis' Woodpecker, Hammond's and Dusky Flycatchers,

Rock and Canyon Wrens, Yellow-breasted Chat, and Sage Sparrow.

Take the North Livermore exit from I-580 in Livermore, go south 3.4 miles to Tesla Road, then east 0.5 mile to Mines Road.

This is a long road, and hot in the summertime, so be prepared. Once you get on Mines Road, there are very few places to get off. You can either drive part way up the canyon and then turn around, or choose a loop trip that covers 105 miles and goes through Del Puerto Canyon, up I-5, and through Corral Hollow back to Livermore.

Mines Road turns into San Antonio Valley Road at the Santa Clara County Line, 20 miles out. There's a small store and restaurant at San Antonio Junction, some 8 miles further south, where Del Puerto Road intersects. Del Puerto Canyon has a nice county campground, with hookups, for those who want to make this a two-day trip.

OAKLAND AREA

Hayward Regional Shoreline

Claiming 817 acres in all, 400 of which are saltwater, freshwater, and brackish-water marshes, this is a remarkably complex restoration project, still in progress, and is the largest of its kind anywhere on the West Coast. Its first phase was completed in 1980, and the area is fast becoming a well-established and recognized marshland, frequented not only by many east bay birders but hikers, cyclists, joggers, and picnickers as well.

A very special bird of this marshland, and one who sojourns in the bay area from April to August, is the endangered California Least Tern, which once occurred by the thousands all up and down the California coast. Its population up from 600 known pairs in the mid-1970's, this species now boasts more than 1,000 breeding pairs, distributed in 28 colonies in the San Francisco area, and from San Luis Obispo County to the border of Mexico.

Shorebirds and marsh dwellers seen here are Great Egret, American Avocet, Black-necked Stilt, Great Blue Heron, Northern Harrier, sandpipers, Forster's Tern, Snowy Egret, Marbled Godwit, Common Moorhen, American Bittern, Eurasian Wigeon, Whimbrel, and rails.

Park gates are open to the public during the hours posted at the entrance. Unless stipulated otherwise, curfew is between 10:00 p.m. and 5:00 a.m. Motor vehicles are restricted to specified parking areas.

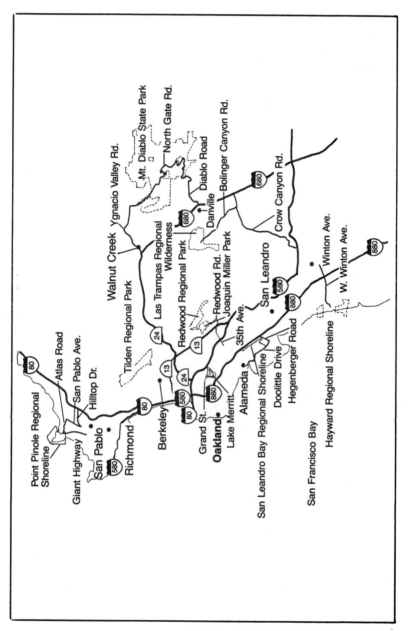

Oakland

For further information about Hayward Regional Shoreline, call (415) 881-1833.

From I-880 in Hayward, take the Winton Avenue exit and go west to the parking lot at the end of Winton Road. There's also access from the end of Grant Avenue in San Lorenzo.

San Leandro Bay Regional Shoreline/Doolittle Drive

This serene 1,218-acre regional park is known for all these features: easy entry from the scenic Doolittle Drive, the very popular Doolittle Beach, expanses of well-kept green lawns, handsome picnic areas, a boat ramp, and a beautifully designed observation platform, complete with wheelchair access, which overlooks 70-acre Arrowhead Marsh.

Burrowing Owls are easily sighted just 100 yards north of the first parking lot on the Swan Road side of the park. This is the road that leads to Arrowhead Marsh, where you can expect Brown Pelican, a variety of egrets, American Goldfinch, House Finch, and a variety of sparrows.

Some birders leave their vehicles in the parking lot at Doolittle Beach and then, instead of birding the park, walk northward toward the bridge to Alameda until they're easy viewing distance from a small islet sometimes covered with birds.

In just five minutes of easy birding on the shoreline near the bridge one day in October, 1989, we sighted 12 Forster's Terns, 75 Marbled Godwits, 20 Black-bellied Plovers, 40 dowitchers, 7 American Avocets, 50 Willets, and 2 Great Egrets.

Ground squirrels are abundant here, easy to mistake for the Burrowing Owls.

Other parts of Doolittle Drive offer good birding also, as for example, the nearby Alameda Municipal Golf Course where Great Blue Herons have often been seen strolling across the greens.

From I-880 in the south part of Oakland, take the Hegenberger Road exit. Go west toward the Oakland Airport 0.5 mile to Doolittle Drive, and turn right. To get to Arrowhead Marsh, turn right on Swan Way, and then immediately left on a good gravel road to the marsh. For the remainder, return to Doolittle Drive and go north.

Lake Merrit/Lakeside Park

Affected by tidal action and bearing about the same level of salinity as the bay, this 150-acre lake, this jewel of downtown Oakland, is a haven for waterfowl and a pleasant place for easy close-up viewing and behavior observation. This is one of the virtues of Lake Merrit: birds who linger here necessarily get used to people and grow tamer in the process.

Lakeside Park, on the eastern shore between two arms of the lake, is the site of display botanical gardens, as well as the oldest wildfowl refuge in the country. There's good birding around the entire lake for water birds, passerines, and some shorebirds, but the park is probably the best place to start. In addition to the tidal input, the lake is fed by four freshwater creeks: two permanent, and two seasonal.

Seen here regularly are Canada Goose, herons, egrets, gulls, grebes, coots, and cormorants, and to the delight of park strollers, occasionally a flock of American White Pelicans appears upon the scene. In the wintertime, look for Tufted Duck, Red-throated Loon, Canvasback, Hooded Merganser, and Redhead. Barrow's Goldeneye is also often sighted here.

The urban passerines are plentiful in the many trees of the parkland: White-crowned, Golden-crowned, and Song Sparrows, Northern Mockingbird, House Finch, Black Phoebe, towhees, and swallows in the summertime.

Lake Merritt is in the center of downtown Oakland, reachable by any number of city streets. One of the easier ways for an out-of-towner, is to take the Grand Avenue exit from I-580, and go west a couple of blocks to the park.

Redwood Regional Park/Joaquin Miller City Park

Although it's just a few minutes from downtown Oakland, Redwood Regional Park has much to offer — most of which is thanks to the creek that winds through its grounds and affords drinking water to many mammals and birds. Here too, Rainbow Trout are known to spawn, fitting, because this famous fish was first identified as a separate species from specimens caught in San Leandro Creek, of which this rivulet is a tributary.

Other than redwood groves, meandering creek, chaparral, and grasslands, this park has picnic sites; grassy play areas; easy access for disabled persons; good trails for joggers, hikers, horseback riders, and birders; access to The East Bay Skyline National Trail, which traverses it for part of its 31-mile course. Besides all this, it borders the Joaquin Miller City Park, a locale recommended by Lake Merrit's naturalist, Dick Kaufmann,

Double-crested Cormorant

as an excellent place to sight Golden Eagles. (Dick reports a nesting pair was here in 1988.) Both of these parks boast occasional sightings of the endangered Peregrine Falcon.

The following is a list of birds identified at Redwood Regional Park in a two hour period, on a clear, warm morning in October, 1988; Sharp-shinned Hawk, Band-tailed Pigeon, Mourning Dove, Scrub Jay, Wrentit, Chestnut-backed Chickadee, Bushtit, Brown Creeper, Red-breasted Nuthatch, Bewick's Wren, Warbling Vireo, Townsend's Warbler, Wilson's Warbler, California Towhee, Song Sparrow, Dark-eyed Junco, and Great Horned, Screech and Northern Pygmy-Owls.

Out-of-towners wishing general information about East Bay parks should call (415) 531-9300.

From I-580 in East Oakland take the 35th Avenue exit and go east. 35th turns into Redwood Road where it crosses SH 13, and goes on into the park. Redwood Road then continues southwest through the length of the adjacent Anthony Chabot Regional Park, a distance of some 10 miles.

Las Trampas Regional Wilderness

Only the birder who is also a serious hiker or rider will ever know what opportunities lie within this undefiled wilderness, what birds are waiting here in these 3,458 acres of unspoiled land that spans parts of the busy, urban Contra Costa and Alameda counties.

Among the natural attractions of this rugged country are wind-sculpted stone outcroppings on Rocky Ridge; a world of wildflowers at Sedum Falls in Devil's Hole; a view from the ridge that's so panoramic you can see Ygnacio, Amador, and San Ramon Valleys, Carquinez Strait, and Mt. Diablo; fully defined geological formations caused by the action of two major bay area faults — Bollinger and Las Trampas; shrubs and small trees such as black sage, chamise, buck brush, manzanitas, gooseberry, toyon, coyote brush and poison oak; eucalyptus trees that tower 100 feet into the sky; plenty of live oak to satisfy the eagles seen soaring overhead.

One of the few signs of civilization are the two picnic areas near the parking lot. Each has 5 tables and 3 barbecue units. Here the facilities are available only on a first-come, first-served basis. One of these, the Corral Picnic area, is a reservable overnight camping area for horseback riders. For further information call (415) 531-9043.

Las Trampas stables offers guided trail rides, boarding stables, overnight rides to Anthony Chabot Regional Park, hayrides, and barbecue rides. Advance reservations can be made by calling (415) 838-7546.

Little Hills Regional Recreation area, which is adjacent to Las Trampas, can facilitate group picnics and other activities by reservation. This area features a swimming pool, two pavilions, barbecue, and picnic areas, and a turfed area for outdoor games. For more information call (415) 837-0821.

The truly special bird of Las Trampas Regional Wilderness and the one that most birders come to see is the Golden Eagle. Among the many other species sighted here are Acorn Woodpecker, Scrub Jay, White-crowned and Golden-crowned Sparrows, American Goldfinch, and House Finch.

Other wildlife seen here includes Raccoons, Opossums, skunks, foxes, and squirrels.

From I-580, take Crow Canyon Road north at Castro Valley, or from I-680 take Crow Canyon Road west from San Ramon to Bollinger Canyon.

Go north 4.5 miles to the parking lot. Foot or horse access is reached via Del Amigo Trail at the west end of Starview Drive in Danville.

Mount Diablo State Park

Experts say that the panorama visible from the summit of Mount Diablo is unsurpassed by that from any other mountain in the world, with the exception only of the wondrous Mt. Kilimanjaro, which reaches all of 19,000 feet into the wide African skies.

Sights viewed from Mount Diablo's summit include the Santa Cruz Mountains, the ethereal Mount Lassen, the Great Central Valley and its winding river delta, the Golden Gate, the Farallon Islands and the ocean beyond for as far as the eye of man or hawk can see.

No wonder this mountain is enshrouded in legends such as the one that William H. Brewer recounted in his journal as he camped at its foot in October of 1861. "The Californians tell us that once in olden time they had a battle with the Indians here," he wrote. "It was going hard with the Spaniards, when the Devil came out of the mountain, helped the Spaniards, and the Indians were vanquished. I cannot vouch for the truth of their story, but the story gave the name to the mountain, and the rocks certainly do look as if the devil had been about at some time. There is a breaking up and roasting of strata on a grand scale."

This "roasted" strata is just one of the many interesting features of this old giant whose geologic story is as fascinating as the legendary devil that dwells in its innards. Experts say that, through forces of the earth bent toward upheaval, a plug of 160-million-year-old red rock came surging upward through miles of overlaying soil. Fossilized remains of mastodons and three-toed horses remain to tell of the tumult.

The following are just a few of the vital statistics of this historic park: elevations that range from 300 to 3,849 feet; broad variations in rainfall and temperature; a wide variety of plant life; an abundance of birds and other wildlife; excellent trails; an area called "Rock City," known for its huge sandstone formations; great rocks to challenge climbers; more than 100 family picnic sites with tables and stoves; group picnic areas equipped to accommodate up to 100 people; developed family campsites; environmental campgrounds; horse group campgrounds with stalls for 84 horses.

Mount Diablo is well-known as a good place for sighting raptors. Here year round are Red-tailed Hawk, American Kestrel, and four species of owl.

Other year-round residents include California Quail, Anna's Hummingbird, Steller's Jay, Plain Titmouse, Scrub Jay, Bushtit, Bewick's Wren, Western Bluebird, House Finch, Band-tailed Pigeon, Chestnut-backed Chickadee, and Acorn, Downy, Hairy, and Nuttall's Woodpeckers. Orange-crowned Warbler is a summer resident, and Golden-crowned Sparrow can be seen in fall, winter, and spring.

Also seen here are Coastal Black-tailed Deer, California Ground Squirrel, Raccoon, Eastern Fox Squirrel, Gray Fox, Striped and Spotted Skunks, Bobcat, Mountain Lion, Badger, Coyote, Cotton-tailed Rabbit, and others. Resident snakes include the rare Alameda Striped Racer and the Northern Rattlesnake.

From Walnut Creek, take Ygnacio Valley Road east through town 3 miles to Walnut Avenue and turn right. After 2 miles Walnut turns into North Gate Road, which goes through the park. From Ygnacio Valley Road, it's about 10 miles to park headquarters, and another 5 to the parking lot for the summit loop trail.

From Danville, take Diablo Road north and east to Mt. Diablo Scenic Boulevard and into the park.

Tilden Regional Park

Here are some of the features that make this so-called "crown jewel" of the East Bay Park System so special: 2,078 acres of land, some highly developed, some surprisingly pristine; fine riparian habitat; two lakes and Wildcat Creek; woods that reach into side canyons rich in birdlife; stretches of grasslands and expanses of chaparral; a child-sized steam train that rides a scenic ridge; an 18-hole golf course with pro shop and coffee shop; a Botanic garden, said to contain the world's most representative collection of California's native plants; a visitor center that offers lectures and tours; the Brazil Building, which contains the Brazilian exhibits of the 1939 World's Fair; a sandy beach offering seasonal swimming; a bathhouse and food stand; year-round fishing; an antique merry-go-round with hand-carved animals; an Environmental Education Center with access for the disabled; and scenic vistas from the crest of the wonderful East Bay Hills. Hiker's maps, bird check lists, and park brochures are available at the visitor center.

Among the many unusual sightings here at Tilden Regional Park are the Hooded Warbler, Calliope Hummingbird, Red Crossbill, Canada Warbler, and Indigo Bunting.

Seen here also are six species of gull, Bald Eagle, Northern Harrier, Red-shouldered Hawk, Golden Eagle, Steller's Jay, Great Blue Heron, California Quail, Rufous-sided and California Towhees, Nuttall's Woodpecker, Scrub Jay, Acorn Woodpecker, and many other species that make this park one of the best places in the bay area to see land birds.

From SH 24 just east of the Caldecott Tunnel, take Claremont Avenue to Skyline Boulevard and turn right. Skyline becomes South Park Drive, and goes into the park. From I-80 in Berkeley, take University Avenue east to the U. C. campus. Turn left on Oxford Street, and after 0.5 mile, follow the road as it jogs to the east, over to Spruce. Take Spruce to Wildcat Canyon Road, which works its way up the hills and into the main entrance to the park.

Point Pinole Regional Shoreline

This park boasts all of the following features: 5.5 miles of shoreline; a 1,250-foot fishing pier; salt marshes that hint of what the Bay area shorelines were like long ago; grasslands where colorful wildflowers flourish; woodlands comprised of the alien Blue Gum; Blue Gum-loving birds uncommon to other shoreline locales; trails in which to stroll, bicycle, or horseback ride; scenic vistas.

Look in the Whittell Marsh for Great Blue Heron, Snowy Egret, Black-necked Stilt, American Avocet, Marsh Wren, sandpipers, Great Egret, and Song Sparrow. In the grasslands expect American and Lesser Goldfinches, Western Meadowlark, Western Bluebird, and a variety of sparrows. Also here are Anna's Hummingbird, Brewer's Blackbird, House Finch, Killdeer, and Band-tailed Pigeon. Western Tanager and Osprey are sighted here as well. A Summer Tanager has been seen at least once.

A check list of birds may be obtained by writing to the Administrative Offices of East Bay Regional Park District at 11500 Skyline Boulevard, Oakland, CA 94619. For further information about Point Pinole call (415) 881-1833.

From I-80 in Richmond, take Hilltop Drive west to San Pablo Avenue, go right, to Atlas Road, and turn left. It's about a mile to the park entrance, just after Atlas Road turns into the Giant Highway.

Chapter 4
Monterey Bay

 This is Steinbeck country, land immortalized in *Cannery Row, Tortilla Flats, East of Eden,* and *The Pastures of Heaven.* It's also the land of the wind-blown cypress, of the fog-shrouded cliffs of Big Sur, of the incredibly fertile fields of the Salinas Valley. The Artichoke Capital of the World is here, as well as the famed boardwalk at Santa Cruz, and the elegant shops of Carmel, and Seventeen Mile Drive showcases the spectacular sea-scapes, stately homes and world class golf courses of Monterey Peninsula.

Rich marine life in the sloughs and tidepools of the bay contrasts with the grassy hills of the San Benito Valley. Pristine redwoods still thrive in the Santa Cruz mountains. Monarch butterflies return by the millions each fall to Pacific Grove. And, Monterey Bay is considered to be one of the finest birding areas in California.

Monterey is also a land of history. It was thriving as the capital of Alta California long before Europeans knew San Francisco Bay existed. Padre Junipero Serra had his headquarters at the mission in Carmel, and is buried there. The largest of the missions is at San Juan Bautista, near Hollister; every month a living history pageant revives its colorful past. Missions also flourished at Santa Cruz, at Soledad, and at San Antonio, in the rolling oak hills and grasslands of what is now Fort Hunter Liggett. It's always a moving experience to visit these restored monuments to our cultural past, but for birders there's yet another dimension: the old buildings and the shrubbery and ancient trees of the courtyards and graveyards are as attractive to a variety of birds today as they were in the days of the Padres.

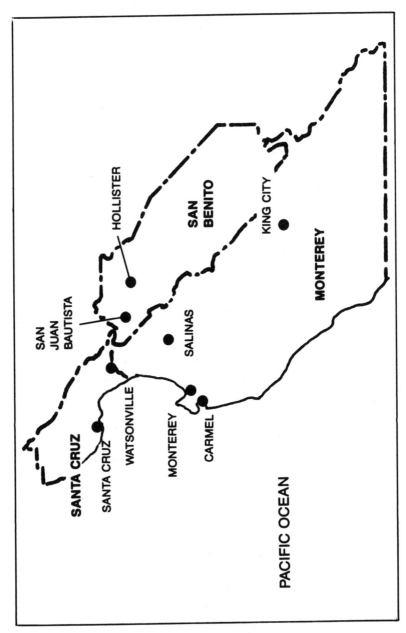

Monterey Bay Region

The Monterey Bay Region, as delineated here, consists of Monterey, Santa Cruz, and San Benito Counties, a total of 5,161 square miles, and represents 6.5% of the area covered by this book.

The population today, as it was in the time of the missions, is concentrated around the bay from Monterey to Santa Cruz, with the largest city, Salinas, some ten miles inland.

The geology is that of the Coastal Range. Salinas Valley extends southeast from the bay and separates the two major ridge systems, Santa Lucia Range on the coast and Cavilan Range inland. The entire area, with the exception of the western coastal slopes, is drained by two major river systems, the San Benito/Pajaro combine and the Salinas, which flow into the bay just seven miles apart.

The major road systems all run north and south. SH 1 from San Simeon to Monterey is known as one of the most spectacular coastal highways in the world; US 101, the major arterial, is the modern day "El Camino Real" through the Salinas Valley; SH 25 handles the sparsely populated San Benito River valley; and in the north, SH 17 runs from the coast to the San Francisco Bay area, through the Santa Cruz mountains.

SUGGESTED CHECK LISTS AND BOOKS
FOR THE MONTEREY BAY REGION

There are several good books and check lists available for the Monterey Bay Region, among them the following:

Checklist of the Birds of the Big Sur Area
Available through Pfeiffer Big Sur State Park
Big Sur, CA 93920
(408) 667-2315
(Send 25 cents and a stamped, self-addressed envelope.)

Two excellent books, *Monterey Birds* ($14.95) by Roberson, and *Pelagic Birds of Monterey Bay* ($2.50) by Stallcup are available through:

The Book Nest
Richardson Bay Audubon Center
379 Greenwood Beach Road
Tiburon, CA 94920
(415) 388-2524

SANTA CRUZ

Castle Rock State Park

This 3,600-acre state park located on the western ridge of the Santa Cruz Mountains, is known especially for its geologic features — caves and holes in its constantly eroding sandstone surface, as well as the odd-shaped formations for which it's named. These ridges were caused by faulting and uplifting movements that began 25 million years ago and continue even today. This is rough land, accessible only by foot, not to be birded by the faint at heart.

There are more attractions at this state park than the namesake rocks so challenging to climbers. History buffs come to reflect upon its colorful past, native plant enthusiasts to revel in its wildflowers, backpackers to hike its network of trails, and birders to view the resident birds, especially a long list of raptors including Northern Pygmy, Western Screech, Barn, and Great Horned Owls.

Common or fairly common here all year long are Band-tailed Pigeon, Belted Kingfisher, Black Phoebe, Pacific Slope Flycatcher (March-October only), Wrentit, Plain Titmouse, Bushtit, California Thrasher, and Acorn, Hairy, and Nuttall's Woodpeckers.

From I-280 in Cupertino, take SH 85 south to Saratoga, turn right on SH 9 and follow it to SH 35 at Saratoga Gap. From here, SH 9 skirts the west side of the park, and there's a parking area at Sempervirens Point, 2 miles down the hill. Or take SH 35 around the east side to park headquarters and Castle Rock.

From the Santa Cruz area, you can pick up SH 9 in Santa Cruz from SH 1, or get on SH 35 from SH 17, 3 miles south of Los Gatos.

Big Basin Redwoods State Park

Big Basin offers many fine examples of its proudest feature, the redwood, *Sequoia sempervirens*, and many other beautiful trees like wax myrtle and California laurel; understory tangles of huckleberry, azalea, and ferns; spring wildflowers such as wild ginger, trillium and the delicate and lovely redwood violet; interesting geological features; environmental campsites; a horse trail camp; riparian woodland; springs and creeks; a marshland boasting 150 species of birds; extraordinary hiking trails (including the

Black Phoebe

famous "Skyline to the Sea") which lead the avid trekker miles from Big Basin Park Headquarters all the way to the sea via Rancho del Oso.

A special species of the park is the Web-footed Marbled Murrelet, which chooses to build its nest 200 feet off the floor of the redwood forest. The first recorded North American sighting of a Marbled Murrelet nest occurred here at Big Basin.

Look for Great Blue Heron, Great Egret, Marsh Wren, American Bittern, Sora, Red-winged Blackbird, Northern Shoveler, and Virginia Rail in the marshland; Brown Pelican, loons, grebes, scoters, sandpipers and the like on the coast; Steller's Jay, nuthatches, California Towhee, Great Horned Owl, and Acorn Woodpecker in the woods; and American Dipper, Belted

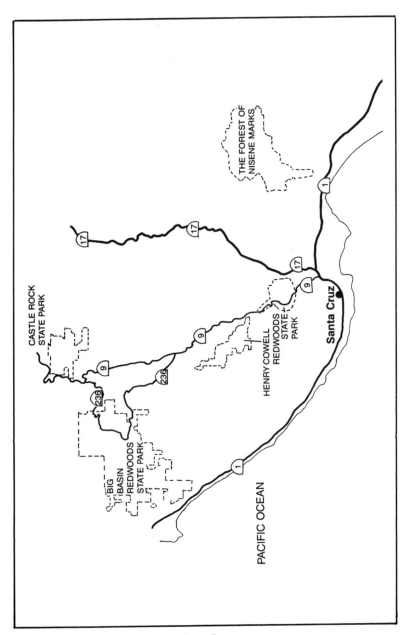

Santa Cruz

Kingfisher, and a variety of sparrows along the creeks. Here too are Pileated Woodpeckers.

Big Basin is home to the Pacific Giant Salamander, the California Newt, the Pacific Tree Frog, and the endangered Western Skink. Mammals common here include Black-tailed Deer, Gray Squirrels, Chipmunks, and Raccoons. Less often sighted are Opossum, bobcat, foxes, Coyote, and Mountain Lion.

Maps and bird lists are available at the park headquarters, as are many fine publications pertaining to the area.

From Santa Cruz, take SH 9 north 13 miles to Boulder Creek, turn left on SH 236 and proceed another 9 miles to park headquarters. SH 236 loops through the park and back to SH 9. From San Francisco, take SH 85 south from I-280 in Cupertino and pick up SH 9 in Saratoga. Turn right and go up over Saratoga Gap to SH 236.

Henry Cowell Redwoods State Park

This beautiful 1,800-acre state park located near Santa Cruz boasts a variety of habitats — virgin redwood forests, canyon streams, pine and oak woods, open meadows, and chaparral — which spell an abundance of birds. Among these are the 187 species listed by the Santa Cruz County 1988 Christmas Bird Count, which centered here in Henry Cowell Redwoods.

The park also boasts 20 miles of fine hiking trails, including a path that's wheelchair accessible; fine picnic facilities; a 120-unit campground complete with tables, fire rings, and modern restrooms; a docent-staffed Nature Center with excellent exhibits, books, maps, and bird lists.

Species common here include California Towhee, Acorn Woodpecker, California Quail, Scrub Jay, White-crowned Sparrow, Great Blue Heron, Belted Kingfisher, and Steller's Jay. Also seen here are Golden Eagle, seven owl species, Nuttall's Woodpecker, American Dipper, and Hermit Thrush.

Look for California Quail, swallows and a variety of sparrows in the meadow by the day use entrance road, ducks, herons, and Belted Kingfisher along the river.

Mammals commonly seen in the park include Black-tailed Deer, chipmunks, and Brush Rabbits. Not often sighted but certainly here, as their footprints testify, are Coyote, Grey Fox, Bobcat, and Mountain Lion.

For further information about Henry Cowell Redwoods call the park office at (408) 335-4598.

From SH 1 in Santa Cruz, you can take SH 9, which runs through the park on the west side of San Lorenzo River. There are parking pull-outs and trailheads along the road, and the day use area, Nature Center, and park headquarters are off this road at the north end of the park. The campground entrance is on the other side of the canyon, off Graham Hill Road, which also is accessed from SH 1 in Santa Cruz or Felton.

The Forest of Nisene Marks State Park

Once ravaged by a logging frenzy, this forest has been renewed and stands as a monument to the Marks family and The Nature Conservancy who worked together to insure its restoration. Today, the trees are thriving; the ridges and canyons are beginning to appear much as they did decades ago; the birds typical to established redwood forests are in residence.

Since many of the park's commonest species are year-round residents, bird counts are fairly constant here from season to season. Expect California Towhee, Red-shouldered Hawk, Acorn Woodpecker, Great Horned Owl, California Quail, Scrub Jay, White-crowned Sparrow, Great Blue Heron, Belted Kingfisher, and Steller's Jay. Also seen here are Golden Eagle, seven species of owl, Nuttall's Woodpecker, American Dipper, and Hermit Thrush.

Mammals include Black-tailed Deer, chipmunks, squirrels, and — though much less frequently sighted — Coyote, Grey Fox, Bobcat, and Mountain Lion.

For further information or for trail camp reservations write: The Forest of Nisene Marks State Park, 101 North Big Trees Park Road, Felton, CA 95018, or call (408) 335-4598.

From the town of Aptos, just off SH 1 between Santa Cruz and Watsonville, take Aptos Creek Road to the park, at the bottom of the canyon. Get to the upper reaches of the park by taking Summit Road/Highland Way from SH 17 in Redwood Estates.

Neary's Lagoon Park and Wildlife Refuge

Although this pleasant, easy-access Santa Cruz park has many attractions, including picnic facilities, modern restrooms, tennis courts, and playground equipment, its most outstanding feature is lovely Neary's Lagoon with its cattails and willows so alluring to birds.

Most conspicuous here, perhaps, are the many swallows who circle the water endlessly, sometimes swooping so low it's as if they're dive bombing their own reflections. But there are many other species to be seen on the water or at its edge, as well as in the nearby foliage — and a trip to Neary's Lagoon is rarely disappointing. Expect Northern Oriole, goldfinches, Golden-crowned and White-crowned Sparrows, House Finch, Northern Mockingbird, Anna's Hummingbird, Ruddy Duck, Common Moorhen, Wood Duck, Marsh Wren, Song Sparrow, Common Yellowthroat, grebes, and Warbling Vireo.

Unusual species sighted in the area include Palm, Nashville, and Lucy's Warblers, and Grasshopper and Chipping Sparrows.

From SH 1 in Santa Cruz, about a mile north of the SH 17 intersection, take Bay Street toward the bay. Cross the tracks, turn left on California, cross the tracks again and immediately turn right to the Nature Area parking lot.

MOSS LANDING STATE BEACH/STATE WILDLIFE AREA

No creature could better serve as symbol for this popular birding spot than the endangered Brown Pelican. According to Bruce G. Elliott, South District Supervisor for the Department of Fish and Game, approximately 7,000 of these great birds roost in the Moss Landing Wildlife Area every winter, more than in any other place on the northern California coast.

Of course, many other species abound at Moss Landing, as for example these listed in the notes we jotted down the last time we birded here:

"Just before the entrance kiosk, pulled off on shoulder. Caspian Terns, about 30, clustered up together over to our right. Maybe 75 Willets. Black Turnstones probing around on an old barge to our left. Head on into the park. Pull off on shoulder about a quarter of a mile past kiosk. Nice place — 200 yards from the ocean on one side, 100 yards from the harbor on the other. Heermann's Gulls, at least a hundred, on a sandbar that points toward the boats in the marina. Half that many Brown Pelicans."

Commonly or fairly commonly seen in the coastal water or tidelands are Common, Pacific, and Red-throated Loons, Horned and Eared Grebes, White-winged Scoter, and Glaucous-winged, Western, Herring, Ring-bil-

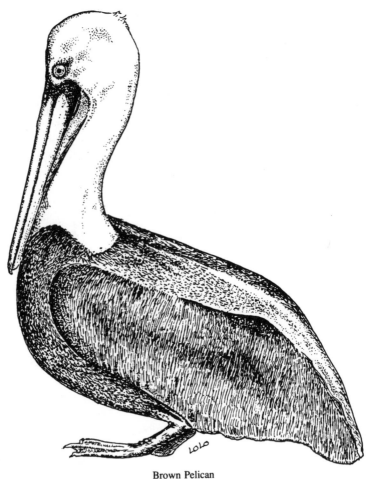

Brown Pelican

led, Mew, Bonaparte's and Heermann's Gulls. Regularly seen on the beach and dunes are Black-bellied Plover, Willet, and Sanderling. Regularly seen in the salt marshes on the wildlife area are Common Goldeneye, Black-necked Stilt, and American Avocet.

Rare or uncommon birds Elliott has sighted in the Moss Landing vicinity include Lesser Golden-Plover, Mongolian Plover, California Clapper Rail, Mississippi Kite, and Black Skimmer.

The Moss Landing State Wildlife Area is managed by the Department of Fish and Game, 2201 Garden Road, Monterey, CA 93940. The phone number is (408) 649-2870.

Birds sighted here are basically the same as those seen at Elkhorn Slough. A bird list, *Checklist of the Birds of Elkhorn Slough*, has been a regular handout at the entrance kiosk of Moss Landing State Beach.

Moss Landing State Beach is just off SH 1, on the north side of the point at which Elkhorn Slough enters the bay. (Moss Landing Marina is on the south side.) It's about halfway between Santa Cruz and Monterey.

Before you plan a trip to Moss Landing State Beach be sure to call ahead and make certain that the park has reopened following a temporary closure of indeterminate length. Write or call California Land Management, 675 Gilman Street, Palo Alto, CA 94301, (415) 322-1181 or California Department of Parks and Recreation, Monterey District, 20 Custom House Plaza, Monterey, CA 93940, (408) 384-7695.

ELKHORN SLOUGH

Just a few decades ago the future of these wetlands was sorely threatened by the urban development that was encroaching on every side. Without human intervention, Elkhorn Slough was destined to share the fate of nearly 90% of California's estuaries — namely, destruction by humans. That it's here today, replete with educational programs, excellent overlooks, tide-dependent waterways, breeding grounds for a variety of lifeforms, scenic beauty, and an extraordinary ambience, is thanks to the combined efforts of many.

The Elkhorn Slough National Estuarine Research Reserve. One of the "saviors" of the slough is the California Department of Fish and Game, which oversees the Elkhorn Slough National Estuarine Research Reserve and operates under an agreement with the Division of Marine and Estuarine Management of the National Oceanic and Atmospheric Administration. Facilities at the reserve include a wheelchair accessible visitor center with book store and interpretive displays, self-guided hiking trails, a pleasant picnic area, modern restrooms, drinking water, and a public telephone. Maps, brochures, and the *Checklist of the Birds of Elkhorn Slough* are available at the Reserve Visitor Center.

For more information write the Department of Fish and Game, Elkhorn Slough National Estuarine Research Reserve, 1700 Elkhorn Road, Watsonville, CA 95076, or call (408) 728-2822.

Elkhorn Slough Preserve, The Nature Conservancy. Another organization whose dedicated efforts preserve this magnificent Monterey County location is The Nature Conservancy, whose private property, the Elkhorn Slough Preserve, is adjacent to the National Estuarine Research Reserve. This preserve covers 388 acres of vital wetland and 3 rare communities: the Northern Eusaline Lagoon, Northern Coastal Saltmarsh, and Coastal Freshwater Marsh. The preserve visitor can walk from one of these to the other with comparative ease and can, in fact, trek all the way from the woodpecker-rife groves of coast live oaks in the uplands to the water's edge at the marsh.

For information about The Nature Conservancy and guided tours of its private preserve, call (408) 728-2822.

The Elkhorn Slough Foundation. This vital, nonprofit organization represents dedicated volunteer workers who perform a variety of jobs ranging from interpretive guide to book sales clerk. These volunteers do all within their power to keep affairs running smoothly everywhere at Elkhorn Slough.

Although summer is generally considered the least exciting time to bird most portions of Elkhorn Slough, each season offers its own particular set of attractions. In fall the migrating birds begin to arrive daily. In winter the population of migratory and resident species is distinctly at its peak, the wetlands literally packed with birds. In spring, when the hills are dotted with the scarlet of pimpernel, the fiery orange of the California poppy, the sun-yellow of lupine, a variety of migrants drop in for a short-term visit, while others linger long enough to breed and nest. Summer is a great time to view and observe the many Brown Pelicans who roost in this area.

Notably, wetlands aren't all that Elkhorn Slough has to offer in the way of wildlife habitat. It is surrounded by acres of cropland and therefore shares some species common to an agricultural habitat. The slough also has grasslands as well as areas wooded by Monterey pines, eucalyptus, and live oaks.

Popular activities at Elkhorn Slough include wildlife photography, hiking, guided tours at both the Nature Conservancy Preserve and the Fish and Game Reserve, educational activities, and special classes.

The many birders who come here especially to see the marshland birds are always stunned to find how many other species meet their eyes. Among year-round residents at Elkhorn Slough are California Quail, Western and California Gulls, Downy Woodpecker, Black Phoebe, Scrub Jay, Chestnut-backed Chickadee, Bushtit, Bewick's and Marsh Wrens, Savannah Sparrow, California Towhee, and Song Sparrow.

Common or fairly common for most of the year are Common and Red-throated Loons, Eared and Horned Grebes, Brandt's Cormorant, Great Blue Heron, Snowy Egret, American Wigeon, Northern Shoveler, Lesser Scaup, Common Goldeneye, Bufflehead, Long-billed Curlew, Willet, Short-billed and Long-billed Dowitchers, and Sanderling.

In fall we suggest birding the South Marsh Loop to scan the marsh for flocks of dowitchers and sandpipers, American Wigeon, Mallard, and Northern Pintail. Take the boardwalk over the mudflats to catch sight of Marbled Godwit and Willet. In winter take the 1-mile hike to Parson Slough to view pintail, shoveler, Double-crested Cormorant, and Red-throated Loon. In spring linger on the flower-bedecked hills. Look for Allen's Hummingbird and California Quail, and scan the skies for Cooper's Hawk and Northern Harrier. Or, take a trek to the wildlife blind on Five Fingers Loop to watch the courtship shows of the pert little Ruddy Duck. In summer, feast your eyes upon the countless Brown Pelicans that roost around the slough.

Take SH 1 south from Watsonville, turn left on Dolan Road just before the town of Moss Landing, and go 3.5 miles to Elkhorn Road. Turn left here and proceed another 2.5 miles until you reach the Visitor Center on the left. The area is clearly marked.

SALINAS RIVER WILDLIFE MANAGEMENT AREA

There's nothing slick or polished anywhere to be seen in these 500 acres of unspoiled Salinas River country. What you will find, however, are sandy dunes upon which the Golden-crowned Sparrows sing, the river's mouth aswarm with gulls, grasslands polka-dotted with the yellow of fennel and the purple of wild asters, lagoon, salt marsh, open space, fresh air, and so many birds you're sure to lose count.

For more information about this wildlife area, write or call The San Francisco Bay National Wildlife Refuge, P.O. Box 524, Newark, CA

94560, (415) 762-0222; or the California Department of Fish and Game, 2201 Garden Road, Monterey, CA 93940, (408) 649-2870.

With its varied habitats — lagoon, seacoast, sandy dunes, and river mouth — this area offers good birding all year long. In just a half hour of leisurely strolling one day in October, 1989, we listed Yellow-rumped Warbler, Northern Flicker, Western Meadowlark, Great Blue Heron, American Avocet, Black-necked Stilt, California Towhee, Northern Harrier, Blue-winged Teal, American Coot, Great Egret, Marbled Godwit, Greater Yellowlegs, Long-billed Dowitcher, Willet, a variety of sparrows, and gulls by the hundreds. Interesting and unusual species reported in this vicinity include Bar-tailed Godwit, Emperor Goose, Hudsonian Godwit, Buff-breasted Sandpiper, and Semipalmated Sandpiper.

The endangered Smith's Blue butterfly feeds and lays its eggs in the wild buckwheat that flourishes on the area dunes.

Salinas River Wildlife Management Area is located 11 miles north of Monterey, on the south side of the Salinas River. Take the Del Monte Boulevard exit from SH 1, go west and stay straight (don't take the right turn) on the unpaved road 0.75 mile to the parking lot.

MONTEREY

Monterey Bay and Peninsula

Extending from the end of the bay into the sea, unseen by the man on the shore, there lies a deep cleft in the sea's floor that might well be described as a kind of sub-marine Grand Canyon. This means that the area lacks a continental shelf, and deep, chilly waters, rich in nutrients, come welling up in the bay like liquid fertilizer to nurture the phytoplankton and initiate the food chains. In a word, this beautiful bay, one of the prime birding locales of California, presents a veritable smorgasbord for migrating seabirds.

Monterey State Beach. This small, local beach offers good drop-by birding. It's an easy-access location, a historic spot, and highly scenic, affording a view that's vaguely reminiscent of Hawaii. Squint your eyes, and the peninsula, from this vantage point, becomes a modified version of Diamond Head.

This is a highly peopled beach, so don't expect peace and solitude. Do expect blue water, pounding surf and some superlative gull watching. If

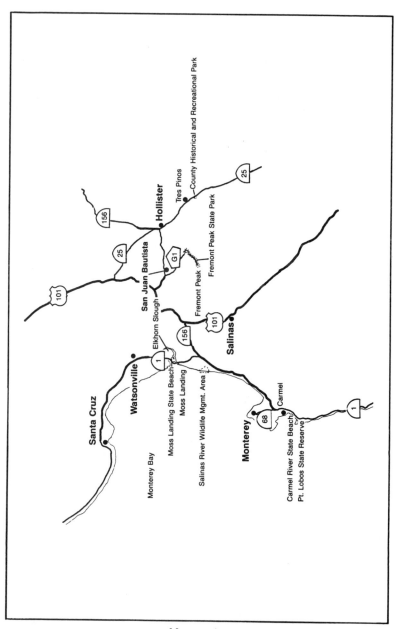

Monterey Area

Heermann's Gull

you're as fond as we are of the colorful Heermann's Gull, with its unique two-tone coloring and its cinnabar-colored beak, here's your chance for some good close-up viewing and behavior observation.

Before you leave, be sure to spend a moment at the Portola-Crespi monument which stands here in plain view. Dedicated in 1969 by the citizens of Monterey in honor of that city's 200th birthday, this cross commemorates a day in the winter of 1769, when the Spanish expedition under the command of Don Casper de Portola and Padre Juan Crespi erected an earlier cross on or near this very site.

Foam Street and Cannery Row. One nice thing about this location is that it's right in town, in an area you're sure to be visiting anyway. It would be sheer folly to pass it by without your binoculars in hand.

There's easy parking in a lot on the corner, at the very beginning of Cannery Row. All you have to do is climb out of your car, walk directly across the street , and there you are — standing before a fine place for some easy drop-by birding, namely a fenced area where you'll see, posted in plain view, a sign that warns of the unevenness of the cement slab you're approaching. The sign is not fooling. As you stand at the fence, scanning the nearby rocks for sightings of Black Turnstone, cormorants, Heermann's Gull, and Brown Pelican, do watch your step.

Municipal Wharf, Monterey Marina. If you're in Monterey in the wintertime, be sure to stroll out on the pier here at Municipal Wharf (not to be mistaken for Fisherman's Wharf) to see the many grebes known to convene in this area. Look too for Northern Fulmars, and, with luck, an Oldsquaw.

Crespi Pond, enroute to Point Pinos. On the way to Point Pinos, stop off for a while at Crespi Pond. Located on Ocean View, just past Asilomar Avenue, it's a good place to see such interesting species as Sora, Virginia Rail, and Common Snipe. Bird the nearby cypresses too, in hopes of sighting warblers, flycatchers, and a variety of sparrows.

Point Pinos. This area of shoreline on the northern point of the Monterey Peninsula is one of the indisputable hotspots of the Pacific Coast. Come here in March or April and you'll see so many migrating loons you'll think you're caught in the climax of some marvelous dream. Here are 3 species of these ancient birds, the Common, the Red-throated, and the Arctic as well, sometimes seen by the thousands.

The swarms of loons notwithstanding, the peak of seabird migration actually comes a little later on, in early May. Bird along Point Pinos at this time of the year and you'll sight virtual clouds of Sooty Shearwaters.

Monterey Bay by Boat. For all its wonders from the shore, there's no question that the best way to bird Monterey Bay is by boat. This way you can expect to see hosts of Black-footed Albatrosses, and hundreds of shearwaters — Pink-footed, Buller's, Sooty, Flesh-footed, and even the much less common Short-tailed. If you're extraordinarily lucky you may even sight such rare and unusual species as the Red-billed Tropicbird, and the Streaked Shearwater from Japan.

You can charter one of the sport-fishing vessels available at Fisherman's Wharf, or better yet, take a Shearwater Journey. The latter is a magnificent trip devised by expedition leader and prominent California birder Debra Love Shearwater, a field ornithologist who's always happy to share her storehouse of knowledge with others. For more information write California Seabirding, Shearwater Journeys, Box 1445, Soquel, CA 95073, or call (408) 688-1990.

It is easy to get to Monterey via SH 1 and SH 68.

Carmel River State Beach/Lagoon and Wetlands Preserve

This state park, which is literally right next door to Point Lobos, is a little gem of the Monterey County coastline known for all these features: 7,900 feet of coastal strand, alluring to anglers, beach combers and tidepoolers alike, gleaming sands, riparian woodland, coastal scrub, bramble bedecked with juicy blackberries, a eucalyptus grove, a river's mouth, willows and cottonwoods, the San Jose Creek wetlands, and a bird preserve.

A flock of fine Canada Geese live here, apparently never giving a thought to moving on. Look for Snowy Plover, Sanderling, and Herring and Heermann's Gull on the shore. Expect to find Brandt's Cormorant and Brown Pelican foraging offshore. Also seen in the park are Black-crowned Night-Heron, Great Blue and Green-backed Herons, American Avocet, Marsh Wren, Great Egret, Purple Finch, Song Sparrow, Black Phoebe, Bushtit, Chestnut-backed Chickadee, Pine Siskin, House Finch, and Red-winged Blackbird. Unusual species such as Baird's and Pectoral Sandpipers have been sighted here too, and sometimes an outright rarity like the Terek Sandpiper, reported in the fall of 1988.

Raccoons are known to dwell in Carmel River State Park. Also seen here are the endangered Smith's Blue Butterfly *(Euphilotes enoptes smithi)* and the Black Legless Lizard *(Annietta pulchra nigra)*, a species considered to be of "special concern" by the U.S. Fish and Wildlife Service.

Restrooms are located at the parking lot, which closes at sunset. The park itself, however, is open to the public from 7 a.m. until 11 p.m. Fishing in either the lagoon or the river is prohibited except between the dates listed in the current Department of Fish and Game regulations.

Carmel River State Beach is on SH 1, about 2 miles south of the town of Carmel.

Point Lobos State Reserve

The names of the trails that wind through this great 1,250-acre complex of coves and inlets, rocky shores and islands, groves of pine and cypress, meadow grasses and wildflowers seem calculated to tantalize: Cypress Grove, Sea Lion Point, Carmelo Meadow, Lace Lichen, Whaler's Cove, Pine Ridge, Bird Island.

These winding pathways lead to natural coastline terraces, a meadow that seems to reel from the color of its wildflowers, unique rock formations, richly inhabited tidepools, and an island literally carpeted with nesting Brandt's Cormorants.

This abode of the cormorants is best seen from Bird Island Trail, as you walk the loop on Pelican Point, where the riot of wildflowers blooming roundabout may vie for your attention. In spring and summer you can watch these prehistoric-looking birds flying down en masse to scoop up kelp near China Cove. Other good vantage points for birding are on North Shore, Whaler's Knoll, South Shore, and Moss Cove Trails.

Unusual species sighted in the reserve include Peregrine Falcon, Brown Booby, and Snow Bunting. More to be expected are the hundreds of cormorants nesting yearly at Bird Island, the shorebirds feeding along intertidal rocks (best sighted on the South Shore Trail), the many raptors seen from Moss Cove Trail, the Western Gull, Pigeon Guillemot, and Pelagic Cormorant found nesting on Guillemot Island and best viewed from a side path off the North Shore Trail.

This is one of California's most fertile habitats for marine wildlife. Seen here are Steller's Sea Lion, Southern Sea Otter, Harbor Seal, California Sea Lion, Gray Whale, and the somewhat less sizable, but nonetheless delightful Beechey Ground Squirrel and Monarch butterfly.

Wintering Monarch butterflies are sighted in the pines along Whaler's Knoll Trail. Expect to see Beechey Ground Squirrels on the boulders at the water's edge at Whaler's Cove, which is also a good place to scan the waters for the otters and seals. Whale watch from the trail near North Point.

A bird list, descriptive brochure, and map are available at the park headquarters. So too is the book, *Interpreting A Primitive Landscape*, which reserve ranger Gerald Loomis recommends to anyone who wants to know more about unique environments such as this one.

Reserve visitors are offered guided tours twice each day in the summer, less often during other seasons.

For further information, write or call Point Lobos State Reserve, c/o Monterey District, #20 Custom House Plaza, Monterey, CA 93940, (408) 624-4909 . Or write Point Lobos Natural History Association, Route 1, Box 62, Carmel, CA 93923.

Point Lobos State Reserve is located on SH 1, about 3 miles south of Carmel and approximately 10 miles south of Monterey.

Andrew Molera State Park

It's said that this beautiful parkland was once a secret landing spot where cargo was brought ashore at the mouth of the Big Sur River so that a fur trader named Juan Bautista Roger Cooper, who owned the land, could avoid the heavy custom fees he'd have otherwise paid at Monterey Harbor. Before Cooper came to California the land was part of the great Mexican land grant known then as Rancho El Sur, or in English, "Ranch of the South." After Cooper, it was a thoroughly upstanding dairy operation, run by the trader's grandson, Andrew Molera, whose delicious Monterey Jack Cheese was as widely known as his constant hospitality. Today this is a beautiful park boasting all of the following: walk-in campground with drinking water, toilets, and fire rings; wonderful hiking trails; a variety of lush and tangled foliage including thimbleberry, honeysuckle, blackberry, willow and California laurel; redwood and eucalyptus trees; an inviting sandy beach; a shallow lagoon teeming with birdlife.

Commonly seen in the Big Sur area are Chestnut-backed Chickadee, Band-tailed Pigeon, Bushtit, Bewick's Wren, Ruby-crowned Kinglet, Hermit Thrush, California Thrasher, Lesser Goldfinch, Golden-crowned Sparrow, Black-headed Grosbeak, White-crowned Sparrow, American Goldfinch, Fox Sparrow, California Towhee, Song Sparrow, Horned Grebe, Green-backed Heron, Northern Harrier, and Black-shouldered Kite.

Also sighted in Big Sur country, though not so commonly, are Golden Eagle, Lewis' Woodpecker, Rufous Hummingbird, Western Wood-Pewee, and Horned Lark. At the mouth of the river are a small beach and lagoon, good for Willets, Sanderlings, and other shorebirds.

A bird list, *Checklist of the Birds of the Big Sur Area*, is available at the park headquarters for 25 cents.

Also seen in the Big Sur area are deer, Raccoon, Gray Squirrel, Opossum, Gray Fox, and the less common Mountain Lion, Bobcat, and Coyote. Sea

Otters frequent the mouth of the Big Sur.

Camping is on a first-come, first-served basis. Fees are collected by a park ranger who drops by the campsites every morning for that purpose.

For further information write: Andrew Molera State Park, c/o Pfeiffer Big Sur State Park, #1, Big Sur, CA 93920, or call (408) 667-2315.

Andrew Molera State Park is 21 miles south of Carmel, via SH 1.

Julia Pfeiffer Burns State Park/Big Sur

This picturesque parkland, which lies atop steep sea cliffs, offers some of the most dramatic scenery in an area widely known for its drama, beauty, and scenic vistas. The highly photogenic McWay Falls slips like a narrow lace curtain over a craggy Big Sur cliffside, directly into the Pacific Ocean. There are 2 miles of splendid coastline, inland reaches graced by the ridges of the imposing Santa Lucia mountains, groves of exquisite redwoods in deep, shaded lowlands, fern-greened canyons, and chaparral-covered slopes.

Equipped with fire pits and food lockers, and located in a bluff-top cypress grove, the park has only two hike-in, primitive campsites. The sea cliffs here provide a comfortable haven to many shorebirds including Brown Pelican, Pigeon Guillemot, and Black Oystercatcher. Also seen on or about the park cliffs are Western and California Gulls, cormorants, and other species who hearken to rugged coastal shorelines. The ferny canyons and the chapparal-covered slopes, of course, are populated by other species entirely. On the slopes are Scrub Jay, Wrentit, towhees, and California Thrasher. In the canyons or in the wooded areas are Chestnut-backed Chickadee, Steller's Jay, and Winter Wren.

Perhaps the most exciting news about Julia Pfeiffer Burns State Park is the fact that the area boasts a nesting pair of the rare and endangered Peregrine Falcons.

Mammals seen here are deer, Raccoon, Gray Squirrel, Opossum, and Gray Fox. Far less frequently sighted are Mountain Lion, Coyote and Bobcat. In December, the observation site above McWay Falls is an excellent whale-watching spot. Up the road 11 miles, at Pfeiffer Big Sur State Park, there's a little beach at the end of Sycamore Canyon Road that's frequented by Sea Otters.

Camping permits are issued at Pfeiffer Big Sur State Park, 11 miles north on SH 1. Advance reservations are advised. A bird list, *Checklist*

Scrub Jay

of the Birds of the Big Sur Area, is available at most area parks for 25 cents.

For further information write Julia Pfeiffer Burns State Park, c/o Pfeiffer Big Sur State Park, Big Sur, CA 93920, or call (408) 667-2315.

Julia Pfeiffer Burns State Park is on SH 1 about 40 miles south of Monterey.

LAKE SAN ANTONIO

This park has all of the following features and more: 5,000 surface acres of water; 60 miles of shoreline; all kinds of boating from houseboating to sailing; swimming; sunbathing; excellent fishing; a grocery store, restaurant, gas station, marina, and rental cabins; more than 500 campsites, some with full hook-ups; a group recreation room and barbecue area; a visitor center; an excellent self-guided nature trail; a plant community that includes wild buckwheat, blue oaks, manzanita, wild lilac, greasewood, coast live oak, squawbush, and valley oak; an outdoor amphitheatre; planned activities and special events; sunset cruises; and most importantly, the park's famous Eagle Watch tours. Bird lists and trail guides are available at the visitor center.

Lake San Antonio Park happens to be one of the largest eagle wintering habitats in central California. Every year a count of these great birds is held in cooperation with the U.S. Fish and Wildlife Service. More than 60 eagles, both Bald and Golden, have been sighted in the vicinity.

Aboard a boat aptly named the *Eagle One*, guided tours take birders to the shallow area at the west part of the lake where the birds can be easily viewed. Tours leave the South Shore Marina on Friday, Saturday, Sunday, and holidays at 10:00 a.m. and 1:00 p.m. Rates are $8.00 per person for regular tours, $17.00 per person for Sunday Brunch Tours, and $6.00 for senior citizens on Fridays only. Reservations are required and may be made by calling (408) 755-4899. Loaner binoculars are provided by the Parks Department.

Seen here also are Western Sandpiper, Wilson's Phalarope, Long-billed Dowitcher, Marbled Godwit, Black-bellied Plover, five species of gull, four species of grebe, Great Blue Heron, Double-crested Cormorant, Snow Goose, Blue-winged Teal, American Wigeon, Wood Duck, American White and Brown Pelicans, Osprey, Northern Harrier, three species of hummingbird and six species of woodpecker.

Coming from the north on US 101, take the Jolon Road exit north of King City. Proceed 45 miles on County Road G14 to the South Shore entrance. From the south, take the Lake Nacimiento/Lake San Antonio exit at Paso Robles. Go 26 miles on County Road G14, past Lake Nacimiento to the South Shore entrance.

HOLLISTER

San Juan Bautista

The old adobe San Juan Bautista Mission is a good place to begin a tour of the best birding spots in this picturesque old town. In the serene, walled confines of the timeless mission garden, hummingbirds streak from olive tree to oleander, from grotto to willow. In the graveyard, listen for Golden-crowned and White-crowned Sparrows, wrens, and the particularly abundant Northern Mockingbird.

Take the self-guided Historic Walking Tour or the El Camino Real Earthquake Walk and watch for Yellow-billed Magpie, Northern Flicker, Black Phoebe, and Chestnut-backed Chickadee.

Other birds seen here include Dark-eyed Junco, Steller's Jay, White-breasted Nuthatch, Western Wood-Pewee, House Finch, Scrub Jay, American Goldfinch, Black-headed Grosbeak, Hermit Thrush, Plain Titmouse, California and Rufous-sided Towhees, and Warbling Vireos.

This beautiful town, with its old-California flavor, has a population of 2,400, an elevation of 200 feet, and a salubrious climate. Located on the San Andreas Earthquake Fault, it's been well-jarred more than once. It was to commemorate these events that the San Andreas Fault Exhibit and the El Camino Real Earthquake Walk (which happens to offer such excellent birding) were dedicated in 1979 by the Chamber of Commerce.

San Juan Bautista is on SH 156, 3 miles east of US 101.

Fremont Peak State Park

The first American flag ever to fly over the state of California was raised here on this picturesque peak, unfurled on the orders of the mountain's haughty namesake, the handsome Captain John C. Fremont, who was here in direct defiance of the Mexican government.

Besides historical interest, the park has all of the following features: wild grasses that grow knee high and ripple like a sea in the wind; an elevation of 3,000 feet; an abundance of wildflowers; interesting geologic features; clear, clean air that renders it the favorite spot of many an amateur astronomer; rolling slopes densely covered with scrub oak, coyote brush, manzanita and toyon; high ridges supporting such foliage as Coulter pine, madrones, and oaks; craggy ridges; deep canyons graced with laurels and willows; 4 miles of hiking trail; an abundance of wildlife; 10 primitive family campsites; 6 group camps for up to 50 people; 40 picnic sites with tables and stoves; pit toilets; drinking water; summertime campfire programs and nature hikes; more than a hundred different species of birds.

The group picnic area is on a first-come, first-served basis, but reservations should be made for the park's six group camps. A small brochure, complete with bird list and map, is available at the park headquarters.

Birds seen here include Western Bluebird, Chestnut-backed Chickadee, Greater Roadrunner, Golden Eagle, Black-headed Grosbeak, Dark-eyed Junco, Yellow-billed Magpie, Northern Oriole, Great Horned Owl, California Thrasher, Varied Thrush, Plain Titmouse, California and Rufous-sided Towhees, Acorn Woodpecker, Wrentit, Golden-crowned Sparrow, and Western Tanager.

Sighted regularly here are Raccoon and deer; less often, Bobcat, foxes, and Coyote.

Reach Fremont Peak State Park via San Juan Canyon Road, an 11-mile, hard-surfaced road which takes off from SH 156 near San Juan Bautista.

San Benito County Historical and Recreation Park

It could well be said that this county park, which lies about 6 miles south of Hollister and near the historic little settlement of Tres Pinos, is one of the best-kept secrets in the state of California. But local birders, who know it well, come often to San Benito County Historical and Recreation Park.

Although plans for enhancement are in the works, none of these include diminishment of the wilderness ambience that renders the area so attractive now. If and when overnight campsites are developed here, they'll be for environmental camping only.

This is not to say that this day-use park bears no signs of civilization whatever. It does have 25 fine picnic sites, modern restrooms, an interesting and historically significant display of fascinating old farm equipment (put together by the San Benito County Historical Society), and a loop trail from which the birding is excellent.

Seen in the park are American Goldfinch, Black Phoebe, Anna's Hummingbird, Steller's Jay, White-breasted Nuthatch, Black-headed Grosbeak, Western Wood-Pewee, California Quail, White-crowned Sparrow, Hermit Thrush, and California Towhee.

Anyone desiring further information about this park or about the nearby San Justo Reservoir (a good place to see grassland birds and waterfowl) should contact the San Benito County Parks Department, at 3220 Southside Road, Hollister, CA 95023.

Seen either here or nearby are deer, foxes, Coyotes, Raccoons, an occasional Bobcat, and wild pigs.

Go south 6 miles from Hollister on SH 25, through the small settlement of Tres Pinos, and continue on SH 25 another mile to the park.

PINNACLES NATIONAL MONUMENT

It's a certainty that the landscape of the Pinnacles is the sort that fixes itself firmly in the mind of the beholder. It must have had that same effect on Teddy Roosevelt, when he declared it a national monument in 1908. And certainly that's how it touches the avid climbers who scale its sheer cliffs, or the geologists who come to reflect upon the forces that shaped it into a virtual monument to the San Andreas Rift Zone, which lies just east of the park.

The area boasts a number of excellent hiking trails ranging from easy to very strenuous. These vary in distance from the one-mile walk to Moses Spring and Bear Gulch Caves to the very strenuous North Wilderness Trail, with its 7.6 mile hike. Here too are fine picnic grounds, an excellent visitor center, campfire programs, modern restrooms, a ranger station, and campgrounds with wheelchair access. A bird list, *A Checklist of the Birds of Pinnacles National Monument*, is available at the visitor center.

There are two campgrounds: the Chaparral Campground on the west side of the monument, which is operated by the National Park Service; and the Pinnacles, a private campground on the east side. The Chaparral sites are available on a first-come, first-served basis. Large group campsites must be reserved in advance at both of these locations. Call (408) 389-4526 to reserve a group site at the Chaparral Campgrounds; (408) 389-4462 for a group site at Pinnacles. For general information about the park call (408) 389-4485.

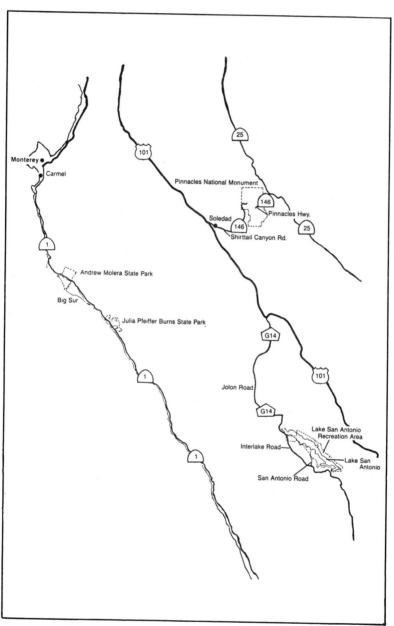

Coastal Monterey County and Pinnacles National Monument

Year-round birds common or abundant in the park include Phainopepla, Prairie Falcon, California Quail, Acorn Woodpecker, Black Phoebe, Scrub Jay, Common Raven, Bushtit, White-breasted Nuthatch, Canyon Wren, Bewick's Wren, Western Bluebird, Wrentit, and Anna's Hummingbird.

Less common year-round residents include Golden Eagle, Sharp-shinned Hawk, Cooper's Hawk, Greater Roadrunner, Barn Owl, Great Horned Owl, and Rock Wren.

Rare and irregular sightings in the area include Chukar, Ferruginous Hawk, and Northern Saw-whet Owl.

When planning a trip to Pinnacles National Monument, first of all make sure which side of the park you want to get to. In the Pinnacles, "East is East, and West is West," and the twain certainly don't meet. We found out the hard way when we set out to join some relatives for a reunion at the park. We went to the west side, they to the east and although we were only 7 miles apart by trail, it was a 67-mile drive by the nearest roads from one set of kin to the other.

To get to the west side, take US 101 to Soledad, turn east on SH 146, and proceed 11 miles to the park. To get to the east side, where the visitor center is, take Highway 25 south from Hollister 30 miles, turn west on SH 146, and go 5 miles to the park. SH 146 *does not meet* in the middle!

Chapter 5
North Country

The North Country of California: remote, expansive, unspoiled. A land of clear skies, snow-capped mountains, vast plateau, volcanic lava beds. White-water rivers and streams cascade through rugged canyons, dense forests, and alpine meadows. Huge lakes and reservoirs provide water for the farms and fields and cities of a California far removed, and recreation for its people. And millions of acres of its magnificent wilderness are protected in national forests, preserves, and parks.

The size of the state of Ohio, this six-county area contains more than 16% of the land area of California, more than 22% of the enclosed water areas, but less than 1% of the population. Eagles and hawks soar over this big country like nowhere else in the state. Bears still wander the forests; coyotes thrive. And huge flocks of waterfowl descend upon the expansive lakes and marshes and wetlands, to feed and rest in their migratory journeys, or to spend the winter, or to breed and raise their young.

The volcanic Cascades, dominated by 14,162-foot Mount Shasta, run through the center of the North Country from Oregon to their convergence with the Sierra Nevada at the Feather River. Mount Lassen, at the range's southern extremity, is still considered an active volcano, last erupting in the early part of this century. The Klamath Mountains and the Trinity Alps, with peaks to 9,000 feet, form the western border of the region; the Warners, in the northeastern corner, rise up from the huge Modoc Plateau which stretches over most of the northeastern portion of the area.

The western mountains are drained by white-water streams that flow into the Trinity and Klamath Rivers. The McCloud and the Sacramento

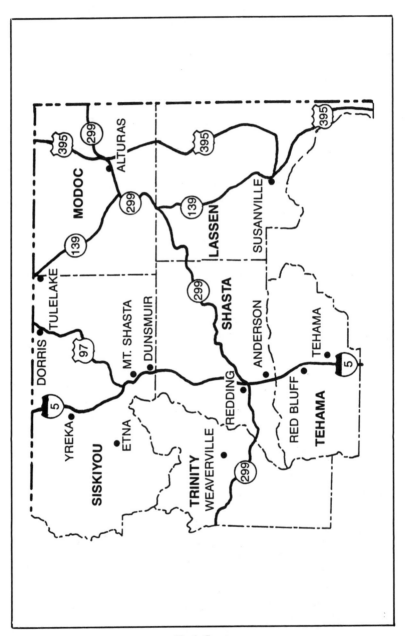

North Country

flow from the central mountains, and are joined by the Pit, after it meanders southwest from the Warners through the Modoc Plateau. The great flat areas of the plateau drain sluggishly, if at all, and form the shallow lakes, marshes, and wetlands that are so vital to migrating waterfowl. Dams on the Trinity and Sacramento impound huge reservoirs, forming Shasta, Trinity, and Whiskeytown Lakes.

The North Country region consists of six counties: Siskiyou, Modoc, Trinity, Shasta, Tehama, and Lassen. Together they encompass an area of 25,398 square miles, which represents 32.2% of the area covered by this book.

Interstate 5, the major West Coast arterial from Mexico to the Canadian border, transects our North Country region from north to south; US 395 skirts the eastern border from Reno to Goose Lake, and US 97 connects the town of Weed with Klamath Falls, Oregon. From east to west, SH 299 extends 300 miles through the entire region, from the Warner Mountains through the Trinity Alps. As for the other state highways, 139 traverses the upper Modoc Plateau, 96 follows the Klamath River through the northwest section, 89 runs southeast from Mount Shasta into the Sierra, and 44 and 36 head east from Redding and Red Bluff, respectively.

SUGGESTED BIRD LISTS FOR THE NORTH COUNTRY REGION

Several fine check lists of bird species of the North Country region are available through the mail.

An excellent booklet, *Wildlife of the Klamath Basin National Wildlife Refuges*, which lists the wildlife and birds of all 6 of the Klamath Basin NWRs and serves well for outlying areas as well, is available as part of a free information packet from:

Refuge Manager
Klamath Basin National Wildlife Refuges
Route 1, Box 74
Tulelake, CA 96134

A free check list, *Birds of Ash Creek Wildlife Area*, which is good for the whole of Big Valley, is available from:

Area Manager
Ash Creek Wildlife Area
P.O. Box 37
Nubieber, CA 96009

Birds of Siskiyou County, a check list compiled by Neal Clark, Raymond Ekstrom, and Michael Robbins, for the Mt. Shasta Area Audubon Society, is available from:
   Michael Robbins
   308 Hillcrest Drive
   Yreka, CA 96097

KLAMATH NATIONAL FOREST

The Klamath National Forest is located in Siskiyou County, California and Jackson County, Oregon. Of its 1,694,597 acres, 1,669,213 are located in California.

A bird list, *Birds of Klamath Basin National Wildlife Refuges*, is available from U.S. Fish and Wildlife Service, Klamath Basin National Wildlife Refuge, Rt. 1, Box 74, Tulelake, CA 96134. The phone number is (916) 667-2231.

Happy Camp Ranger District. Located in the scenic Klamath River Valley, the area covered by the Happy Camp Ranger District is known for its abundant wildlife, its "fighting steelhead" and rainbow trout, its many beautiful places to hike; wonderful rockhounding; and river rafting.

Birders visiting this part of the Klamath National Forest may choose to headquarter in the historic little town of Happy Camp — once a mecca for gold miners — where they'll doubtless take the time to soak up the old-west ambience and photograph the rustic buildings, which still wear their ancient iron doors like badges. Besides stores, restaurants, motels, and service stations, the historic old mining town boasts river boat guide services, which offer fine opportunities for some riparian birding.

The area that surrounds this quaint little town is genuinely spectacular. Here are narrow valleys, conifer-covered mountains, and the truly photogenic Klamath River that gives this national forest its name.

The climate is generally mild in the Happy Camp area. Snowfall is generally light in the valley, and of short duration.

For more information write Happy Camp Ranger District, Klamath National Forest, P.O. Box 337, Happy Camp, CA 96039, or call Steve J. Anderson at (916) 493-5301.

The town of Happy Camp is located 70 miles west of Yreka, 104 miles south and west of Medford, Oregon, and 40 miles south of O'Brien,

Oregon. Year-round access is provided from Medford and Yreka on paved highways I-5 and SH 96.

Ukonom Ranger District. The Ukonom Ranger District offers all of the following: more than 100 miles of maintained trails, many more miles of less-traveled older trails; winter sports in the area's higher elevations; two developed campgrounds with daily fees of $4.00; undeveloped sites at four locations; rafting and kayaking on both the Salmon and Klamath Rivers.

Some of the more common species in these ranger districts include Mountain Quail, Band-tailed Pigeon, Anna's Hummingbird, Acorn Woodpecker, Western Wood-Pewee, Hairy Woodpecker, Olive-sided Flycatcher, Common Raven, Steller's Jay, Chestnut-backed Chickadee, Red-breasted Nuthatch, Winter Wren, Great Blue Heron, Common Merganser, and Purple Finch.

Less often seen, but definitely here, are Northern Goshawk, Peregrine Falcon, Spotted Owl, Pileated Woodpecker, Gray Jay, Cassin's Finch, and Yellow-breasted Chat. Here too are both Golden and Bald Eagles.

For further information write Ukonom Ranger District, 99300 Highway 96, Somes Bar, CA 95568 or call (916) 469-3331.

Salmon River Ranger District. Known for its 430,000 acres of mountainous terrain, including a large portion of the famous Marble Mountain Wilderness, the Salmon River Ranger District offers endless opportunities for hiking, fishing, and cross-country skiing, as well as a good chance for a much-coveted sighting of the controversial Spotted Owl. Species more common to the area are Band-tailed Pigeon, Western Screech-Owl, Common Nighthawk, Vaux's Swift, Anna's Hummingbird, Belted Kingfisher, Hairy and Downy Woodpeckers, Hermit Thrush, Orange-crowned Warbler, and Steller's Jay. Found on the streams, ponds, and lakes of the district are Eared, Western, and Pied-billed Grebes, Northern Pintail, Cinnamon Teal, Ruddy Duck, and Common Merganser.

Sawyers Bar is 25 miles from Etna, over Etna Summit on a dirt road that reaches on elevation of 6,000 feet. Some snow in winter, but generally the road is open. From Somes Bar on SH 96 take Salmon River Road southeast 17 miles to Sawyers Bar Road. Turn left and go about 15 miles to the Ranger Station.

Scott River and the Marble Mountain Wilderness. Besides the river for which it's named, its many tributaries, and the shimmering lakes that render Scott Valley a haven for anglers, this section of the Klamath National Forest boasts 7 campgrounds: 3 situated in fine riparian habitat by the river, 1 at the Lovers Camp entryway to the Marble Mountain Wilderness, 1 at Kangaroo Lake at the south end of the district, another along the Callahan-Cecilville road, and one at Etna. Jones Beach has a popular picnic area right along the Scott River, a pleasant place to spread a meal, swim, or bird.

The headquarters of the Scott River Ranger District is located in the small town of Fort Jones in the northern part of Scott Valley. The area is largely ranchland, but has four small towns and a population of 8,000. The valley has an average elevation of 2,900 feet, and a climate that's generally mild. Winter snows melt quickly.

Birders who enjoy backpacking won't want to leave Klamath National Forest without spending some time in the spectacular 226,000-acre Marble Mountain Wilderness. Anyone entering the area from May through October must have a valid campfire permit, which is obtainable in any of the national forest headquarters. No other permits are necessary.

Although the wilderness area is entered most often from this Ranger District, via the Lover's Camp entryway, access is possible from other ranger districts as well.

Birds sighted in this area include Spotted and Flammulated Owls, Bald and Golden Eagles, Common Snipe, and Black-backed Woodpecker.

For further information write to the Scott River Ranger District, Klamath National Forest, 11263 N Highway 3, Fort Jones, CA 96032, or call (916) 468-5351.

Scott River Ranger District is in Fort Jones, on Highway 3, 17 miles southwest of Yreka and I-5.

Goosenest Ranger District. Located in Butte Valley near the famous Tule Lake, an area widely known for its natural beauty and resident wildlife, the Goosenest Ranger District of the Klamath National Forest is comprised of woodlands, grasslands, agricultural, and riparian habitats which serve as fulltime or part-time homes to the following common bird species: Eared, Western and Pied-billed Grebes, Northern Pintail, Cinnamon Teal, American Wigeon, Ruddy Duck, Band-tailed Pigeon, Western Screech-

Golden Eagle

Owl, Common Nighthawk, Vaux's Swift, Anna's Hummingbird, Belted Kingfisher, Hairy and Downy Woodpeckers, Hermit Thrush, Orange-crowned Warbler, and Dusky Flycatcher.

Rare or uncommon birds which can be *regularly* viewed in the Butte Valley area are Bald and Golden Eagles, Swainson's and Ferruginous Hawks, Prairie Falcon, Goshawk, Spotted, Burrowing, and Long-eared Owls, Sandhill Crane, American White Pelican, White-faced Ibis, Bank Swallow, Northern Shrike, Pinyon Jay, Gray Flycatcher, and Sage Thrasher.

Animals common to Butte Valley include Black Bear, Mule Deer, Striped Skunk, Gray Fox, California Ground Squirrel, Bottas' Pocket Gopher, Belding's Ground Squirrel, Dusky-footed Wood Rat, California Vole, Black-tailed Jackrabbit, Nuttall's Cottontail, Brush Rabbit, Douglas Squirrel, Western Skink, and Pond Turtle. Less common to the area but certainly here are Pronghorn, Raccoon, Badger, Spotted Skunk, Coyote, Red Fox, Mountain Lion, Porcupine, Pika, and Elk.

For further information, write to Klamath National Forest, Goosenest Ranger District, 37805 Highway 97, Macdoel, CA 95058, or call (916) 398-4391.

Goosenest Ranger District is at Macdoel, on US 97, about 40 miles northeast of Weed and I-5.

CASTLE CRAGS STATE PARK

This park boasts all of the following and more: a wide variety of trees and shrubs, including valley oak, red fir, Jeffrey pine, western yew, incense cedars, and ponderosa and sugar pines; altitudes that range from 2,000 feet along the winding Sacramento River to more than 6,000 feet at the tip of those rough-hewn crags for which the park is named; wildflowers galore — azalea, tiger lily, and pitcher plant among them; towering spires of granite formed some 70 million years ago; views of the spectacular, snow-garbed Mount Shasta, which reaches 14,162 feet up into a clear and smogless sky.

Castle Crags State Park is known for its summer campfire programs, good fishing, fine hiking trails, post-snowmelt swimming holes, and equestrian trails. There are 64 family campsites here, each with table, stove, and food cupboard.

Birds of the area include Steller's Jay, Western Screech-Owl, Northern Pygmy-Owl, Cooper's Hawk, Great Blue Heron, and Pileated Woodpecker. A checklist, *Birds of Siskiyou County*, sponsored by the Mt. Shasta Area Audubon Society and compiled by Neal Clark, Raymond Ekstrom, and Michael Robbins, is available at the park office.

Also seen here are Coyote, Bobcat, Black Bear, Gray Fox, Raccoon, California Ground Squirrel, Gray Squirrel, and Mountain Lion.

During the winter months campsites are available on a first-come, first-served basis. In the summer, however, advance reservations are advisable.

Castle Crags is on I-5 at Castella, about 45 miles north of Redding.

KLAMATH BASIN NATIONAL WILDLIFE REFUGES

The Klamath Basin, which spans part of Oregon, is best known for its lakes, ponds, and reservoirs. Some of these waters glitter sapphire blue;

some wear skins of organic green ooze. Some were the bailiwick of Indian anglers centuries ago; some are the handiwork of latter-day man. Some, the best known, the ones to which birders travel from all over the world, lie within areas designated as national wildlife refuges, which are protected and succored, replenished and regulated by humankind, and favored by millions of birds.

Of these designated areas, which comprise one vast complex known as the Klamath Basin National Wildlife Refuges, three lie in Oregon's "Upper Klamath" area and three in California's "Lower Klamath."

Oregon's sector of the complex includes the Upper Klamath, Klamath Forest, and Bear Valley National Wildlife Refuges. California's portion is comprised of the Lower Klamath, Tule Lake, and Clear Lake National Wildlife Refuges. The Visitor Center for all of the refuges is located at Tule Lake and is well-staffed and well-stocked, and features a fine assortment of specimen exhibits, interpretive displays, educational programs, books and literature, including the fine bird and wildlife list entitled *Wildlife of the Klamath Basin National Wildlife Refuges.*

The Klamath Basin National Wildlife Refuges all offer peerless opportunities for wildlife observation, bird photography, and avian behavior studies. Two refuges feature auto tour routes which wind their way over easily traversed, improved dike roads; two boast canoe trails which afford a unique opportunity to experience the birds from a different vantage point.

Because so many Bald Eagles (between 500 and 800) are here in the winter when other species are less evident, birding is truly spectacular at the Klamath Basin National Wildlife Refuges all year long. Waterfowl migration begins in late August and September when the Northern Pintails and the White-fronted Geese arrive. In March, April, and May the refuges are teeming with waterfowl and shorebirds as they stop off to refuel on their way north to their breeding grounds in Alaska and Canada. In summer, large numbers of juveniles can be sighted from the vantage points of the tour roads. According to official estimates, 45,000 ducks, 2,600 Canada Geese, and thousands of shorebirds are hatched and raised here in the Klamath Basin refuges every year.

Common or abundant for a portion of the year at these three California refuges are Bald Eagle, Northern Harrier, Ring-necked Pheasant, Great Blue Heron, Great and Snowy Egrets, Black-crowned Night-Heron, Snow, Ross', and Canada Geese, Canvasback, Redhead, Lesser Scaup, Common Goldeneye, Ruddy Duck, California Quail, Black-necked Stilt, American

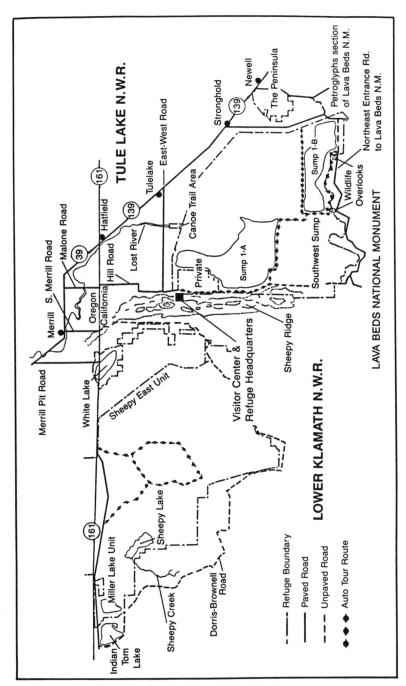

Klamath Basin National Wildlife Refuges
Lower Klamath and Tule Lake

Avocet, Willet, Long-billed Curlew, Wilson's Phalarope, Western Kingbird, Bewick's and Marsh Wrens, as well as Barn, Long-eared, and Great Horned Owls.

Species known to nest locally include Bald and Golden Eagles, Prairie Falcon, Pied-billed, Eared, and Western Grebes, American and Least Bitterns, Great Blue Heron, Black-crowned Night-Heron, Great and Snowy Egrets, Canada Goose, Green-winged Teal, Mallard, Northern Pintail, Blue-winged Teal, Northern Shoveler, Gadwall, American Wigeon, Canvasback, Redhead, Ring-necked Duck, Lesser Scaup, Northern Harrier, Sharp-shinned Hawk, California Quail, Virginia Rail, Sora, Snowy Plover, American Avocet, and Black-necked Stilt.

Mammals sighted at one locale or another within the confines of the refuges include Mountain Lion, Bobcat, Elk, Mule Deer, Pronghorn Antelope, Coyote, Raccoon, Marten, Ermine, Least and Long-tailed Weasels, Mink, Badger, Western Spotted Skunk, and River Otter. Smaller and more ordinary species of the area are Northern Flying Squirrel, California Kangaroo Rats, Nuttall's Cottontail, White-tailed and Black-tailed Jack Rabbits, Yellow-pine, Allen's, and Least Chipmunks, and Belding's, California, and Golden-mantled Ground Squirrels.

For further information write to Refuge Manager, Klamath Basin National Wildlife Refuges, Route 1, Box 74, Tulelake, CA 96134, or call (916) 667-2231.

Tule Lake National Wildlife Refuge. Since its establishment in 1928, Tule Lake has become practically synonymous with northern California birding. To mouth the words "Tule Lake" is to instantly envision thousands of Canvasback ducks taking to the air, Bald Eagles winging their way through the vast blue sky, or Sandhill Cranes strutting proudly about on their thin, gangly legs.

Notably, this is the only one of California's three Klamath Basin National Wildlife Refuges that offers a self-guided canoe trail, a marvelous adventure open to any hardy, canoe-owning birder from July through September. For those without canoes there is an excellent self-guided auto tour along a good dike roadway that affords a marvelous vantage point for sighting the countless birds who blanket the waters.

The Tule Lake National Wildlife Refuge encompasses 38,908 acres of croplands and open water. Approximately 15,000 acres of these are leased by farmers through a program administered by the Bureau of Reclamation. Another 1,400 acres are farmed by refuge personnel with the crops grown thereby used to help provide food for migrating winter waterfowl.

The town of Tulelake is on SH 139, 4 miles south of the Oregon border. To get to the visitor center, go west on East-West Road from Tulelake, to its junction with Hill Road, and turn left. The Visitor Center is 0.5 mile down Hill Road.

Lower Klamath National Wildlife Refuge. Established by President Theodore Roosevelt in 1908, this 47,600-acre site bears the honor of being our nation's very first waterfowl refuge. A fine potpourri of open water, shallow marshes, grassy uplands, and croplands, it's been popular with nature lovers ever since. The area is meticulously managed to provide appropriate nesting sites and brood-rearing habitat for the thousands of birds to whom it's homeland, either part-time or year-round.

This refuge is one of two in the Klamath Basin that features an auto tour along its improved dike roads.

To get to Lower Klamath, continue north from Tulelake on SH 139 for 4 miles, to SH 161. Then turn left and go about 10 miles to the entrance. From US 97, turn east on SH 161 and go 7 miles to the first entrance.

Clear Lake National Wildlife Refuge. This 33,400-acre area is almost as notable for its grassland, sagebrush, and juniper habitats as it is for the 20,000 acres of lake which serves as the main source of water for the agricultural program of the eastern portion of the Klamath Basin. Besides that, it harbors a number of small islands, which provide nesting sites for pelicans, cormorants, and other colonizing species.

Upland areas of the refuge provide needed habitat for the many Mule Deer, Sage Grouse, and Pronghorn Antelope that flourish here. This is wildlife country indeed, a place to cherish, a place to guard, a fragile habitat where the rights of nesting birds come first. This being true, for the sake of the wildlife, the Clear Lake National Wildlife Refuge is closed to the public from spring through fall.

To get to Clear Lake, take SH 139 for 25 miles south from Tulelake, turn east on Clear Lake Road, and proceed 10 miles to the refuge.

LAVA BEDS NATIONAL MONUMENT

At the visitor center here at Lava Beds National Monument, sightseers will find a number of interesting displays, some devised to depict the

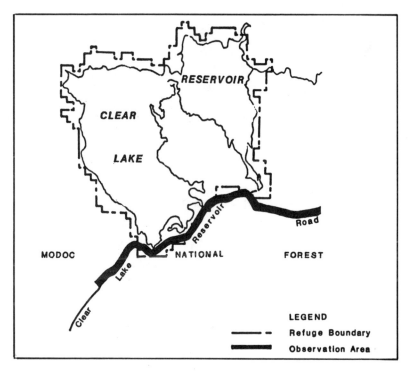

Klamath Basin National Wildlife Refuge
Clear Lake

prehistoric volcanic upheavals that shaped this rough terrain, some the battles that ensued many centuries later when Modoc Indians sought to defend it against encroaching settlers. Here too is plenty of literature about the park, maps, brochures, nature and history books for sale, and flashlights available on loan to those venturesome sightseers who want to explore the many fascinating volcanic caves here in this rugged parkland.

With elevations that range from 4,000 to 5,700 feet, this area can be formidably cold in winter. The weather is lovely in other seasons, however, and in summer the park is a popular destination of geologists, history buffs, folklorists, spelunkers, mammal watchers, and birders, as well as casual tourists.

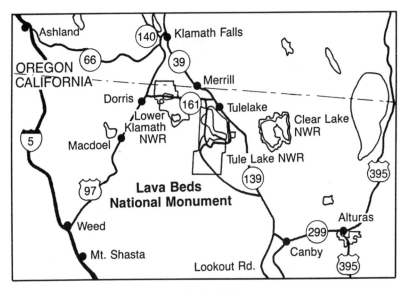

Lava Beds National Monument

Other than the thousands of migrating waterfowl often seen from the vicinity of the northwest entrance of the park as they fly to and from Tule Lake, Lava Beds National Monument is best known to birders for its many raptors. Chief among these is the Bald Eagle. This splendid bird winters here in numbers greater than anywhere outside the state of Alaska! At least 23 other species of raptors are sighted here too. Expect Northern Goshawk, Golden Eagle, Northern Harrier, Merlin, Prairie Falcon, Sharp-shinned, Cooper's, Red-tailed, Swainson's, Rough-legged, and Ferruginous Hawks, and Western Screech, Great Horned, Northern Pygmy, Burrowing, Long-eared, Short-eared, and Northern Saw-whet Owls.

In addition to all of the above, a variety of land birds dwell here as well. These and the waterfowl are the same as those found at Tule Lake.

For more information about this National Monument write to: Superintendent, Lava Beds National Monument, Box 867, Tulelake, CA 96134.

Entrance to Lava Beds National Monument is from SH 139. Watch for the signs 5 miles south of Tulelake or 26 miles north of Canby.

MODOC NATIONAL FOREST

Medicine Lake Highlands

Characterized by the highly scenic Medicine Lake, which got its name from the "big medicine" rites the Indians used to hold near its shores, this land of "rocks that float and mountains of glass" is volcanic country — 200 square miles of it — located in Modoc and Siskiyou Counties and covering portions of Modoc, Klamath, and Shasta-Trinity National Forests. The scenery is spectacular, the geological features endless, the archaelogical attractions many, the fishing good, the hiking great, the water sports many, and the history of the area fascinating to ponder.

Although best known for lava flows and craters, the highlands boast several scenic fish-stocked lakes and a variety of plants including sugar pine, red and white fir, lodgepole pine, bitterbrush, manzanita, and snowbrush. All these features, of course, insure the presence of a number of interesting birds, especially raptors — Bald Eagles, nesting Prairie Falcons, and (newly introduced here) Peregrine Falcons and Golden Eagles.

Less dramatic than the raptors, but also seen in the highlands are Common Nighthawk, Anna's Hummingbird, Lewis' Woodpecker, Plain Titmouse, Mountain Chickadee, Pygmy Nuthatch, Winter Wren, Hermit Thrush, Western Bluebird, Bewick's Wren, Steller's Jay, Hairy Woodpecker, Ash-throated Flycatcher, Black-billed Magpie, Common Raven, Clark's Nutcracker, and Mountain Bluebird. Rarities sighted here include Black Skimmer and Pinyon Jay.

Camping is available in the highlands on a first-come, first-served basis at Hemlock, Headquarters, and Medicine Lake Campgrounds. For further information write or call either one of the following: Doublehead Ranger District, P.O. Box 818, Tulelake, CA 96134, (916) 667-2246; Modoc National Forest, Supervisor's Office, 441 N. Main St., Alturas, CA 96101, (916) 233-5811.

From SH 139, take Tionesta Road to the west. (This is the same turn-off as the one for Lava Beds National Monument. Watch for the signs 26 miles

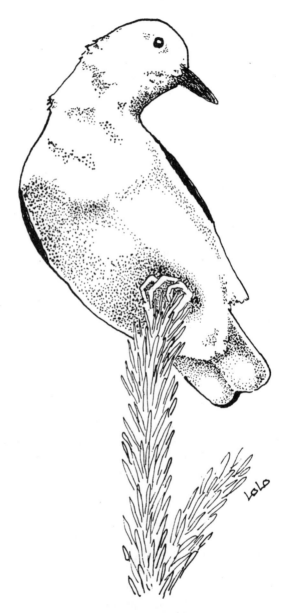

Clark's Nutcracker

north of Canby, or 5 miles south of Tulelake.) Stay straight on this same
road when Lava Beds Road veers off to the right, about 3 miles from the
highway.

From SH 89, turn north on Pioneer Hill Road in the town of Bartle.
Medicine Lake can also be reached from the visitor center at Lava Beds.
It's 14 miles by good dirt road.

Ash Creek Wildlife Area, Big Valley

According to Jim Gordon, wildlife biologist with the Big Valley Ranger
District of the Modoc National Forest, this high plateau located in the
northeastern section of California is "the best kept secret in California."
Here the summers are clear and breezy, the winters harsh and biting, the
scenery beautiful all year long. Here too — if your timing is right — the
birds are plentiful. In the springtime you may see as many as 500 Sandhill
Cranes. Golden Eagles may be sighted all year long, Bald Eagles in the
spring and winter.

Birding can be good at many locations in Big Valley, for example, in
the meadows and sweeping hayfields between the towns of Beiber and
Lookout, where Canada Geese sometimes convene, or at valley edges
where eagles are often sighted. But the best spot to bird in the valley is a
3,000-acre wetland, the Big Swamp. Once a favored haunt of the Pit River
Indians, it's still fed by the flow of a half-dozen seasonal streams, still
visited by thousands of waterfowl, still throbbing with life. And today it's
known as the Ash Creek Wildlife Area, a most remote and pristine designated wildlife area.

This prime area offers little in the way of amenities. There are two short
roads and five well-situated parking lots, and that's about it. You'll find
no picnic benches here, no modern restrooms, no formal hiking trails. This
is prairie-like country, however, which means easy walking.

One special feature of the area is a historic old structure, the picturesque
and photogenic Wayman Barn. Held together with wooden dowels instead
of nails, it hearkens back to the days when barn building was an art. Even
if old buildings aren't your forte, you'll want to stroll around the periphery
of this one just to view the many American Kestrels that favor this area.

The calendar of avian events here in Big Valley is an impressive one.
In fall look for Sandhill Cranes as they arrive at the marsh and gather in
the areas around Wayman Barn. Gadwalls, and other waterfowl can be

American Kestrel

very visible at this time too. In February, when the wintering Bald Eagles are already very much in evidence, Cackling Goose (a subspecies of the Canada Goose), Ross', and Snow Geese begin to arrive in great, showy flocks. In March and April, the Sandhill Cranes are strutting and dancing, and the Sage Grouse gurgling and thumping, as they go about the business of their extraordinary breeding displays. In July Swainson's Hawks come winging in from their winters in Argentina.

Abundant or common here all year round, apparently thriving even in the biting cold, are Pied-billed Grebe, Canada Goose, Northern Harrier, Ring-necked Pheasant, Barn and Great Horned Owls, and Black-billed Magpie.

Common or abundant for all seasons *except* winter are Great Blue Heron, Great Egret, Redhead, Sandhill Crane, American Avocet, Willet, Common Snipe, and Forster's Tern.

Among the many species nesting in the area are Pied-billed Grebe, Northern Pintail, Cinnamon Teal, Northern Shoveler, Gadwall, American Wigeon, Canvasback, Redhead, Ruddy Duck, Northern Harrier, Swainson's Hawk, Sage Grouse, Virginia Rail, Sora, American Avocet, Spotted Sandpiper, and Great Horned, Burrowing, and Short-eared Owls.

Sandhill Cranes are common all seasons excepting winter, whereas Bald Eagles are common in spring and winter.

Mammals sighted in the Big Valley area include Cottontail, Jack Rabbit, chipmunks, Coyote, Raccoon, Marten, Ermine, Weasel, Badger, Western Spotted Skunk, River Otter, Mountain Lions, Bobcats, Elk, Mule Deer, and Pronghorn Antelope.

A bird checklist, *Birds of Ash Creek Wildlife Area*, available at the Ash Creek headquarters, serves well for the whole of Big Valley.

Maps of the Big Valley area can be obtained at the headquarters of the Big Valley Ranger District of the Modoc National Forest in Adin, or by writing: Big Valley Ranger District, Modoc National Forest, Adin, CA 96006. Call (916) 299-3215.

For further information about Ash Creek Wildlife Area write: Department of Fish and Game, Ash Creek Wildlife Area, P.O. Box 37, Bieber, CA 96009, or call (916) 294-5326.

Visitors wishing to explore Big Valley may want to headquarter in either one of two small towns, Beiber or Adin, or in one of the Modoc National Forest campgrounds.

The Ash Creek Camp, which has tent sites, is located 8 miles southeast of Adin. Lava Camp, located 9 miles north of Adin on U.S. Highway 299, then east 0.5 mile on Rush Creek, has trailer sites, as does Upper Rush Creek, located north of Adin on Rush Creek and 3 miles beyond the lower camp. Willow Creek Camp, 16 miles south of Adin on SH 139, has trailer sites as well. All of these camps are equipped with tables, benches, stoves, and toilets.

Ash Creek and the Big Swamp lie directly west of Adin. The south entrance is off SH 299, about 10 miles southeast of Adin. From the north, take the Adin-Lookout Road (County Road 87) and go west 8 miles to Elkins Lane. Turn left and go 0.25 mile to the park's unattended entrance. There's also a parking area on Bieber-Lookout Road, off SH 299 about 0.5 mile north of Bieber. This is a closed area, so observation must be done from the parking area.

The Big Valley Ranger District headquarters is located in Adin.

Devils Garden Ranger District

Points of interest in the Devils Garden Ranger District include the largest stand of junipers in the western U.S., located on the west side of Goose Lake, seven miles from McGinty Point; several old emigrant trails, dating back to the mid 1800's; Indian petroglyphs and other prehistoric artifacts in Fairchild Swamp, approximately nine miles west of Big Sage Reservoir.

Raptors of the area include Sharp-shinned, Cooper's, and Rough-legged Hawks, as well as Screech, Flammulated, Great Horned, Northern Pygmy, Long-eared, and Saw-whet Owls. Local woodpeckers are Lewis', Downy, and Black-backed. Also seen here are Blue Grouse, Sage Grouse, Purple Finch, Townsend's Solitaire, Clark's Nutcracker, Evening Grosbeak, Hermit Thrush, Cedar Waxwing, Mountain Quail, and Chukar, as well as Willow, Hammond's, Dusky, Gray, and Pacific Slope Flycatchers.

Species common or abundant throughout the Modoc National Forest include Western Tanager, Dark-eyed Junco, California Quail, Burrowing Owl, Hairy Woodpecker, Mountain Chickadee, Loggerhead Shrike, and Solitary Vireo.

Rare sightings include Peregrine Falcon, Spotted Owl, Great Gray Owl, Pileated Woodpecker, Ash-throated Flycatcher, Gray Jay, Black-capped Chickadee, Swainson's Thrush, Northern Shrike, Yellow-breasted Chat, Red Crossbill, and Fox and Lincoln's Sparrows.

Mammals of the Modoc National Forest include Coyote, Badger, Bobcat, Marten, Weasel, Rocky Mountain Mule Deer, Porcupine, and a variety of rodents.

There are three campgrounds in the Devils Garden Ranger District: Big Sage, 4 miles west and 10 miles north of Alturas; Howard's Gulch, 6 miles northwest of Canby; Cottonwood Flat, a hunter's camp, located 5 miles south and 8 miles west of Canby.

For further information and/or to obtain an area map (at a cost of $2.00) write: District Ranger, Devils Garden Ranger District, Modoc National Forest, Canby, CA 96105.

Devils Garden Ranger District headquarters is in Canby, at the junction of SH 299 and SH 139.

Modoc National Wildlife Refuge

It was a fair September morning when we birded here in the Modoc National Wildlife Refuge. We saw the Warner Mountains off in the distance, shrouded in fog; ponds set like gemstones in gently rolling, scrub-covered hills; grasslands that ranged in hues from pale, greenish-beige to the gold of saltwater-taffy; curious deer ogling us from every side; 22 species of birds in just twice that many minutes. And what we heard, like background music, was the peculiar gurgling-liquid call of the Sandhill Cranes.

Established in 1960, the Modoc National Wildlife Refuge covers 6,280 acres, and contains an extensive system of ponds, dikes, and control structures devised to regulate water levels by sytematically flooding and draining the meadow and marsh.

The refuge offers a fine auto tour route, wonderful opportunities for wildlife observation and photography, hunting in season, fishing at the Dorris Reservoir, and excellent educational programs. Public use areas are open every day from sunup to sundown.

To give you a fair idea of what you can expect to see at this fine refuge, the following is a list of species we sighted in less than an hour of early morning birding one day in mid-September: Greater Sandhill Crane, Canada Goose, Tundra Swan, Red-winged Blackbird, Snowy Egret, Marsh Wren, Great Blue Heron, Great Egret, Cinnamon Teal, Common Moorhen, Northern Pintail, American Wigeon, Redhead, Ring-necked Pheasant, Sage Grouse, American White Pelican, Northern Harrier, and Song Sparrow.

Mammals common to the area include Mule Deer, Cottontails, and Black-tailed Jackrabbits. Less often sighted but here nonetheless are Rac-

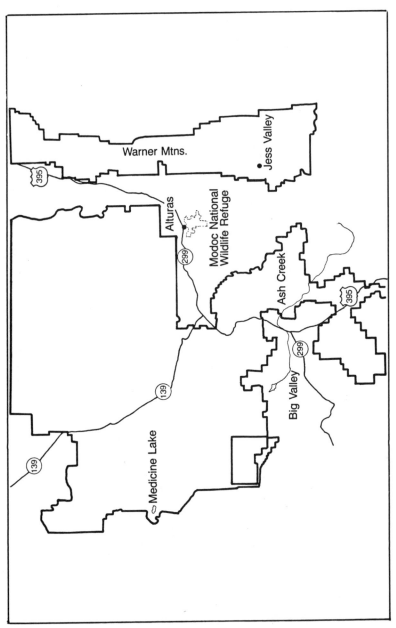

Modoc National Forest

coon, Mink, Muskrat, skunks, and a variety of squirrels and mice.

A brochure and maps are available at the headquarters, as is an excellent bird list, *Birds of Modoc National Wildlife Refuge*.

For further information write: Refuge Manager, Modoc National Wildlife Refuge, P.O. Box 1610, Alturas, CA 96101, or call (916) 233-3572.

From the south, take County Road 115 to the right from US 395, about 8 miles south of Alturas. There are parking areas along this road on the left side for observations, but to reach the refuge headquarters, continue north on 115 and watch for the sign on the right. From Alturas, come east on County Road 56 and turn south on 115. To get to the Dorris Reservoir area of the refuge, continue east on 56 for a couple of miles past Road 115.

Warner Mountains/Jess Valley Area

Nine miles east of the town of Likely, at the foot of the Warner Mountains, lies Jess Valley, an area that offers some very good birding. The Warner Range is 80 miles long by about 10 miles wide and rises up fairly moderately from the Devils Garden portion of the Modoc Plateau at Likely, to elevations approaching 10,000 feet, then plunges precipitously down on the eastern side to the Surprise Valley. This is wilderness country, largely undiscovered, but a haven for the hunter, fisherman, hiker, geologist, and historian, as well as the birder.

Mountain lakes, rushing streams, reservoirs, wetlands, forests of mixed conifers and quaking aspen, scrublands of sagebrush, rabbitbrush, juniper, grasslands and meadows: these are the varied habitats that provide sustenance and shelter for a great number of bird species.

Jess Valley is usually fairly wet in spring and early summer, and depending on the amount of dampness, may attract many of the species that occur in another (and even better known) northern California hotspot, Sierra Valley. To the southeast is Blue Lake, at an elevation of 6,000 feet, surrounded by mixed conifer woods and meadows; and beyond that, on Patterson Sawmill Road, Parsnip Springs with its meadows and aspen trees, and Patterson Meadow, at 7,200 feet.

In addition to some very good birding, the Warners offer hunting, fishing, beautiful campsites, and hiking on a number of picturesque trails. There's a campground at Blue Lake with 48 sites and a small one at Patterson Meadow with 5 sites. Both have piped in water, vault toilets, tables, and fire pits. There are nine other campgrounds in the Warner Mountains, which vary in accessibility and accommodations. Further information is available at Warner Mountain Ranger District, Cedarville, CA 96104, (916) 279-6116. A bird list is available.

Eared Grebes breed in Jess Valley, as do Sandhill Cranes. You'll find Black Tern, Common Snipe, Red-winged Blackbird, loons, and a good assortment of geese and puddle ducks. At Parsnip Springs you can expect all these woodpeckers: Downy, Hairy and White-headed, along with Williamson's and Red-breasted Sapsuckers. And with luck you may see the nesting Willow Flycatchers that have been sighted here.

Other birds to look for are Gray Jay, Vaux's Swift, Lazuli Bunting, Mountain Bluebird, Cordilleran Flycatcher, Clark's Nutcracker, Townsend's Solitaire, Loggerhead Shrike, American Dipper, and a variety of chickadees, nuthatches, vireos and warblers.

Bighorn Sheep roamed these mountains until the late 1800s, when their population declined rapidly. They were reintroduced, but disease struck again in 1988. The rangers request that any sightings be reported.

Mule Deer, Pronghorn, Porcupine, Coyote, and a whole slew of rodents are all common. Occasionally there's Mountain Lion and Bobcat.

Likely is on US 395, 19 miles south of Alturas and about a three hour drive from Reno, Nevada. From Likely, go due east on Jess Valley Road.

SUSANVILLE

Susanville. Coming into Susanville from the south, you're on SH 36; just continue on until you come to a Bank of America building in the north end of town, turn right, and walk the backroads among the houses and apple trees where you can expect good sightings of all the usual montane birds not apt to be seen further south. This is also one of the most likely places in this part of California to spot the Bohemian Waxwing.

Leavitt Lake. Leaving Susanville on SH 36 southbound takes you again to US 395. If you take US 395 north (which happens to go east here for quite a little way) you'll come to Leavitt Lake Market, on the corner of Buffum Lane. Take Buffum to the south, along the west side of Leavitt Lake. Raptors such as Red-tailed Hawk, Northern Harrier, and Rough-legged Hawk are abundant here in the wintertime, and you've got a good chance of seeing a Bald Eagle down at the end of the road.

Then go back out to 395, go east about 6 miles to County Road A3, and turn south again. Winding through the grasslands in this area, you'll find a number of roads that offer good birding. Any one of these will afford you excellent hawk watching and a good chance to see the Northern Shrike.

Honey Lake Wildlife Area

Near the Diamond Mountains, a favorite haunt of migrating Sandhill Cranes, lies the Honey Lake Wildlife Area, a locale that's lauded for unusual species such as Tree Sparrows and Sage Grouse, colonies of breeding terns and gulls, a heron rookery, and high concentrations of migrating waterfowl.

According to Dave Shuford of the Point Reyes Bird Observatory, this area offers especially good birding in May and June when California Gulls, Caspian Terns, and Ring-billed Gulls are nesting on the islands in the lake and ponds. Also here are breeding Canada Geese, Snowy Egrets, and Black-crowned Night-Herons, and Snowy Plovers nesting along the shoreline.

Certainly the breeding season is an excellent time to bird at Honey Lake. Thanks, in part, to the efforts of an organization called Ducks Unlimited — and the carefully devised island nesting sites that hold predators at bay — the success rate of birds breeding here is better than ever. (Consider, for example, the 93% success rate of Canada Geese nesting on islands, as opposed to the 31% of those on levees.) Obviously there are many birds to see in spring and early summer, but it's good to know that the Honey Lake area offers good birding at other times too.

When Wildlife Habitat Supervisor Chuck Holmes gave us a tour of the Dakin Unit one September afternoon in 1988, a list of species we sighted included Horned Lark, American Avocet, Black-necked Stilt, Ring-necked Pheasant, grebes, Canada Goose, Gadwall, Red-winged Blackbird, Double-crested Cormorant, Barn Owl, and Lewis' Woodpecker. Rarities seen by Chuck include Baikal Teal, Peregrine Falcon, and, on one occasion, 12 Bald Eagles perched in one cottonwood tree!

Mammals seen in the area are Pronghorn Antelope, Muskrat, skunks, Coyote, and Mule Deer.

When visiting Honey Lake it's advisable to check with the ranger regarding temporary closures or restrictions such as those that occur during critical breeding periods or hunting season. From the 15th of March until the first of May, for example, the unit is closed for the protection of nesting Canada Geese. And for three days a week, during the hunting season, the area is open to hunters only. During the other four days, birders are welcome but must park at the ranger's house near the entry and hike in. When hunting season is over, visitors may drive directly into the unit, park in a designated lot, and scout about from there on foot.

Coming from the south on US 395, turn right on Standish-Buntingville Road (County Road A3) at Buntingville. Go about 6 miles, keeping an eye out for raptors, turn right on Mapes Road, go 3 miles and look for the sign on your right.

To get to the Dakin Unit from Susanville, take US 395 north to Standish, turn right on A3, go to Mapes Road, and turn left.

To reach the Fleming Unit, continue east on Mapes Road, past the Dakin Unit turnoff, another 4.5 miles.

Janesville

This charming little Sierra town is unique in the Eastern Sierra for its mix of black oak and yellow pines, and for the birds these trees bring to its quiet streets, the local cemetery, and the surrounding stream-studded countryside. Look for Golden Eagle, Merlin, Evening Grosbeak, Lewis' and Acorn Woodpeckers, Mountain Chickadee, Scrub and Steller's Jays, nuthatches, juncos, and sometimes even Red Crossbills.

Janesville is just to the west of US 395, 12 miles south of Susanville. To find the Janesville cemetery turn east on Christie Street 2 blocks north of the center of town.

Red Rock Canyon

Shades of Canyonlands in Utah; that's how this area struck us when we dropped by Red Rock Canyon for an hour of birding one warm summer day. The sun shone on rock walls of stark white, plum, rose red, cinnabar-orange, and deep rust, and the buzzing trill of a Rock Wren rose up like an anthem to rocky western places.

This is very desert-like country. Except for the dramatic splashes of color from flowers and canyon walls, the world seems entirely beige, a bit forbidding, and in summer and fall as dry as the old bare coyote bones we saw lying behind a clump of rabbitbrush.

Besides the Rock Wren, which is best sighted along the base of the cliffs, look for Pinyon Jay, Black-chinned Hummingbird, Say's Phoebe, Cassin's Finch, Townsend's Solitaire, Bushtit, Golden Eagle, and Common Raven.

Mammals seen in the vicinity include Coyotes, foxes, deer, and rodents enough to keep the resident raptors well-fed.

Red Rock Canyon Road goes east from US 395, about 12 miles north of Halleujah Junction (SH 70 and US 395).

WHISKEYTOWN LAKE/WHISKEYTOWN-SHASTA-TRINITY NRA

Eight lush, year-round creeks wind through this parkland that lies in country that once was home to the Wintu Indians. Those were quieter times, those days when disc beads served as money, acorns for food, woven baskets for storage bins. Nowadays, the manmade lake devised to divert water to the Sacramento River draws such crowds that in some areas, where the noise of power boats and jet skis prevail, it's hard to believe quiet ever reigned. Yet there are other spots, like along the lake's arms and coves, or in the surrounding valleys and canyons, or on the banks of the creeks, where a nature-loving visitor can find peace and solitude such as the Wintu knew.

With its balance of bustling places and quiet hideaways, this is a good place to come if you're traveling with nonbirding friends or family members, for there's plenty to do for everyone. The park offers fine sailing, canoeing, powerboating, and jet skiing; swimming, wading, and sunning on fine sandy beaches; boats for rent at Oak Bottom Marina; excellent fishing in season; fine hiking trails; lots of backcountry land to explore on foot or horseback; opportunities for nature study; gold panning; RV camping for self-contained units; walk-in tent campsites with picnic tables and modern restrooms; permit camping in designated backcountry locations; ranger-guided walks; a variety of educational programs; a visitor center; bird check lists.

Birds common or fairly common here all year long are Red-breasted Nuthatch, Bewick's Wren, Hutton's Vireo, Lesser Goldfinch, Rufous-sided Towhee, Song Sparrow, California Quail, Great Horned Owl, Black Phoebe, Northern Pygmy-Owl, Steller's Jay, Mountain Chickadee, Bushtit, and Plain Titmouse. Less common residents are Townsend's

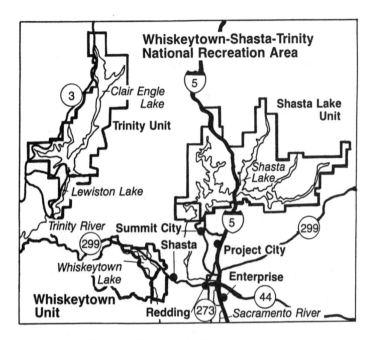

Whiskeytown-Shasta-Trinity National Recreation Area

Solitaire, Cassin's Finch, Great Blue Heron, Spotted Sandpiper, Northern Saw-whet Owl, and Pileatd and Downy Woodpeckers.

In spring or summer look for Solitary and Warbling Vireos, Western Tanager, Lazuli Bunting, and Red-winged Blackbird as well as Orange-crowned, Black-throated Gray, and MacGillivray's Warblers. In winter expect Wood Duck, Canvasback, Lesser Scaup, Common Goldeneye, Bufflehead, Ruddy Duck, and other waterfowl.

Unusual species sighted here include Osprey, Pileated Woodpecker, Spotted Sandpiper, Long-eared Owl, and Peregrine Falcon.

For further information write to Whiskeytown Unit, Whiskeytown-Shasta-Trinity NRA, P.O. Box 188, Whiskeytown, CA 96095-0188.

The Visitor Information Center is at the eastern end of the lake, on Highway 299, eight miles west of Redding.

Garner's Trinity Wilderness Campground/Trinity Alps

This private campground lies in the Trinity Alps, a land of Indian pink, tiger lilies, ponderosa pine, and Port Oxford cedar. It's literally in the thick of excellent mountain birding country and surrounded by a National Forest, a good place to see Osprey, eagles, and a variety of owls.

The campground offers all these features: easy access; a secluded and sandy beach with a shallow swimming area; comfortable, private, wooded campsites; flush toilets and hot showers; water hookups; close proximity to Weaverville (13 miles away), Junction City at 4 miles, and the Big Bar Ranger Station at 20; nearby attractions, such as the ghost town of Helena; and Trinity Lake, a riparian habitat that ensures the presence of many mountain birds.

Species sighted in these Shasta-Trinity forests include Wood Duck, Osprey, Bald Eagle, Screech and Spotted Owls, Red-shouldered Hawk, Allen's Hummingbird, Steller's Jay, Red-winged Blackbird, Rufous and Anna's Hummingbirds, Dark-eyed Junco, Western Tanager, Hermit Thrush, Rufous-sided Towhee, Cedar Waxwing, and Great Blue Heron, as well as Acorn, Hairy, Downy, Pileated, and Lewis' Woodpeckers.

Garner's Campground is generally open from the first of April until the first of December, depending, of course, on weather conditions. For reservations or further information write: Garner's Campground, Box 368, Dutch Creek Road, HC2, Box 90, Junction City, CA 96048.

Just east of Junction City, about 60 miles west of Redding on SH 299, turn south at the Forest Service Guard Station. Cross the Trinity River, turn left, and follow the signs. It's about 4 miles from the highway.

McARTHUR-BURNEY FALLS MEMORIAL STATE PARK

McArthur-Burney Falls Memorial State Park. Theodore Roosevelt called the waterfalls here "the eighth wonder of the world." We'll let his description suffice and be content to list a few unembellished facts: the park covers 875 acres: its elevation is 3,000 feet; it includes roughly 2 miles of frontage along Burney Creek; it boasts a portion of the shoreline of PG&E's beautiful Lake Britton, complete with boat ramp; it offers good swimming, boating, and fishing.

Here too are campsites, picnic tables, a self-guided nature trail, lovely flora, an available bird check list, and, of course, a goodly share of birds, including those waterfall-loving aerial performers, the Black Swifts, very much in evidence in the park, and the Bald Eagles for which its neighbor, Lake Britton, is famed. The swifts dwell here in the summer, the eagles all year long.

Common in the vicinity for at least two of the four seasons of the year are Pied-billed Grebe, Double-crested Cormorant, Great Blue Heron, Canada Goose, Common Merganser, Barn Owl, Great Horned Owl, Belted Kingfisher, and Purple Martin. Less often sighted are Common Loon, Bufflehead, Common Nighthawk, Pacific Slope Flycatcher, and Western Wood-Pewee. Rare or occasional sightings include American Wigeon, Wood Duck, Sandhill Crane, American Avocet, and Pileated Woodpecker. A bird list is available and serves for Lake Britton as well as for the state park.

Fifty-eight miles east of Redding, SH 89 crosses SH 299. Go 4 miles north on SH 89 and watch for the signs on the left.

Lake Britton. This lake seems so pristine it's hard to believe its very existence is the direct result of a manmade contrivance, namely, Pit River Number Three, one of several turn-of-the-century dams constructed for the purpose of generating hydroelectric power. Fortunately the Bald Eagles are oblivious to its origins. They're very much at home here, and frequently sighted. Although Lake Britton is the property of PG&E, it's looked upon by many visitors as a part of McArthur-Burney Falls Memorial State Park.

Birds seen at Lake Britton are the same as those listed for the state park.

Get to Lake Britton through McArthur-Burney Falls State Park or continue on SH 89 past the McArthur-Burney turn-off. There's a boat dock and campground where SH 89 crosses the upper arm of the lake. Or take Clark Creek Road to the left at Old Four Corners before you get to the McArthur-Burney exit; this leads to Lake Britton dam.

LASSEN VOLCANIC NATIONAL PARK

Until Washington's restive Mount Saint Helens erupted in 1980, Lassen Peak was the scene of the most recent volcanic fury in the 48 contiguous states. It's last outburst occurred as recently as 1915. It was then that the peak exploded in a great mushroom-shaped cloud that rose seven miles into the stratosphere, like a smoke signal sent to inform the world that here, in this part of California, change was in order; the landscape was

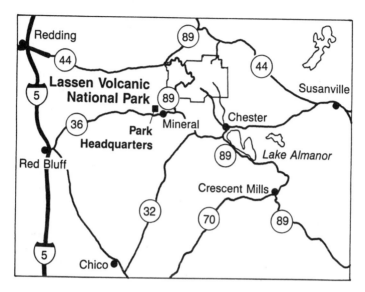

Lassen Volcanic National Park

being redone; nothing would ever be the same again.

There was nothing garbled about the message. It was only the terrain that was all awry, peppered as it was with cinders, lined with ribbons of lava, pock-marked, rutted, and venting steam. Nonetheless, it was still beautiful, as dramatically mountainous as ever, still blessed with crisp and rarefied air, bearing deep-green conifers, dotted with lakes and meadow-land, adorned with spring flowers, and ringing with birdsong. It was at once a curiosity and a wonderland, a monstrosity and a beauty. It was a place so incredibly scenic, in fact, so obviously significant, so bound to serve as a kind of laboratory of volcanic phenomena, that scarcely had the lava cooled — in 1916 — than was it set aside as a national park, a place where people could always come to see what Mother Nature wrought in this southernmost part of the Shasta Cascades.

This is one park where even the most singleminded of birders is apt to give equal time to some concentrated sightseeing, in which case, customary "musts" on lists of places to see usually include Little Hot Springs Valley, Bumpass Hell, the Painted Dunes, and Cinder Cone. But carry your binoculars with you wherever you go: there are nesting Bald Eagles here and you never know when one might go soaring through the sky above.

Besides the peerless scenery and the endless geologic features, Lassen Volcanic National Park boasts all of the following features: 150 miles of great hiking trails, including a seventeen-mile section of the Pacific Crest Trail; an excellent auto tour; good fishing and non-power boating in beautiful, blue waters; wilderness backpacking and rough-it camping (permit required); horse corrals at Butte, Summit and Juniper Lakes; a park information center; educational programs offered by the superb Loomis Museum, where books, bird lists, maps, and an assortment of descriptive material are available; seven campgrounds, all of which are operated on a first-come, first-served basis.

Interesting species nesting here at Lassen Volcanic National Park include Bald Eagle, Gray Jay, Goshawk, Ring-necked Duck, Sharp-shinned Hawk, Prairie Falcon, Cooper's Hawk, Mountain Quail, Common Snipe, Spotted Sandpiper, Great Horned Owl, Common Poorwill, Common Nighthawk, Calliope Hummingbird, Blue Grouse, and Clark's Nutcracker.

Common year-round residents include American Dipper, Canada Goose, Steller's Jay, and White-breasted and Red-breasted Nuthatches.

Look in the forests for Blue Grouse, Pileated Woodpecker, Great Horned Owl, Clark's Nutcracker, and White-headed Woodpecker. Expect to see Western Bluebird, Fox Sparrow, Rufous Hummingbird, Common Nighthawk, and Wilson's and Yellow Warblers in the meadows, shrubs, and on open slopes. Scan the streams and lakes for American Bittern, American Dipper, American Wigeon, Canada Goose, and Belted Kingfisher. Keep an eye on the skies for Bald Eagles and other raptors.

Residing in the parklands are Mountain Lion, deer, foxes, and a variety of rodents.

For a list of informative publications pertaining to the park and offered for sale at the museum, write: Loomis Museum Association, Lassen Volcanic National Park, P.O. Box 100, Mineral, CA 96063-0100.

For further information write: Superintendent, Lassen Volcanic National Park, P.O. Box 100, Mineral, CA 96063-0100, or call (916) 595-4444.

SH 89 runs through the park, but there's a good chance the central portion will be closed during the winter. SH 89 at the south entrance is reached by a 44-mile drive east on SH 36 from Red Bluff. To get to SH 89 and the north entrance, take SH 44 east from Redding, about 47 miles.

YOLLA BOLLY WILDERNESS

"A wilderness . . . is an area where the earth and its community of life are untrammeled by man, where man himself is a visitor who does not remain." This description of an area that inspires many to poetry comes not from the poet, but straight from the bureaucracy. It's taken verbatim from the Wilderness Act of 1964.

In the Trinity Alps, between the northern end of the Great Central Valley and the coastal hills of the Pacific, lies one of the most remote, rugged, and undeveloped regions in California. Two national forests, Six Rivers and Trinity, cover practically all of this territory. This is the Yolla Bolly Ranger District of Trinity National Forest, which includes a good portion of the Yolla Bolly - Middle Eel Wilderness, an area covered by the 1964 Act. There are *no* roads within the Wilderness. Narrow foot trails are the interior transportation system.

This area is comprised of high peaks (to 8,000 feet), a lot of creeks, some small lakes, conifer and mixed conifer-hardwood forests, some grasslands, wet and dry meadows, and chaparral. It's fascinating country with interesting birding opportunities. An information sheet put out by the Forest Service probably depicts it most aptly when it lists solitude as its number one attraction.

Many of the forest birds can be observed along SH 36, which transects this area and offers the amenities of National Forest camping, even as it serves as staging area for the more remote parts of the district. In these locations, as elsewhere in the area, the best birding is from May to November. In view of seasonal weather conditions, this is understandable, for winters here can be rough indeed. In fact, the name "Yolla Bolly" is derived from the Indian words meaning "snow covered" and "high peak."

Woodpeckers abound here: White-headed, Acorn, Pileated, Hairy, Downy, Red-breasted Sapsucker, and Northern Flicker. Not as common but here nonetheless are Peregrine Falcon, Spotted Owl, Goshawk, Bald Eagle, and Golden Eagle. A February 1989 publication of Shasta-Trinity National Forests (covering both forests) noted the presence of 17 pairs of nesting Bald Eagles and 5 pairs of nesting Peregrines in 1988.

Active birding in the Yolla Bolly should produce excellent counts of the woodland species: chickadees, nuthatches, creepers, warblers, sparrows, and hummingbirds. Western Tanager, Clark's Nutcracker, Mountain Quail, American Dipper, and Belted Kingfisher are frequently sighted.

Headquarters for the Yolla Bolly Ranger District is at Platina, CA 96076, telephone (916) 352-4211. Contact them for more information about both the regular areas of the National Forest and about the wilderness area.

Yolla Bolly Ranger District headquarters is in Platina, on SH 36, about 50 miles west of Red Bluff.

WOODSON BRIDGE STATE RECREATION AREA

Notable for its fine riparian habitat and more than 100 species of plants including black walnut, Oregon ash, black cottonwood, sycamore, willow, wild grape, and blue elderberry, the Woodson Bridge area is one of the last California strongholds for the Yellow-billed Cuckoo. It is largely this bird (seldom seen and generally found only in Butte, Glenn, and Colusa Counties, further south) that renders this popular Sacramento River park fascinating to birders.

The allure of the cuckoo notwithstanding, there are many other species to be seen here at Woodson Bridge. Expect Steller's Jay, Western Screech-Owl, Anna's and Rufous Hummingbirds, Northern Flickers, Willow Flycatcher, Western Meadowlark, Bewick's and Winter Wrens, Hermit Thrush, and Blue-gray Gnatcatcher. Scour the park's oak woods for these species that regard acorns as either snack food or staple: California Quail, American Crow, Scrub Jay, Acorn Woodpecker, and White-breasted Nuthatch. Scan the wild grape vines, in season, for Western Bluebird and Purple Finch. Amidst the elderberries, look for California Towhee, White-crowned Sparrow, Northern Oriole, Northern Mockingbird, Ruby-crowned Kinglet, Black-headed Grosbeak, Ring-necked Pheasant, Yellow-breasted Chat, and House Finch. Focus on the Oregon ash and you may espie Evening Grosbeaks or a flock of Cedar Waxwings. Then, of course, look to the river for Great Blue Heron and Wood Duck, to the sky for Sharp-shinned and Red-shouldered Hawks.

Besides pleasing birders and botanists, this park has plenty of allure for anglers, boaters, and campers. Nestled invitingly under the oaks are 46 campsites with tables, piped drinking water, modern restrooms, and hot showers. A boat-launching ramp is available at adjoining Tehama County

Park, and a store and cafe are not far away.

For further information write Woodson Bridge State Recreation Area, 25340 South Avenue, Corning, CA 96021, or call (916) 839-2112.

From I-5 (1.5 mile south of Corning), take South Avenue (County Road A9) to the east for 6 miles.

BLACK BUTTE LAKE

Created by the damming of historic old Stony Creek, a Corps of Engineers project that was completed in 1963, Black Butte Lake is situated on land most notable for the jet-black buttes of volcanic rock clearly visible from the lake. Once a haunt of the Nomlaki Indians, the area is best known today for its fishing, boating, and family camping.

There is probably no bird more typical of this Tehama/Glenn County lake than the Yellow-billed Magpie. Out-of-staters who've failed to sight this bonafide Californian elsewhere are almost sure to see it at Black Butte. Other species common here are Barn Owl, Scrub Jay, Great Blue Heron, Acorn Woodpecker, Western Kingbird, Plain Titmouse, and California Quail. Western Meadowlarks are so nearly ubiquitous here they deserve mention if for no other reason than abundance alone.

Important species occasionally sighted in the area include Bald Eagle, Peregrine Falcon, Swainson's Hawk and Yellow-billed Cuckoo. Considering the status of these birds, the sighting of any one of them makes a trip to Black Butte well worthwhile.

A checklist, "Birds Of Black Butte Lake," put out by the US Army Corps of Engineers, is available at the park.

Mammals seen here include Bobcat, Mule Deer, Raccoon, Opossum, and an abundance of rodents.

The park has 100 family campsites that include parking spurs, tables, and fire pits. Restroom facilities complete with showers and flush toilets are located nearby.

Reservations may be made ahead of time for group camping by calling (916) 865-4781. General family camping is strictly on a first-come first-served basis.

Black Butte Lake is in the western foothills of both Tehama and Glenn counties. From Orland on I-5, take County Road 200 (Newville Road) to the west. The road splits after 5 miles, but both branches lead to different campgrounds on the lake.

Central Valley

Chapter 6
Central Valley

 The central valley of California — the Great Valley — stretches nearly 500 miles through the heartland of California, between the foothills of the Sierra Nevada on the east, and the Coastal Ranges on the west. From Redding to Bakersfield, it's the richest agricultural region in the world, and from time immemorial its fields and wetlands have succored and nourished the huge flocks of migrating birds that travel the Pacific Flyway, and provided wintering and breeding grounds for countless others.

Agricultural reclamation of the wetlands and marshes has very seriously diminished these vital habitats over the past century, an item of critical importance to those concerned with the preservation of our planet, its environs, and its species. In recent years this trend has been curtailed, and even reversed; the reclamation is being reclaimed.

The Central Valley is actually two valleys — the Sacramento, and the San Joaquin. They are drained, sluggishly because of the flatness of the land, by rivers bearing the same names, which join together into the rich habitats of the Sacramento Delta before flowing into San Francisco Bay and the Pacific Ocean.

For the purposes of this book, northern California's portion of the Central Valley encompasses Glenn, Butte, Colusa, Yuba, Sutter, Yolo, Sacramento, San Joaquin, Stanislaus, and Merced County, and part of Madera County. The area is 13,502 square miles, or 17.1% of the area covered by this book.

Interstate Highway 5 speeds along the less populated western side of the valley, while State Highway 99 follows the route that has connected the major population centers since settlement began. These two major north-south routes are connected by a whole series of state highways and county roads that traverse the valley from east to west.

SUGGESTED CHECK LISTS AND BOOKS
FOR THE CENTRAL VALLEY

There are several good books and check lists available for the Central Valley Region.

Birds of the Sacramento Area
Published by the Sacramento Audubon Society
$4.95 plus tax and $3.00 for shipping and handling

Birds of the American River Parkway
Published by the American River Natural History Association
$3.95 plus tax and $3.00 for shipping and handling

Sacramento's Outdoor World
Published by the American River Natural History Association
$7.95 plus tax and $3.00 for shipping and handling

These three books are available from:
The Nature Center
2580 Fair Oaks Blvd.
Sacramento, CA 25958

Field Checklist of Butte County Birds
Available from:
Altacal Audubon Society
P.O. Box 3671
Chico, CA 95927
10 cents. (Please include a self-addressed, stamped, legal-sized envelope when placing your order.)

Birds of Stanislaus County California
By Harold M. Reeve

Available from Stanislaus Audubon Society
P.O. Box 4251, Modesto, CA 95352
or directly from
Harold Reeve
1404 Bandera Lane
Modesto, CA 95355

LAKE OROVILLE

From dam-building Beavers to nesting Bald Eagles, from strutting Wild
Turkeys to the big male Mountain Lion prowling at the foot of Kelly
Ridge, the wildlife of this area is rich and varied. Here too are Osprey,
Wood Duck, Great Horned Owl, Western Screech-Owl, California Quail,
Ring-necked Pheasant, Pinyon Jay, Scrub Jay, California Thrasher, North-
ern Mockingbird, House Finch, Northern Oriole, Acorn Woodpecker,
Evening Grosbeak, California Towhee, Plain Titmouse, Yellow-billed
Magpie, and White-breasted Nuthatch.

Here's what else Lake Oroville State Recreation Area has to offer: easy
access from its neighbor, Chico, a stone's throw away; four multi-level
boat launching ramps equipped with floats; plenty of parking; 167 miles
of shoreline; 18 miles of established hiking trails; access to the Feather
Falls hiking trail, which leads to the 7th highest waterfall in the United
States; 75 campsites with full hookups; beaches for swimming; secluded
areas, away from the crowds; 137 family campsites, fine picnic areas; an
active fish-planting program; 6 group campsites, a visitor center and
museum; 89 boat-in campsites; the tallest earth-fill dam in the nation; two
full-service marinas offering houseboat rentals; enforced noise control.

This is a popular park, so advance reservations are distinctly a good
idea. For any further information write: Lake Oroville State Recreation
Area, 400 Glen Drive, Oroville, CA 95966, or call (916) 538-2200.

From SH 70 in Oroville, turn east on SH 162 and proceed about 6 miles
to the lake.

SACRAMENTO VALLEY NATIONAL WILDLIFE REFUGES

Forewarned or not, birders visiting California's Great Valley wetland
areas for the first time are always astonished at the number of birds that
meet their eyes. As awesome as they are today, however, these protected

lands that comprise the Sacramento Valley National Wildlife Refuges give only a hint of what the Sacramento Valley was like in its halcyon days.

"On the vast plains roamed tens of thousands of antelope," wrote a newspaper editor who came here first in 1851. " Skirting the foothills and the timber were great bands of elk. In the hills and along the river were an abundance of deer and grizzley bear by the way, and here too I found primitive man. He had not progressed even to the fig leaf. This digger Indian has but to gather the grass and acorns that grew in such abundance for bread. He had to but set his nets to catch the finest fish in the world, but to bend his bow to kill all sorts of game. He was as happy as Adam could have been before he had knowledge of good and evil."

This valley is and always has been, an important wintering area for the millions of migrating waterfowl of the Pacific Flyway. Long ago, before it was inhabited by anyone other than native Americans, it was covered with vast marshlands that served the birds well. As civilization encroached, however, the wetlands shrank, and so too the natural food supply they represented. Until these important refuges were set aside, the situation was drastic.

The entire four-refuge complex, which includes the Sacramento, Delevan, Colusa, and Sutter NWRs, is comprised of approximately 23,500 acres of marshes, uplands, ponds, and agricultural fields, and covers sections of Glenn, Colusa, and Sutter counties.

When birding this area, remember that each refuge habitat that lies within the four Sacramento Valley National Wildlife Refuges boasts its own particular list of species. It's in the seasonal marshes, for example, those areas that are flooded intentionally during the fall and winter, that one can expect to see such species as Greater White-fronted Goose, American Wigeon, and American Avocet. In the refuge's permanent ponds one is more apt to sight Great Blue Heron, Pied-billed Grebe, and the very abundant Red-winged Blackbird. Species such as Belted Kingfisher, Green-winged Teal, Wood Duck, and American Bittern prefer the riparian lands, either the rivers, canals, and ponds themselves or the trees that line their banks. Food production lands, areas where rice and barley have been planted for their consumption, are apt to be populated by Sandhill Cranes, and Snow and Canada Geese. The grasslands, on the other hand, are home to such species as California Quail and Northern Harrier.

Mammals common to the Sacramento Valley National Wildlife Refuges are Opossum, Black-tailed Jackrabbit, California Ground Squirrel, Musk-

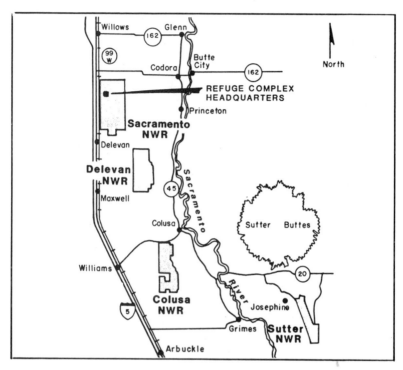

Sacramento Valley National Wildlife Refuge

rat, Black Rat, Norway Rat, House Mouse, Raccoon, Striped Skunk, Black-tailed Deer, and Beaver. Also seen are Desert Cottontail, Deer Mouse, Coyote, and Gray Fox.

All of the areas in the complex allow hunting and fishing in season. For further information write: Sacramento National Wildlife Refuges, Route 1, Box 311, Willows, CA 95988, or call (916) 934-2801.

Sacramento National Wildlife Refuge. Of the four refuges in this vast complex, none is more popular than Sacramento NWR, located in Glenn County in an area that's dotted with sunflowers and blooming chicory. This is the only refuge in the complex that boasts a walking trail, a photo blind, and a calendar of excellent group programs. Here too, as at Colusa

NWR, is an auto tour route that offers easy observation of the many species that abound in this productive valley.

During the peak population months of November and December there are approximately 200,000 geese and 500,000 ducks at this refuge alone. More than 212 species of birds have been recorded here. Among these are such notable species as Bald Eagle, Peregrine Falcon, and the Aleutian race of the Canada Goose.

A check list, *Wildlife of the Sacramento Valley National Wildlife Refuges*, is available.

Public use areas are open every day during daylight hours except when schedules are modified by hunting regulations.

Sacramento National Wildlife Refuge lies just to the east of I-5, five miles south of Willows. Take the Norman Road exit and go north on the frontage road 2 miles to the entrance.

Delevan National Wildlife Refuge. Although Delevan NWR lacks some of the facilities available at two of its sister refuges, it is nonetheless a vital link in a chain of designated areas that helps to insure the preservation of America's wildlife heritage. And of course, like the others it's teeming with wildlife.

Portions of Delevan are open to the public for wildlife observation as well as for fishing and hunting. Anglers and hunters should contact the Sacramento Refuge headquarters or the California Department of Fish and Game for current regulations.

The most representative species here is the Northern Pintail, which is seen here in great number. Here too are grebes, coots, teals, wigeons, egrets, herons, and many other species.

Delevan National Wildlife Refuge is located 10 miles south of the town of Willows, off I-5: from I-5, turn east at Maxwell and continue 4 miles on Maxwell Road to the entrance of the refuge.

Colusa National Wildlife Refuge. This refuge and Sutter NWR were created in 1944 and 1945, adding 6,633 acres to the Sacramento National Wildlife Refuge, which was established in 1937. Through the interim years, Sacramento Valley farming had continued to expand, the vital wetland feeding areas to shrink, and the ducks and waterfowl, of course, to steal from the cropland that was stolen from them. Colusa and Sutter refuges were established especially for the purposes of combatting an ecological problem that was both moral and economic.

An excellent auto tour route makes observation easy at this popular birder's haven, which counts among its special birds the White-faced Ibis. This fascinating species, which nests in the refuge, is listed by the U.S. Fish and Wildlife Service as a sensitive species in California. It meets the sensitive species criteria in accord with Criteria 4, which means its ". . . populations are small or restricted to a few localities such that any significant reduction in population or deterioration of habitat could cause federal listing as a threatened species."

Although the best opportunities for birding at the Colusa NWR exist from fall through early spring, birders are encouraged to visit throughout the year.

To get here from the town of Colusa, drive 0.5 mile west on SH 20 to the refuge entrance.

Sutter National Wildlife Refuge. According to Bruce Deuel, assistant Waterfowl Coordinator of the California Department of Fish and Game and himself a resident of Sutter County, this area is "used largely by fisherman and hunters." He goes on to note, however, that birding is good here from the public road that runs through the refuge.

The most typical bird at Sutter NWR is unquestionably the Mallard, seen here by the thousands. Also here are many other birds sighted in the Sacramento Valley National Wildlife Refuges and listed previously, among them the White-faced Ibis.

Sutter National Wildlife Refuge is located 5 miles south of the town of Sutter in the Sutter bypass. From SH 99, 5 miles south of Yuba City, turn west on Oswald Road, go about 5 miles to Schlag Road and turn left into the parking lot.

MARYSVILLE

Gray Lodge Wildlife Area

This is truly a phenomenal refuge, one of the most widely used and developed marshlands on the whole Pacific Flyway, an area visited by more than a million hungry ducks and 100,000 swarming geese, home to thousands of other birds and many other kinds of wildlife. With its wetlands, towering cottonwoods, and stands of non-native bamboo, it's a favorite locale for birders, wildlife photographers, botanists, and hikers — with doubtless a few amply-inspired poets thrown in for good measure.

Gray Lodge was named for a certain gray clubhouse, haunt of hunting club members whose suggestion it was that the Department of Fish and Game purchase this extraordinary wildlife habitat as a refuge for migrating waterfowl. It's operated to preserve and provide habitat for fowl and other wildlife; to produce feed for these creatures and thereby lessen crop damage; to provide carefully controlled public shooting and other recreational activities.

The area boasts 8,400 acres of land and water; an excellent specimen museum that features species sighted here; many miles of fine, level hiking trails; organized walks led by the area naturalist; dog trials by advance approval; bicycling; fishing in season; public restroom; free literature and maps; group overnight camping under special permit.

Many species of birds make Gray Lodge their home, either on a part-time basis or year-round. Winter is the time to see flocks of ducks and geese so large they actually dim the sky. The herons are at their liveliest in January, when the rookery's great cottonwoods are festooned with nests. In spring, as the migratory birds begin to leave, the ponds are drained, and the shorebirds have their heyday in the food-rich mud. In early March the resident Wood Ducks are ready to nest in the 200 boxes placed for them in riparian trees.

A bird list, "Field Checklist of Butte County Birds" may be purchased from the Altacal Audubon Society at P.O. Box 3671, Chico, CA 95927.

Also seen at Gray Lodge are Coyotes, Black-tailed Deer, and many rodents. Occasionally an albino Black-tailed Deer appears on the scene.

The entrance fee at Gray Lodge Wildlife Area is $2.00 per person for anyone over 16 years of age. There is no cost for entry for those possessing a valid California fishing or hunting license. Annual passes, which serve for eight other state wildlife areas as well, may be purchased for $10.00.

For further information call (916) 846-5176.

From SH 99 in Gridley, go west on Colusa Road to Pennington Road. Turn left, go 1 mile, and watch for the entrance sign.

Colusa-Sacramento River State Recreation Area

An excellent example of the transforming powers of humankind (for it lies on land that once served as the city dump), nowadays this popular

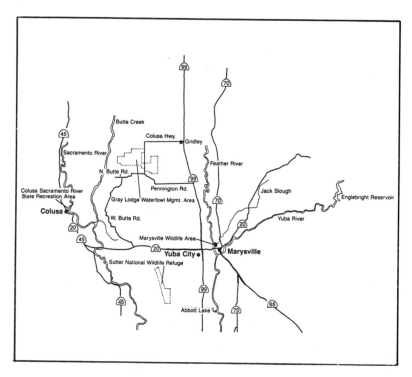

Marysville

State Recreation Area offers lush riverbanks graced with cottonwoods, willows, wild grape, and figs; excellent fishing in this largest of California rivers; boat launching ramps; 22 developed campsites equipped with tables, barbecue stoves, and food storage lockers; piped drinking water; modern restrooms and hot showers; tree-shaded picnic sites; 5 acres of lovely green lawn.

The Yellow-billed Magpie is a special bird of the Colusa-Sacramento River State Recreation Area. Other species commonly seen here are Ring-necked Pheasant, California Quail, Canada Goose, Wood Duck, House Finch, American Goldfinch, Cedar Waxwing, Scrub Jay, Western Bluebird, Black-headed Grosbeak, Northern Mockingbird, and Northern Oriole.

Campsite reservations are advisable from April through September. For further information write: Colusa-Sacramento River State Recreation Area, P.O. Box 207, Colusa, CA 95932, or call (916) 458-4927.

The city of Colusa is at the junction of Highway 20 and 45 in Colusa County. Take Levee Road north from the town.

Sutter Butte Area

One of northern California's most unusual geologic features, the Sutter Buttes are extinct volcanoes that rise up incongruously from the flat valley floor. Once believed sacred by the Indians and still looked upon with awe not only by birders but geologists, anthropologists, ethnographers, photographers, and venturesome sightseers, the buttes and the surrounding land support a large variety of mammals and birds.

Butte Slough Wildlife Area. This little-known wildlife area, which was acquired from State Reclamation Board in 1977, lies right at the foot of Sutter Buttes. The Butte Slough area consists of 178 acres of undisturbed riparian vegetation with an overstory comprised of valley oaks, western sycamore, Fremont cottonwood and black walnut. The understory is a labyrinthian tangle of rye grass, blackberry, and elderberry. The western edge of the area is largely valley oak savanna.

The Butte Slough area offers good fishing and upland hunting in season, and affords some excellent birding.

Regular residents here on the Feather River floodplain include Wood Duck, Great Blue Heron, Great and Snowy Egrets, Green-backed Heron, Cooper's and Red-shouldered Hawks, California Quail, Ring-necked Pheasant, Barn Owl, Western Screech and Great Horned Owls, Wrentit, House and Bewick's Wrens, Northern Mockingbird, Western Bluebird, Phainopepla, Loggerhead Shrike, Hutton's Vireo, Orange-crowned Warbler, Common Yellowthroat, Yellow-headed, Red-winged, and Brewer's Blackbirds, Anna's Hummingbird, and Belted Kingfisher.

Summer visitors include the rare Yellow-billed Cuckoo, Lesser Nighthawk, White-throated Swift, Black-chinned Hummingbird, Swainson's Thrush, Yellow-breasted Chat, Northern Oriole, Lewis' Woodpecker, Western Kingbird, Willow and Pacific Slope Flycatchers, Purple Martin, and Lazuli Bunting. Lewis' Woodpecker can be seen in winter.

Mammals present are California Spotted Skunk, Striped Skunk, Raccoon, Long-tailed Weasel, Virginia Opossum, Ring-tailed Cat, Beaver, River Otter, Muskrat, Mink, Gray and Red Foxes, Coyote, and Black-tailed Jackrabbit.

To reach Butte Slough Wildlife Area take SH 20 west from Yuba City for 10 miles to West Butte Road. Turn right and go 3.8 miles to the access road.

Sutter Buttes. This peculiar volcanic cluster, widely known as a mecca for raptors, is largely private property and the roads that traverse it not generally open to the public. They are open, however, to some very special, exciting, and educational tours which are planned and conducted by a non-profit organization and led by various experts in the fields of natural and cultural history. This is a great adventure and we highly recommend it. There are many raptors to be seen in this area — Prairie Falcons, Bald Eagles, and nesting Golden Eagles.

Realize that a Sutter Buttes trip is not to be considered a drop-by birding excursion. This is an in-depth experience and one that should be well planned. For information about special events and pre-organized charter groups write: Ira Henrich, Executive Director, Middle Mountain Foundation, Forest Ranch, CA 95942. Or call Ira at (916) 343-6614.

Marysville Wildlife Area

Since the floodplains of the Sacramento Valley that lie adjacent to intensely developed agricultural lands and residential areas often form important ecological niches that support a variety of wildlife species, it's no surprise that the Marysville Wildlife Area is so rich in avifauna.

This area is part of the floodplain of the Jack Slough and the Feather and Yuba Rivers. Here are cottonwood, honey locust, button willow, blue elderberry, white alder, box elder, sycamore, and valley oak. Here too are tangles of blackberry bramble, wild grape, sweet clover and California mugwort.

Most of the parcels of land in the Marysville Wildlife Area are riparian forests, with dirt roads and trails running around or through them. Originally used as borrow pits to build the levee around Marysville, these properties are easily accessible from Marysville city streets.

One representative species of this area is the handsome Black-shouldered Kite. Other birds you can expect to sight include Red-shouldered Hawk,

Great Horned Owl, California Quail, Wrentit, Rufous-sided Towhee, Hermit Thrust, Common Yellowthroat, Orange-crowned Warbler, Hutton's Vireo, Cedar Waxwing, Anna's Hummingbird, Black Phoebe, Willow and Pacific Slope Flycatchers, Scrub Jay, Plain Titmouse, Bushtit, White-breasted Nuthatch, Acorn Woodpeckers, and White-crowned, Golden-crowned, and Savannah Sparrows.

Mammals dwelling in this area are Raccoon, Long-tailed Weasel, Virginia Opossum, Ring-tailed Cat, Coyote, Gray Fox, and Spotted and Striped Skunks. In the rivers and sloughs are Beaver, River Otter, Muskrat, and Mink.

The wildlife area is the floodplain of Jack Slough and the Yuba River. It can be reached from any one of several city streets in the northwest section of Marysville.

Englebright Lake

This shimmering, 815-acre, man-made body of water is set like a gemstone in rolling, scrub and oak-dotted land. The park boasts a variety of picnic sites, some overlooking the marina, others providing easy access to the shore, all affording a grand view of this dam-created lake; a group picnic area located next to the dam; picnic tables and barbecues; good fishing for Catfish, Sunfish, Kokanee Salmon, and Rainbow Trout; two paved boat-launching ramps near the park's entrance; a marina that offers slips, gas docks, boat rentals, and a small store; boat-in camping along 24 miles of shoreline.

Seen here are Wild Turkey, Bald and Golden Eagles, Peregrine Falcon, Wood Duck, California Quail, Lesser and American Goldfinches, White-crowned Sparrow, House Finch, Northern Mockingbird, Scrub Jay, Canvasback, and Canada Geese.

Mammals sighted in the area include Black-tailed Deer, Raccoon, Opossum, Bobcat, Ring-tailed Cat, a variety of rodents, and occasionally a Mountain Lion.

For further information write: Corps of Engineers, Englebright Lake, P.O. Box 6, Smartville, CA 95977-0006, or call (916) 639-2342.

Englebright Lake is located 21 miles east of Marysville on SH 20.

Abbott and O'Connor Lakes Ecological Reserves

Both of these lakes lie on the floodplain of the river named for the feathers that the Indians once hung in the trees along its banks as tangible prayers to the spirits they worshipped. It's a lush area, thick with willow, cottonwood, button willow, honey locust, blue elderberry, white alder, Oregon ash, western sycamore, and valley oak. The less wooded areas are covered with blackberry, raspberry, wild grape, mugwort, ragweed, sweet clover, and perennial grasses such as wild rye and Bermuda.

If plans for the future materialize, these two ecological reserves will soon be one, and since Abbott Lake is the more prominent landmark of the two, its name will be affixed to the whole.

This is an outstanding wintering area for Turkey Vultures. If you've never had occasion to see these big funereal-looking birds in great throngs, then it's time to put a winter trip to the Abbott and O'Connor Lakes on your agenda. This is a birding experience you won't forget.

Other birds you should expect to see are Great Egret, Green-backed Heron, Wood Duck, Red-shouldered Hawk, Band-tailed Pigeon, Western Bluebird, Yellow-breasted Chat, House Finch, Ash-throated Flycatcher, Black-headed Grosbeak, Scrub Jay, Yellow-billed Magpie, Northern Mockingbird, Northern Oriole, White-crowned Sparrow, California Towhee, Wrentit, and Rufous-sided Towhee.

For more information about these reserves contact wildlife biologist Dale L. Whitmore at (916) 743-5068.

Where SH 99 makes the right angle turn a mile east of Tudor, go north on Garden Highway. A permanent road easement to Abbott Lake exists from the general location of 7327 Garden Highway to the levee. This road is partially paved and leads to a levee ramp. Levee gates are locked by the local maintenance district, therefore the nearest public parking is along Garden Highway. Access to the O'Connor Lakes property is by parking on the road shoulders of Star Bend Road and walking the levee to the property.

Bobelaine Ecological Reserve

This designated ecological reserve with its cottonwood forest ecosystem, oak woods, and impenetrable thickets is the property of the Audubon Society. Open to the public, complete with maintained trails and good observation points, it's predictably a wonderful place to bird.

One hundred and forty-four species have been recorded in the Sanctuary. California Quail can be seen on the grasslands or in and about the rose thickets. Northern Pintail and Wood Duck, which nest here, can be found in large flocks on Ringtail Slough and Lake Crandall, as well as on the aptly named Duck Slough.

Hundreds of waterfowl visit the Feather River in the winter, especially in years of flooding. Great Blue Herons can be found in the ponds and at the river's edge, and during spring and winter many migrants pass through.

Rare birds have been sighted here too, including a Northern Parula seen in 1987, and there is recent evidence of nesting Swainson's Hawks and Yellow-billed Cuckoos. Also seen are Bald Eagle and Peregrine Falcon.

Wildlife is abundant. Expect Columbian Black-tailed Deer, California Striped and Spotted Skunks, California Raccoon, California Badger, Virginia Opossum, California Valley Coyote, Townsend Gray Fox, California Ringtail, California Jackrabbit and Audubon Cottontail. Abundant in the river and the sloughs are Golden Beaver and Muskrat. Occasionally Lowland Mink and California Otter are sighted as well.

Bobelaine is located on the west side of the Feather River about 15 miles south of Marysville/Yuba City. From SH 99, take Laurel Avenue east to the preserve.

DAVIS

Capay Valley/Cache Creek

The same Cache Creek which flows out of Lake County's Anderson Marsh flows into Yolo County's Capay Valley. As Bald Eagles are seen at the marshland in that neighboring county, so too they are in Capay Valley — but in even larger numbers. The astonishing fact is that 70 or 80 of these splendid, endangered birds, the pride of our nation's avifauna, seem to hold this single California creek in special favor. At any place along its winding route, especially in the Capay Valley, the eagle watching is superb.

Other birds in the vicinity include Yellow-billed Magpie, House Finch, Common Raven, Lesser and American Goldfinches, Swainson's Hawk, Black Phoebe, Western Kingbird, and many other species common to this western portion of the Central Valley.

To reach this area, take SH 16 south from SH 20 or west and north from I-505 in the Sacramento Valley. Cache Creek runs alongside SH 16 for approximately 5 miles in the very northwestern tip of Yolo County.

Davis and Vicinity

With a population of 43,000, Davis is a charming town, known for the excellence of its university, its outdoor-loving citizenry, its bicycle-riding young people, its conferences and sport camps, and its excellent birding. According to Allen Fish, the director of the Golden Gate Raptor Observatory, it's especially notable for raptors and for many easily accessible locations from which to sight them.

U.C. Davis Campus. The popular specialty of Davis is the Burrowing Owl, which is frequently sighted in the vicinity of the veterinary hospital on the grounds of UC Davis. Also seen in this part of town are many other species common to the Great Central Valley, among them the colorful Yellow-billed Magpie. So abundant here as to rate mention despite their commonplace status are Western Meadowlark, Brewer's Blackbird, and American Crow.

Entrances to the campus are clearly marked on I-80 in the city of Davis, 15 miles west of Sacramento.

Hunt-Wesson Spray Fields. This rural locale, another Davis hotspot that comes highly recommended by Allen Fish, is right on the outskirts of town. In Allen's words: "There's a place known as the Hunt-Wesson spray fields, a wastewater release valve for the Hunt tomato plant in Davis. It's very popular. In fact, it's referred to as the Hunt-Wesson Hawk and Owl Preserve. It's green all summer and all winter, and it turns out to be a great spot for Short-eared Owl, kites, harriers, and Red-tailed Hawk."

When we scanned this field one day in October, 1989, a mere 30 minutes of birding from the shoulder of the road earned us a count of 6 Northern Harriers, 1 Swainson's Hawk, approximately 25 Western Meadowlarks, a flock of blackbirds, 50 American Crows, and 15 Ring-necked Pheasants.

Also seen in this area are Vesper Sparrow, Yellow-billed Magpie, Lark Sparrow, Black-shouldered Kite, and American and Lesser Goldfinches.

The spray fields are directly north of the Hunt-Wesson plant in Davis, off Road 29.

Putah Creek at Stevenson's Bridge. Winding Putah Creek serves as a boundary line between Yolo and Solano Counties, and the concrete, graffiti-covered bridge that spans it on Stevenson Bridge Road is a notable landmark

Burrowing Owl

in an area that offers some very pleasant and fruitful birding. Expect to see Belted Kingfisher, Winter Wren, Warbling Vireo, Song Sparrow, Lewis' Woodpecker, Common Yellowthroat, Blue Grosbeak, *Empidonax* flycatchers, Western Tanager, and a variety of warblers including Black-throated Gray, Yellow-rumped, Nashville, Townsend's, Hermit, Orange-crowned, Wilson's, and MacGillivray's. Also reported at Putah Creek are Red-shouldered, Cooper's, and Sharp-shinned Hawks.

We prefer to bird Putah Creek along its southwestern bank. Others may choose to follow one of the several trails that lead down to the water's edge to see some of the species that may only be *heard* from higher up.

For 75 cents, a bird list which serves well for this and other area parks, *Checklist of the Birds of the Sacramento Area*, may be purchased at the Effie Yeaw Center in Ancil Hoffman County Park.

The Putah Creek 1988 Christmas Bird Count, which centered west of the intersection of Putah Creek Road and Pleasants Valley Road approximately 15 miles from Stevenson's Bridge, had a species count of 199, and an individual count of 101,888 birds.

To reach the bridge from I-80 in Davis, take SH 113 north 2 miles to Russell Road. Go west on Russell 5 miles to Stevenson's Bridge Road (County Road 95A), turn left and proceed about a mile to the bridge. There are places to pull off on the south side.

SACRAMENTO

A historic place, the capital of the state, a river town, a city that boasts fine restaurants, tree-lined streets, water sports and cultural opportunities, Sacramento also has much to offer the nature lover. Even discounting its promising parks, of which there are several, there's excellent riparian habitat right in the city limit. If you never set foot outside town at all, you'd still sight much in the way of wildlife — birds such as the handsome Wood Duck, mammals like the playful River Otter. Scout the surrounding countryside, of course, and your list will grow.

The elevation of Sacramento is 17 feet, the population for the city 335,000, and for the entire metropolitan area, 1.2 million.

Cal-Expo Floodplain. To many Sacramento residents, the name Cal-Expo calls to mind the site of the 133-year-old California State Fair, a popular event held every year through the 18 days preceding Labor Day. To others, however, it's just as apt to evoke thoughts of the floodplain that lies behind it. Verdant and jungle-like, this portion of the famous American River Parkway is a favorite haunt of Sacramento hikers, joggers, and cyclists. It's highly endorsed by many local nature lovers too, like avid birder Sydney G. Hibma, who's observed more than 121 species in this area alone.

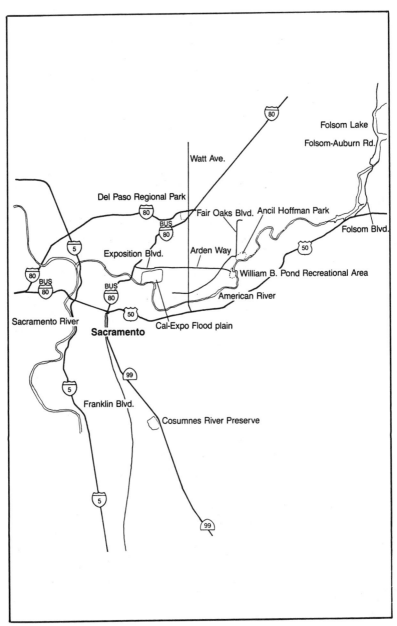

Sacramento

Among the many birds common to the Cal-Expo floodplain are Green-backed Heron, Black-shouldered Kite, Scrub Jay, Yellow-billed Magpie, Swainson's Hawk, and Tricolored Blackbird.

The American River Parkway, of which this area is a part, is a unique, nationally recognized open-space corridor which extends from the confluence of the Sacramento River to Folsom Lake and is rich in avifauna all the way.

From I-80 — Business Route in Sacramento, take Exposition Blvd. east past the racetrack and turn right on Ethan Way. Go straight where Ethan veers left. The parking area and entrance are right there.

Del Paso Regional Park. This easy-access park boasts a rare habitat that renders it well worth visiting, namely one of the land's few remaining, unspoiled riparian woods. Today streamside woodlands like this one (narrow bands of forest on the banks of valley rivers and streams) comprise less than 1% of the 1,000,000 acres they covered in the valley's early days.

Besides the habitat here on Arcade Creek, this park boasts an information kiosk, a nature trail, and a bridle path.

Birds seen here include Belted Kingfisher, Red-shouldered Hawk, Wrentit, Bewick's Wren, Varied Thrush, Northern Oriole, California Quail, and American Goldfinch as well as Lewis', Nuttall's, Downy, and Hairy Woodpeckers. Nesting in the vicinity are Yellow-billed Magpie, Bushtit, Plain Titmouse, Acorn Woodpecker, and Scrub Jay.

Del Paso Regional Park is located near the convergence of I-80 and Business I-80 on the north side of Sacramento. Take the Watt Avenue exit from either freeway.

William B. Pond Recreation Area. The green lawns, small ponds, river inlets, and trails of this popular park are home to many birds. Seen here and common all year long are Great Blue Heron, Eared Grebe, Great Egret, Ruddy Duck, Black-shouldered Kite, and California Quail. Seasonal residents include Tundra Swan, Canada Goose, American Wigeon, Northern Pintail, Canvasback, Common Merganser, and Spotted Sandpiper.

Seen in the vicinity of this American River parkland are Raccoon, Spotted Skunk, a variety of rodents, and occasionally, River Otter.

From SH 50 in Sacramento, take Watt Avenue north to Fair Oaks Blvd., turn right to Arden Way, turn right again and follow Arden Way into the park. Continue to the last parking lot.

Effie Yeaw Nature Center/Ancil Hoffman Park. This nature center is named for Effie Yeaw, a Sacramento woman, a lifelong conservationist, a teacher of children whose classroom was nature, whose chosen text consisted of wild animals, flowers, birds, and trees. As did Effie Yeaw, the center exists to promote greater appreciation and understanding of the natural wonders of the Sacramento Valley and to preserve them for the future.

The center has all of the following to offer: a modern visitor center; live animal exhibits; instructive programs; weekend walks and talks; publications; self-guided trails; group tours; school outreach; an excellent staff always ready to answer questions, supply information, or point the way to good places to bird in Sacramento County.

The Effie Yeaw Nature Center is a part of the Ancil Hoffman County Park, which boasts an expanse of green lawn, towering oaks, extensive picnic facilities, a game field, and a popular golf course and driving range. The county park, in turn, is a part of the magnificent American River Parkway.

Acorn Woodpeckers are abundant here. You can stand in the oak woods and count 6 or 7 without so much as turning your head. Other birds of the vicinity include Yellow-billed Magpie, Wild Turkey, Red-shouldered Hawk, California Quail, Great Horned Owl, Anna's Hummingbird, Red-breasted Sapsucker, Western Wood-Pewee, Bewick's Wren, Scrub Jay, and Nuttall's and Hairy Woodpeckers.

From SH 50 in Sacramento, take Watt Avenue north to Fair Oaks Blvd., turn right and follow Fair Oaks around to Van Alstine Avenue. Turn right again, to California Avenue, left one block to Tarshes Drive, and right into the park.

Folsom Lake State Recreation Area

This shimmering lake, located on the hinterlands of the oak-dotted Sierra foothills and the Great Valley, has all the following features: 1,010,000-acre feet of water, 75 miles of shoreline, boat ramps and slips, a tow service, a snack bar, a gas dock, more than 160 family campsites, 12 environmental camps, overnight mooring for self-contained sail or power boats, 80 miles of trails for hikers and riders, an equestrian camp that can accommodate 50 horses and riders, a bicycle path, and a visitor center with plenty of free literature and a small specimen exhibit.

Seen here are Great Blue Heron, Snowy Egret, California Quail, Bushtit, California Towhee, Belted Kingfisher, American Bittern, Gadwall, Scrub Jay, Wood Duck, Redhead, Black-shouldered Kite, Northern Harrier, Virginia Rail, Sandhill Crane, and Common Moorhen.

Mammals seen in the area include Opossum, Gray Fox, Bobcat, and Raccoon.

From SH 50 east of Sacramento, take Folsom Blvd. north 3 miles to the city of Folsom, and follow the signs. Folsom-Auburn Road goes around the west side of the lake, Green Valley Road around the east.

Cosumnes River Preserve

Here's some of what you'll find if you come birding here on this fascinating eastern edge of the Sacramento-San Joaquin delta: 1,454 acres of pristine land and waterways; a climate that's best described as Mediterranean; wetlands and grasslands extraordinarily rich in nutrients that keep the wildlife thriving; interesting plant communities, including a rare riparian valley oak forest; six species of willows thriving in the shady woodland canopy; wild grape growing so rampantly the area looks like a jungle; freshwater marshes supporting such flora as marsh primrose, swamp knotweed, tules, and cattails; a variety of birds and mammals.

Once widespread in the Sacramento area, riparian forests like this one at the Cosumnes River Preserve are now practically extinct. Today they cover less than 1% of the one million acres they claimed long ago.

To those who hearken to the giants of the avian kingdom, there may be no better place to bird in northern California than The Nature Conservancy's Cosumnes River Preserve in the fall and winter. Here are not only Sandhill Cranes, but also Great Blue Heron, Greater White-fronted Goose, Turkey Vulture, and large flocks of Tundra Swans. This is not to say smaller birds don't dwell here too; they do indeed. In fact, more than 200 species of birds have been recorded in the vicinity of Consumnes River Preserve.

Also seen here are River Otter, Muskrat, Raccoon, Mule Deer, Ring-tailed Cat, Opossum, Mink, and Pacific Tree Frog.

This unique preserve lies between SH 99 and I-5 on the eastern edge of the Sacramento-San Joaquin delta, not far from the town of Walnut Grove. From I-5, take Twin Cities Road east to Franklin Blvd., and turn right to the preserve.

STOCKTON

San Joaquin County lies in the very heart of the Central Valley, where the Sacramento and San Joaquin Rivers come together to form the vast maze of waterways that are the Sacramento River Delta. The Mokelumne and Calaveras Rivers flow through the county, and the Stanislaus forms its southern border. This is flat, rich farm country, prototypical of the agricultural lands of the Central Valley. Stockton and Lodi together form the hub of a very substantial viticulture region that has been producing wines for more than a century. Valley oaks used to cover this countryside; a few groves remain yet today.

Woodbridge Road Ecological Preserve. Once a pastureland, now a marsh, this fine preserve is a popular locale with many birders, some of whom come especially to see the throngs of Sandhill Cranes that arrive in late September and stay until early March. Others come in hopes of sighting some of the unusual species reported here. Consider these exciting accidentals: Ruff, an Old World species and casual migrant throughout North America, Swamp Sparrow seen in the berry bramble in 1988 and 1989, and Eurasian Wigeon.

More common to the area are herons, egrets, Black-shouldered Kite, Cedar Waxwing, Northern Pintail, Green-winged Teal, Tundra Swan, Greater and Lesser Yellowlegs, Black-necked Stilt, American Avocet, Bald and Golden Eagles, Peregrine and Prairie Falcons, and Rough-legged Hawk, as well as Snow, Ross', Greater White-fronted, and Canada Geese.

To reach the preserve, get off I-5 at SH 12, go north on Thornton Road to Woodbridge, turn left and proceed about 2 miles to the parking area.

Lodi Lake. This park, with its wilderness area and handsome lake, located within the city limits of Lodi and on the Mokelumne River, can make several claims that endear it to birders. It's one of the few areas on the valley floor that has a remnant population of Wrentits; it attracts large numbers of migrants (for example, 50 Warbling Vireos sighted *at one time)* including Solitary Vireo and Western Tanager; it's visited by many vagrant species including Orchard Oriole, Rose-breasted Grosbeak, and Chestnut-sided, Black-and-white, and Blackpoll Warblers.

The Willow Flycatcher is common in here in the fall, Osprey in the winter. Common Merganser, and Winter Wren winter here as well, and you're practically guaranteed to spot a White-throated in among the many Golden-crowned and White-crowned Sparrows that are fairly teeming here. Raptors include Swainson's, Cooper's, and Sharp-shinned Hawks; Screech, Barn, and Great Horned Owls.

Deer, Raccoon, Opossum, and River Otter are seen in the confines of this city park.

Lodi Lake is on the north side of town. From I-5, take Turner Road east to the park.

White Slough Water Treatment Facility. These sewer ponds, visible from I-5, are a haven to many birds. Most notable of these are two rarities, the Little Gull, the presence of which has lured many a birder to Lodi, and the Common Black-headed Gull. Seen here too are Franklin's Gull, Canvasback, Common Goldeneye, Northern Shoveler, Ruddy Duck, Lesser Scaup, and Ring-necked Duck. This is also an excellent spot for shorebirds including unusual species like the Semipalmated, Baird's, and Pectoral Sandpipers seen here in August and September.

To reach these ponds, take the SH 12 exit from I-5, go south on Thornton Road 1 mile, and then west under the freeway.

Oak Grove Regional Park. This 180-acre park, which derives its name from a fine grove of valley oaks, has a Nature Center, a 500-seat outdoor amphitheater, picnic sites, a 10-acre, man-made lake, excellent trails, and a special feature, the Johnston Bird Oasis, a "dripping faucet" watering hole for birds.

Swainson's Hawks nest here. Other species seen include Yellow-billed Magpie, Red-shouldered and Red-tailed Hawks, Acorn and Nuttall's Woodpeckers, Lazuli Bunting, Plain Titmouse, and Great Horned and Barn Owls, as well as many migrant warblers, vireos, and flycatchers, and an occasional vagrant.

Oak Grove Regional Park is north of Stockton, at the corner of I-5 and Eight Mile Road.

Lewallan Properties. California conservationist Alberta Lewallan has two separate pieces of private property which she's established as wildlife preserves. She graciously accommodates serious and conscientious birders, and also hopes to inspire others to consider setting aside private land for

Lesser Scaup

the use and protection of wildlife.

According to stipulations in Alberta's contract with the Fish and Game Department, these properties can be used for anything related to agriculture in perpetuity, but are not to be developed or used for hunting.

Remember that these exemplary preserves are private property and should be respected as such. For directions and permission to enter the sites, serious birders may call Alberta Lewallan or her son at (209) 887-3360.

The first Lewallan site is near the town of Linden, east of Stockton. There are four ponds on the property, other than the one by the house, which reach a maximum of 50 acre-feet in the wintertime. The second site is in Calaveras County near New Hogan Lake.

At the Linden Property Great and Snowy Egrets, as well as Great Blue Heron and Black-crowned Night-Heron are year round residents. In the wintertime look for Common and Hooded Mergansers, Ring-necked Duck, Bufflehead, American White Pelican, Canada Goose, Western Bluebird, and Yellow-billed Magpie. This is also a great spot for Bald and Golden Eagles, Peregrine and Prairie Falcons, Merlin, Northern Harrier, Black-shouldered Kite, and Barn Owl, as well as Cooper's, Red-tailed, Ferruginous, and Swainson's Hawks. Nesting species include Mallard and Gadwall.

The Calavaras property is an outstanding place to see the Lewis' Woodpecker, which is common here in the winter. Western and Mountain Bluebirds, Phainopepla, and Ferruginous and Rough-legged Hawks are also seen in the area, but the main reason birders visit this location is to see the wintering Bald Eagles from late December through late February.

Jack Tone Road. This is largely a single species locale. It is, in fact, one of the state's prime hawk watching spots, and one that's highly endorsed by Allen Fish of the Golden Gate Raptor Observatory. 'Most any time between July and September one can witness the convergence of enormous numbers of Swainson's Hawks as they feed on the migrating insects that await them here, an awesome sight to any birder with an eye for raptors.

Jack Tone Road is at the corner of SH 4 and SH 99 near Stockton.

Caswell Memorial State Park

Besides 138 acres of fine old valley oaks, a remnant of the woodlands that once were commonplace on Central Valley river banks, this state park has all these attractions: a world of other foliage including cottonwood, ash, and alder trees, wild roses, currants, and tangles of rambling blackberry; a trail that winds along the scenic Stanislaus River; an observation point from which to view a heron rookery; swimming and fishing; day-use facilities; inviting riverside campgrounds with 66 sites, complete with tables, stove, food lockers, piped water, restrooms and hot showers; brochures, maps, and a bird list, *Field Checklist of the Birds of San Joaquin County*.

Birds commonly sighted at Caswell State Park include Wood Duck, Great Blue Heron, California Quail, Great Egret, Black-shouldered Kite, Western Bluebird, Red-winged Blackbird, Northern Oriole, Black-headed Grosbeak, Plain Titmouse, and White-breasted Nuthatch.

Nesting in the vicinity are Great Horned Owl, Nuttall's and Downy Woodpeckers, Scrub Jay, Plain Titmouse, Bushtit, White-breasted

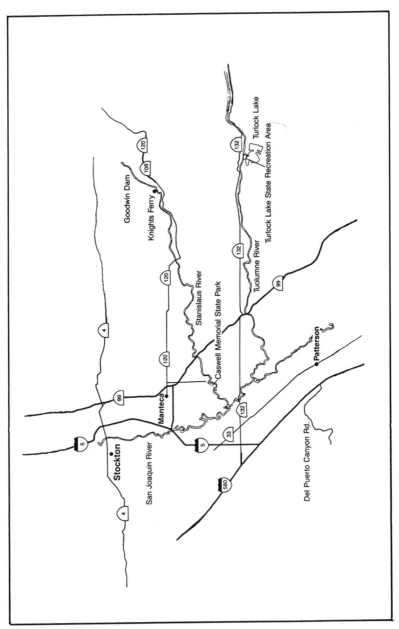

Stockton

Nuthatch, Bewick's Wren, Loggerhead Shrike, Rufous-sided Towhee, House Finch, and Lesser and Lawrence's Goldfinches.

In the winter months it's usually easy enough to find a vacant campsite here. Summers, however, can be quite crowded, especially on the weekends, and advance reservations are highly advisable.

For futher information about this area write: Caswell Memorial State Park, 28000 South Austin Road, Ripon, CA 95366, or call (209) 599-3810.

From SH 99 in Manteca, take Austin Road south about 5 miles to the park.

Stanislaus River Parks

This system of Stanislaus River Parks covers 59 miles of lush river country and parts of Stanislaus, Tuolumne, and San Joaquin counties, with 9 separate recreation areas overall. You'll find good hiking trails, kayaking, canoeing, whitewater rafting, and fishing at the New Melones Dam and reservoir; an information center in the historic town of Knights Ferry; and for those who want to stay a while, motels in nearby Oakdale, and a private campground in Knights Ferry.

Wood Duck is often sighted here. Also seen are Great and Snowy Egrets, Golden Eagle, Prairie Falcon, Red-shouldered Hawk, Great Blue Heron, California Towhee, and Yellow-billed Magpie.

The Stanislaus River Parks are under the jurisdiction of the Army Corps of Engineers. Anyone seeking information about the area should contact the U.S. Bureau of Reclamation, 16805 Peoria Flat Road, Jamestown, CA 95327, or call (209) 984-5248.

The parks extend along the Stanislaus River from the Goodwin Dam, east of Knights Ferry, to River's End, where the Stanislaus joins the San Joaquin River.

Del Puerto Canyon

This scenic canyon still bears some of the features by which it was known in decades past, as for example when the explorer, Professor William H. Brewer, camped here in June of 1861 and penned his impressions on the pages of his journal.

"We came on about fifteen miles to Camp 74, in the Canada del Puerto, or, to translate, 'Door Canyon'," he wrote. And after recounting the rigours of the journey, a tedious ride on which he and his cohorts had to make their way "across the trackless plain," he went on to describe the *canada* itself. "The Puerto Canyon breaks through the ridges, which are made by strata of rocks tilted up at a high angle. The outside ridge is of hard rock, and the canyon comes through by a very narrow 'door,' which gives the name to the valley behind, which widens out. There is a fine stream now — soon it will be dry, however — with cottonwoods growing along it. We camped in a beautiful spot just within the 'gate.'"

Today this fascinating area is one of the highlighted sites on the inimitable Mines Road Loop, a well-known birders' tour.

Visitors with tents or RVs who wish to spend more than a day scouring this prime area may want to spend the night at Henry Raines campground. It's a comfortable park, fully developed, complete with picnic tables, water, electricity, modern restrooms, and a group picnic area. It's a fine place to stay from the first of May all through the month of October, but from early November until April 30th the immediate area is teeming with off-road vehicles.

Birds seen in Del Puerto Canyon include Prairie Falcon, Costa's and Rufous Hummingbirds, Cassin's Kingbird, Rock Wren, Black-throated Gray Warbler, Black-headed Grosbeak, California Quail, Black Phoebe, Lesser and Lawrence's Goldfinches, House Finch, Nuttall's Woodpecker, Common Raven, Bewick's Wren, California Towhee, Scrub Jay, and Red-winged Blackbird, as well as Great Horned, Western Screech, and Barn Owls.

Del Puerto Canyon Road takes off from I-5 in Patterson. For the entrance from the other side, see the Mines Road entry in the San Francisco Bay chapter.

Turlock Lake State Recreation Area

A popular place, especially in the summertime when it's teeming with people, this fine Stanislaus County park offers 3,500 acres of grass-caped hills; spreading shade trees; great tangles of lush blackberries; fine boating facilities; group picnic areas; great opportunities for wildlife photography (especially in the wintertime); a secluded campground bounded on one side by a sheer cliff, on the other by the river; picnic tables, stoves, and food lockers; modern restrooms and hot showers.

The park is visited most in the summer, at which time advance reservations are advisable, but the best time for birding is from December through mid March, when the crowds of people are gone but the birds are here in great flocks.

Commonly seen in the vicinity are Yellow-billed Magpie, Ring-necked Pheasant, Great Blue Heron, Great Egret, Wood Duck, Northern Shoveler, Gadwall, Belted Kingfisher, House Finch, Black Phoebe, Scrub Jay, American Crow, Wrentit, California Towhee, Lesser Goldfinch, and a variety of sparrows.

In the winter, take your eyes off the multitudes of waterfowl long enough to scan the oak woodlands around the lake for Bald Eagle and Osprey.

Also seen here are deer, Beaver, Raccoon, Opossum and skunk.

For further information about this parkland write: Turlock Lake State Recreation Area, 22600 Lake Road — Star Route, La Grange, CA 95329, or call (209) 874-2008.

Turlock Lake State Recreation Area lies 21 miles east of Modesto and approximately the same distance north and east of Turlock. It's a short drive off SH 132. Conspicuously posted intersection signs clearly show which turnoff to take from the highway.

MERCED COUNTY

George J. Hatfield State Recreation Area

The same Merced River that formed the dramatic geologic wonders of Yosemite National Park winds by this San Joaquin Valley park where the land is flat as a prairie and the scenes are all pastoral.

This is a fine riparian habitat and well it should be, for the river borders the park on three sides. Predictably, cottonwoods thrive here, as do box elders, valley oak, maple, and Modesto ash. The park has more than a mile of river frontage; 7 developed family campsites with tables, grills and food lockers; 27 family picnic sites; drinking water; restroom; a group camping area for up to 200 persons (reservations are advisable); interpretive programs on summer weekends.

Species you can expect to see include Sandhill Crane, Ring-necked Pheasant, Yellow-billed Magpie, Barn Owl, Swainson's Hawk, American Goldfinch, Western Bluebird, California Quail, Scrub Jay, Rufous-sided and California Towhees, Black Phoebe, Bewick's Wren, White-crowned Sparrow, Ruby-crowned Kinglet, Plain Titmouse, Belted Kingfisher, and

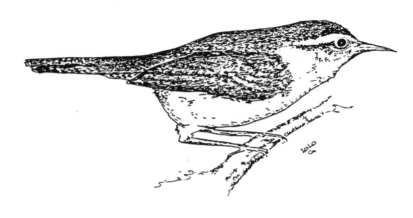

Bewick's Wren

less frequently, Purple Finch, Northern Oriole, and Black-headed Grosbeak.

Birds known to nest in the park include House and Bewick's Wrens, Tree Swallow, Ash-throated Flycatcher, and Nuttall's Woodpecker. Black-shouldered Kite, American Kestrel, Barn Owl, and Western Bluebird are thought to nest as well.

For more information write: George J. Hatfield State Recreation Area, 4394 Kelley Road, Hilmar, CA 95324, or call (209) 632-1852.

From SH 99 near Turlock, take SH 165 (Lander Avenue) south to County Road J18. Turn right and follow J18 to Kelly Rd. Turn right on Kelly and the park is on the right.

McConnell State Recreation Area

This area, surrounded by croplands, nut trees, and cattle ranches, spells leisure-time pleasures to 35,000 people every year and offers spacious sweeps of green lawn, sunning and swimming, a group picnic area for up to 150 people, overnight campsites complete with tables and stoves, and an outdoor theater where Saturday night interpretive programs are held in summer.

Birds seen here include Ring-necked Pheasant, Wood Duck, Band-tailed Pigeon, California Quail, Lesser Goldfinch, Northern Shoveler, Gadwall, Belted Kingfisher, House Finch, Black Phoebe, Scrub Jay, California Towhee, and a variety of sparrows.

Mammals seen here include Opossum, Black-tailed Deer, Muskrat, Raccoon, as well as rabbits and squirrels.

For further information, write: McConnell State Recreation Area, McConnell Road, Ballico, CA 95303, or call (209) 394-7755.

From SH 99 in Livingston, take Livingston-Cressey Road east 2 miles to the park.

Santa Fe Grade Road

This site, on the outskirts of the town of Gustine, is located on a narrow, dirt road that offers little or nothing in the way of shoulders on which to pull off and park but affords some excellent drop-by birding. In 15 exciting minutes of birding this road from the car, we counted 1 Great Blue Heron, 6 Snowy Egrets, 2 Black-shouldered Kites, 1 Great Egret, 30 Long-billed Curlews, approximately 400 Black-necked Stilts, about 300 Long-billed Dowitchers, 8 American Avocets, 6 Savannah Sparrows, 1 Spotted Sandpiper, and 1 Northern Harrier.

Santa Fe Grade Road takes off to the south from SH 140 about 2.5 miles east of Gustine. The road is marked by a sign that reads "Wilbart Farms, Gustine." The pond is near the southeast corner.

Central San Joaquin Valley National Wildlife Refuges

West of Merced, on both sides of SH 165 are Kesterson, San Luis, and Merced National Wildlife Refuges. San Luis NWR is famed for its large concentrations of waterfowl and resident Tule Elk, Merced NWR for Sandhill Cranes, Ring-necked Pheasants, and Ross' Geese, while Kesterson — regrettably — is best known currently for the misfortunes that have befallen it in recent years.

Bird lists, fishing and hunting regulations, descriptive brochures, and maps for these refuges may be obtained by visiting the refuge headquarters, located at 535 J Street, Los Banos. For information by mail or telephone, contact: Refuge Manager, Central San Joaquin Valley National Wildlife Refuges, P.O. Box 2176, Los Banos, CA 93635, or call (209) 826-3508.

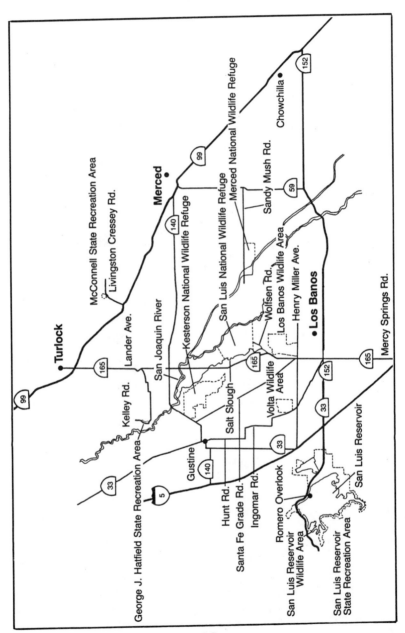

Merced County

Kesterson National Wildlife Refuge. Ironically, ever since it fell prey to the ecological nightmare that thrust it into the limelight, this newest of the three Central San Joaquin Valley National Wildlife Refuges is probably the one best known to the public. "Oh, I remember all about it," cries the man on the street when he hears the name mentioned. "That's the place where all the ducks started dying off!" He's right, of course. The natural trace element selenium, leached from the soil by agricultural runoff, gathered and concentrated in Kesterson's evaporation ponds, much to the peril of fish and waterfowl.

What happened at Kesterson, incidentally, could happen elsewhere. According to Karen Garrison, of the Natural Resources Defense Council, "there isn't anything of an enforceable nature to prevent future Kestersons." Grim news like this is food for thought and good reason for active concern.

Despite the troubles here, it's good to remember that Kesterson NWR hasn't been abandoned by people or by birds, or incidentally, by wildflowers. In fact, there are few places where you'll find California's colorful wildings blooming more beautifully than here.

Although birding is better at the other Central San Joaquin Valley NWRs, we urge you *not* to skip by Kesterson when you're visiting Merced County. This is a place that deserves your attention for several reasons — for consideration of its sobering past, for respect to its brighter future, for the beauty of its wildflowers, and for the birds that can be seen here and enjoyed: for what their presence represents.

Kesterson Refuge is located 18 miles north of Los Banos, and can be reached by driving 4 miles east from Gustine on SH 140.

San Luis National Wildlife Refuge. "Cottonfield right next door. Land as flat as any ironing board. Creekside willows. Grasslands. Telegraph Weed growing here and there. Biggest Elk we've ever seen. Rack so huge it looks like his head sprouted an oak tree." So go the notes in our Birder's Diary.

The lush grasslands here are rather like an island, enclosed as they are by tree-rimmed slough and the rambling San Joaquin River. While year-round wetlands are guaranteed by canals and control devices carefully regulated to maintain the right water levels, elsewhere on the grassy "island" itself every little shallow basin or swale spends at least part of the year as pond or marshland.

Of the three San Joaquin Valley National Wildlife Refuges this one is

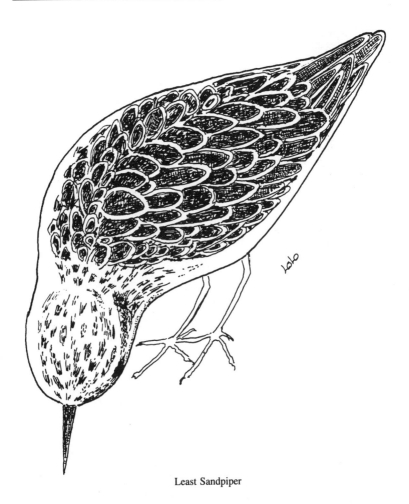

Least Sandpiper

the most highly recommended for large concentrations of ducks. Northern Pintail, Green-winged Teal, Mallard, Gadwall, Cinnamon Teal, and Northern Shovelers are abundant and easy to sight. It's also a good place for raptors and perching birds.

Waterfowl concentrations are most dramatic from the middle of October until February. December is the best time to view large concentrations of ducks, while geese are most numerous in January. The nesting season for most species, however, is in April, May, and June. Common or abundant here all year long are Pied-billed Grebe, Northern Harrier, Red-tailed Hawk, Great Blue Heron, Great Egret, Snowy Egret, Gadwall, Ring-necked Pheasant, Northern Pintail, Black-necked Stilt, American Avocet, Scrub Jay, Loggerhead Shrike, Red-winged and Tricolored Blackbirds, Northern Mockingbird, and House Finch.

Common or abundant in fall or winter but *not* during other seasons are Canada Goose, Black-shouldered Kite, and Common Snipe as well as Greater White-fronted, Snow, and Ross' Geese.

Other species sighted here regularly are American Bittern, Cinnamon Teal, Greater Yellowlegs, Long-billed Curlew, Least and Western Sandpipers, Long-billed Dowitcher, Marsh Wren, and Water Pipit.

Here also are Coyote, Longtailed Weasel, Raccoon, Opossum, Striped Skunk, Badger, Black-tailed Jackrabbit, California Ground Squirrel, and a small herd of Tule Elk.

San Luis Refuge is located about 10 miles north of Los Banos. From Los Banos, take County Road J14 (also called North Mercy Spring Road) north for 8 miles, then go northeast 2 miles on Wolfsen Road to the refuge.

Merced National Wildlife Refuge. There's little doubt that this 2,561-acre wildlife refuge wins favor on the basis of its large population of Ring-necked Pheasants, for literally hundreds of these handsome game birds convene in the grasslands every fall.

Of the three designated Central San Joaquin Valley National Wildlife areas, this refuge also offers the best opportunities for sighting Sandhill Cranes and Ross' Goose.

Other species sighted here include Northern Harrier, Snow Goose, Bald Eagle, Black-necked Stilt, Yellow-billed Magpie, Marsh Wren, Savannah Sparrow, and more than 175 others.

Mammals sighted in the refuge include Coyote, Raccoon, Striped and Spotted Skunks, Muskrat, Badger, Black-tailed Jackrabbit, and Desert Cottontail.

Merced Refuge is reached by driving 8 miles south of Merced, California, on SH 59, and then west on Sandymush Road.

San Luis Reservoir SRA/Romero Overlook

Inside the modern visitor center at the Romero overlook, you may view the wall displays, slide shows, movies, and videotape presentations that tell the story of the San Luis reservoir. You may scan the grassy hills and the shimmering water through the center's telescope, discuss native flora and fauna with staff member, Eva McCleland, or with luck, gaze directly into the eyes of the Greater Roadrunner that sometimes posts itself on the other side of the center's one-way window glass.

With 13,800 surface acres, 65 miles of shoreline, and storing as much as 2,038,771 acre-feet of water, the San Luis is the largest off-stream reservoir in the United States. Even so, it's only a part of one great complex that includes the O'Neill Forebay, the San Luis Pumping-Generating Plant, and 103 miles of the California Aqueduct.

The Basalt Area at the south end of the reservoir's main dam has parking lots; boat launching ramp; picnic area; a developed 79-site family campground with picnic tables and cupboards, and restrooms with showers.

In addition to the Greater Roadrunner, birds frequently sighted in the overlook area include a variety of finches, sparrows, and raptors. Species sighted at the reservoir are Eared Grebe, American Wigeon, Black-necked Stilt, California Gull, Ross' Goose, Northern Pintail, Cinnamon Teal, Ring-necked Duck, Western Bluebird, Cedar Waxwing, Belted Kingfisher, Yellow-billed Magpie, and others.

A bird list, *Birds of San Luis, Merced and Kesterson National Wildlife Refuges,* which applies also to many locations at the San Luis Reservoir State Recreation Area, is available at the Romero Overlook visitor center.

Campsite reservations for this area as well as the O'Neill Forebay can be made at Ticketron outlets anywhere in California, or by mail from Ticketron, P.O. Box 26430, San Francisco, CA 94126.

The San Luis Reservoir State Recreation Area is located in the eastern foothills of the Diablo Mountain Range, off SH 152, near Pacheco Pass, approximately 12 miles west of Los Banos.

San Luis Reservoir Wildlife Area

This 900-acre wildlife area is owned by the U.S. Bureau of Reclamation and the California Department of Water Resources and is operated by the California Department of Fish and Game. There is no charge for use but registration is required and permits are available at a self-registration booth.

Especially abundant here are Western Bluebird, Nuttall's Woodpecker, Black-shouldered Kite, Great Horned Owl, Plain Titmouse, Bushtit, Bewick's Wren, Loggerhead Shrike, and Scrub Jay. Also seen at San Luis Reservoir are a wide variety of waterfowl.

A bird checklist, "Birds of San Luis, Merced and Kesterson National Wildlife Refuges," is available at the Romero Overlook visitor center nearby.

The San Luis Reservoir Wildlife Area is located in Western Merced County on Dinosaur Point Road between the west end of the San Luis Reservoir and SH 152.

Los Banos and Volta Wildlife Areas

Los Banos Wildlife Area. The California Fish and Game Commission purchased 3,000 acres of river overflow lands in 1929, and this salvaged wetland in an area once peopled by the Yokut Indians became the heart of California's very first waterfowl refuge.

Here's what visitors can expect to see on a tour of this great wildlife area: 5,586 acres of lush and nutrient-rich land; 55 fields that are managed to encourage the growth of smartweed and watergrass and other feed for wildlife; levees on which to walk or drive over the winding wetlands; graveled roads that lead to Ruth and Buttonwillow lakes; photography blinds; restrooms, drinking water; maps, literature, and bird lists.

Fall is an exciting time to come to Los Banos. In mid-September the Greater White-fronted Geese come charging down, and not long afterward come the Sandhill Cranes, whose melancholy, liquid-sounding cries can be heard from great distance. By October you can expect every pond and lake in the refuge to be liberally covered with Northern Pintail, Mallard, Northern Shoveler, Cinnamon Teal, and Gadwall. You might find as many as 40,000 individual birds on Buttonwillow Lakes all at one time. In December you can see Canada Goose winging down in great flocks. Some years there are as many as 500,000 birds here. But although the birds are everywhere, and wherever you are there's plenty to see, we suggest a drive to Field 60 or to the bird mound between Buttonwillow Lakes for a spectacular sighting of thousands of Snow Geese. From a distance they look like fields of great white flowers in full bloom.

Any time of the year expect Pied-billed Grebe, American Bittern, Snowy Egret, Black-crowned Night-Heron, Cinnamon Teal, Northern Harrier, Ring-necked Pheasant, Common Moorhen, American Avocet, Black Phoebe, Yellow-billed Magpie, Northern Mockingbird, Loggerhead

Shrike, and Red-winged Blackbird. Nesting species include Pied-billed and Western Grebes, American Bittern, Great Blue Heron, Great and Snowy Egrets, Black-crowned Night-Heron, Mallard, Northern Pintail, Redhead, Ruddy Duck, Black-shouldered Kite, Northern Harrier, Swainson's and Red-tailed Hawks, American Kestrel, Ring-necked Pheasant, Virginia Rail, Sora, Common Moorhen, American Coot, Killdeer, Black-necked Stilt, and American Avocet.

In season, hunting (waterfowl, doves, raccoons, and rabbits) is legal, as is fishing for black bass, catfish, striped bass, and crappie. Department of Fish and Game and local regulations are strictly enforced.

For further information write: Department of Fish and Game, Los Banos Wildlife Area, 18110 West Henry Miller Avenue, Los Banos, CA 93635, or call (209) 826-0463.

To reach the Los Banos Wildlife Area take SH 165 north from Los Banos, toward Turlock. After 3 miles, turn right (east) on Henry Miller Road. Continue 1 mile and there you are.

Volta Wildlife Area. This 3,000-acre area was puchased by the Bureau of Reclamation to be used as a holding reservoir in case it were ever necessary to dump large quantities of water out of the Delta-Mendota Canal. The Department of Fish and Game leased the area in 1952 and has developed about 2,800 acres of emergent marsh as a habitat for waterfowl and a hunting ground for sportsmen. Also developed here are 50 acres of permanent water devoted to fishing. Department of Fish and Game and local regulations are strictly enforced. The birds here are the same as those found at Los Banos.

For further information regarding the Volta Wildlife Area write: The California Department of Fish and Game, Los Banos Wildlife Area, 18110 W. Henry Miller Ave., Los Banos, CA 93635.

The Volta Wildlife Area lies approximately 0.5 mile north of the town of Volta, which is 5 miles northwest of Los Banos on Ingomar Grade Road.

Chapter 7
High Sierra

 The majestic Sierra mountains stretch along two thirds of the eastern border of California from the Cascades in the north to the Tehachapis in the south, from the Great Basin in the east to the Great Valley in the west. In the confines of the Sierra Nevada are towering Mount Whitney, the highest peak in the contiguous states; magnificent Tahoe, the largest alpine lake on the continent; and Yosemite, in John Muir's words ". . . the grandest of all the special temples of Nature I was ever permitted to enter." Here also are the largest living things on earth, and the oldest: the giant Sequoias, and the Bristlecone Pines, respectively. These peaks and valleys, stretching forests, lakes, streams, and high meadows offer some of the prime birding habitat in the state.

The High Sierra region, as delineated in this book, also includes the Mono Basin, a haunting country of lunar-like terrain and alkaline lake on the eastern side of the range which provides unique support to an abundance of avifauna; and the western foothills of the Sierra where James Marshall's discovery of gold in 1848 altered the course of history.

This area is composed of Plumas, Sierra, Nevada, El Dorado, Amador, Alpine, Calaveras, Tuolumne, Mono, and Mariposa counties, and parts of Placer and Madera counties. These spectacular 18,088 square miles represent 22.9% of the area covered in this book.

The snowmelt rivers of this westward-tilting range, the Feather, Yuba, American, Consumnes, Mokelumne, Calaveras, Stanislaus, Tuolumne,

High Sierra

and Merced, flow into the Central Valley. Most are dammed to provide water for the huge agricultural production of the valley, and the ever-increasing population of the cities.

The highway systems are oriented generally east-west through the range. By far the major traffic loads are carried by I-80 and SH 50, from Sacramento to the north and south sides of Lake Tahoe, respectively. State Highways 89 and 70 handle the northern counties; State Highways 88, 4, and 120, which are closed in the winter, traverse the high country to the south. North to south, US 395 skirts the eastern side of the range, while SH 49 runs through all of the Gold Country from Madera County, over Yuba Pass, into the Sierra Valley.

SUGGESTED CHECK LISTS AND BOOKS
FOR THE HIGH SIERRA REGION

There are several good books and check lists available for the High Sierra Region.

The following publications, as well as a catalogue listing many others, are available through the Mono Lake Committee: *Field Checklist of the Birds of Mono Basin*, compiled by Terry Hart and David Gaines (75 cents); *Birds of Yosemite and the East Slope* by David Gaines ($16.50); *Discovering Sierra Birds*, by Edward C. Beedy and Stephen L. Granholm ($9.95). Include sales tax plus $2.50 for postage and handling.

Order from:
Mono Lake Committee
P.O. Box 29
Lee Vining, CA 93541

The illustrated checklist, *Preliminary Checklist of the Birds of the Sierra Valley and Yuba Pass Area*, compiled by "Mac" McCormick, Dave Shuford, and Jim Steele, is available from:
Jim Steele
Sierra Nevada Field Campus
School of Science
San Francisco State University
San Francisco, CA 94132

INDIAN VALLEY

Highly scenic Indian Valley lies in the Greenville District of the Plumas National Forest. Some of the 162 species sighted commonly in this area include Pied-billed Grebe, Great Blue Heron, Canada Goose, Mountain Quail, Black-crowned Night-Heron, Bufflehead, American Wigeon, Eared Grebe, Ruddy Duck, Canvasback, and Northern Pintail. More unusual species are Osprey, Spotted Owl, Pileated Woodpecker, Hooded Merganser, Black-backed Woodpecker, Sandhill Crane, and Barrow's Goldeneye.

Spring and summer are especially good birding seasons but there's probably no such thing as a bad time to bird in Indian Valley. The 1988 Christmas Bird Count was 84 species, 4,370 individuals.

Also seen here are Rocky Mountain Mule Deer, Badger, Golden-Mantled Squirrel, and other rodents. Occasionally Black Bear are sighted in the area.

Literature of the area, including bird lists, may be obtained at any district office of the Plumas National Forest.

For more information about Indian Valley, its lakes and recreation areas, and/or the town of Greenville, write to Indian Valley Chamber of Commerce, P.O. Box 516, Greenville, CA 95947, or, The Plumas National Forest, P.O. Box 329, Greenville, CA 95947, or call (916) 284-7126.

The town of Greenville, which is the hub of Indian Valley and the site of the Greenville Ranger District, is on Highway 89, 9 miles south of Lake Almanor.

Lake Almanor. This largest of Plumas County's lakes boasts 26,600 surface acres, good trout fishing, boating, swimming, and picnicking. Access is easy. Just 9 miles away is the town of Greenville, and closer still are private trailer parks, and resort motels, as well as a public campground. Lake Almanor Campgrounds, operated by the Pacific Gas and Electric Company and located on the west shore, boasts 100 units.

For information about camping in the Lake Almanor Campgrounds contact PG&E, 814 Main Street, P.O. Box 340, Red Bluff, CA 96080, or call (800) 624-8087.

Round Valley Reservoir. Many an angler is fooled by this Sierra reservoir, for situated at 4,500 feet and rimmed with conifers, it looks like a good place for catching trout. This is actually a warm water fishery, however,

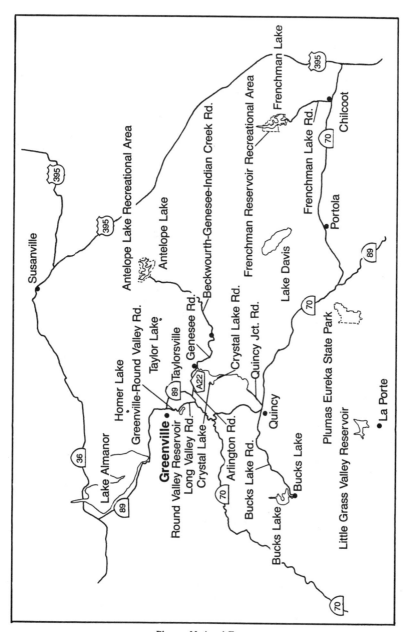

Plumas National Forest

teeming with large-mouth bass and so many bluegills that if you toss in your line here you can hardly fail to catch one. There's good birding here too, with more than 100 species possible.

Also a pleasant place for boating and camping, the area is complete with campgrounds, running water, sanitary and shower facilities, and a seasonal boating concession.

Taylor, Homer, and Crystal Lakes. These small alpine lakes offer anglers the trout fishing they expected — but didn't find — at Round Valley Reservoir. Here too: beautiful scenery, quietude, and excellent birding in remote locations far from the swarming crowds.

Taylor Lake lies directly below the Forest Service Lookout outpost on a peak called Kettle Rock. It's more remote than many areas in the valley, and access isn't always easy. Be sure to inquire about road conditions before you set off.

Another angler's haven, Crystal Lake is nestled below the Mt. Hough Fire Lookout. Access isn't easy here either; you have to take a rough road leading up from Taylorsville, or another that originates in Quincy.

There are two ways to reach the equally lovely and even more secluded Homer Lake. One is by foot, up a trail that branches off a logging road that leads up from Setzer Camp near Greenville. The other is via a rough four-wheel trail that climbs the eastern side of the ridge.

UPPER FEATHER RIVER LAKES

These 3 recreation areas, Antelope, Davis, and Frenchman's Lakes, each a part of a multipurpose State Water Project, lie in the Plumas National Forest, an area known for beautiful scenery, good fishing, inviting campsites, and a large variety of waterfowl and raptors. Here are Osprey, Bald and Golden Eagles, Red-tailed and Cooper's Hawks, Canada Goose, Hairy Woodpecker, Common Raven, Hermit and MacGillivray's Warblers, Pine Siskin, and Red Crossbill, as well as Western Screech, Flammulated, Great Horned, Northern Pygmy, Spotted, Long-eared, and Northern Saw-Whet Owl.

Several area bird lists are available and may be obtained at any district office of the Plumas National Forest.

For more information about the area write Plumas National Forest, Beckworth/Mohawk Ranger District, Mohawk Road, P.O. Box 7, Blairsden, CA 96103, or call (916) 836-2575 or (916) 832-5161.

Lake Davis. This prime recreation area boasts 4,030 acres of surface area, 32 miles of shoreline, excellent trout fishing, a two-lane boat launching ramp, 180 campsites, a trailer dump station, restrooms, and drinking water. No reservations are necessary, but campsites are closed during the winter. To make sure the area is open, call (916) 283-2050.

For more information about this area write Plumas National Forest, Beckworth/Mohawk Ranger District, Mohawk Road, P.O. Box 7, Blairsden, CA 96103, or call either (916) 836-2575 or (916) 832-5161.

Grizzly Valley Dam and Lake Davis can be reached by taking Lake Davis Road north from Portola on SH 70.

Antelope Dam and Lake. This is the smallest of the Feather River Lakes, with only 15 miles of conifer-rimmed shoreline. Its features include educational programs; ranger-guided nature walks; a historic pioneer log cabin; good fishing; water skiing, swimming, boating, hunting, and hiking; a beaver pond; and 209 family campsites with picnic tables, stoves, water, and toilets. Facilities are open from May through November.

Antelope Lake and Dam can be reached by taking Arlington Road from SH 89, 6 miles southeast of Greenville, to Genesee Road, which turns into Indian Creek Road. Travel 34 miles northeast to the lake.

Frenchman's Lake. With a shoreline 21 miles long, and a capacity of 55,480 acre-feet of water, this scenic, high country lake, well stocked with Rainbow Trout, is popular with anglers, boaters, campers, and birders alike. Recreation facilities include 199 campsites, a boat launching ramp with four lanes; two group campsites, a trailer dump station, drinking water, and full sanitary facilities.

On your way to or from Frenchman's Lake, stop off at Wiggins Trading Post in "downtown" Chilcoot, an old-fashioned general store so fully stocked with practically everything that you'll think you've been transported back in time.

To reach Frenchman's Lake from SH 70 in Chilcoot, take Highway 284 north 7 miles to the dam.

BUCKS LAKE

Fortunately for birders, hikers, and winter sports lovers, who have good reason to stay a while at Bucks Lake, the area has plenty of overnight accommodations. For those who like to camp, PG&E operates the 65-unit Haskins Valley Campground, and the National Forest Service manages the 19-unit Sundew campgrounds on the lake's west shore, the 5-unit Lakeview RV Campsites on the south shore, and the Hutchins Meadow Group Camp northeast of Lower Bucks Lake.

Other overnight accommodations are available at Bucks Lake Lodge and Lake Shore Resort. These establishments are open to the public all year, although during the winter months, when weather closes the roads, there are only two ways to get in — by snowmobile or skis.

Bald Eagles are regularly sighted in the Bucks Lake area. Here also are Canada Goose, Osprey, Goshawk, Spotted and Northern Pygmy-Owls, Cassin's and Purple Finches, Lazuli Bunting, White-breasted and Red-breasted Nuthatches, Mountain Chickadee, Ruby-crowned Kinglet, Bohemian and Cedar Waxwings, Blue Grouse, California and Mountain Quail, Cooper's Hawk, Common Merganser, Hermit Thrush, Olive-sided Flycatcher, Western Wood-Pewee, Song and Fox Sparrows, Calliope Hummingbird, Pileated and Lewis' Woodpeckers, and Red-breasted and Williamson's Sapsuckers.

For information about Bucks Lake Lodge, call (916) 283-2262. For the Lake Shore Resort, call (916) 283-2333. Anyone desiring more facts about the PG&E sites should call (415) 973-5552. For further data about the National Forest campgrounds write: Plumas National Forest, Oroville Ranger District, 875 Mitchell Ave., Oroville, CA 95965, or call (916) 543-6500.

To reach the Haskins Valley campgrounds take Bucks Lake Road from SH 70 at Quincy, and travel 16.5 miles further. To reach Sundew, proceed as mentioned and go south from the campground on Bucks Lake Road 0.2 miles, to a fork in the road, take the road to the right and drive 1.1 miles to the next fork. Again bear right and go 1.5 miles to Bucks Lake Dam. Follow this road past the dam, turn right onto the road just west of the dam and proceed 0.5 mile, cross over the stream, and continue 0.2 mile to the intersection. Drive through the intersection up the hill 0.6 mile, turn right, and continue 0.1 mile.

To reach the main recreation area of the lake, just continue on Buck's Lake Road.

LITTLE GRASS VALLEY RESERVOIR

The clarity of the sky is as outstanding a feature of this lovely Plumas County lake as the Bald Eagle often seen silhouetted up against it, or the

Cedar Waxwing

winds that render sailing so superb. At an altitude of 5,000 feet, far from the distraction of city lights, the Little Grass Valley Reservoir is a haven for astronomers and casual stargazers alike.

The area also offers excellent fishing, picnic facilities, 191 campsites with tables and stoves, gently sloping beaches equipped with change pavilions, and superb sightings of nesting Bald Eagles. Also seen here are Clark's Nutcracker, Great Blue Heron, Great Horned Owl, Northern Pintail, Common Merganser, American Wigeon, Canvasback, Common Goldeneye, Bufflehead, Ruddy Duck, Osprey, Northern Goshawk, California and Mountain Quail, Belted Kingfisher, Hairy Woodpecker, Steller's and Pinyon Jays, Common Raven, Mountain Chickadee, Red-breasted Nuthatch, Pygmy Nuthatch, Red-breasted Sapsucker, Golden-crowned Kinglet, Song Sparrow, Dark-eyed Junco, Cassin's Finch, Red Crossbill, Pine Siskin, and Evening Grosbeak.

Located in the La Porte Ranger District of the Plumas National Forest, the Little Grass Valley Reservoir is outside of La Porte, 50 miles northwest of Oroville, on County Road E21.

PLUMAS-EUREKA STATE PARK

Located only 80 miles from Lake Tahoe on the spectacular eastern slopes of the Sierra Nevada and near the headwaters of the Yuba and Feather Rivers, this scenic park has two lakes of its own, the Eureka and the Madora. Here too are many scenic acres of Douglas fir, ponderosa, incense cedar, and Jeffrey pine forests; old mining roads that serve now as hiking trails; good fishing in nearby lakes and streams; 67 creekside campsites in a forested canyon; skiing nearby; an opportunity to scout about the partially restored Plumas-Eureka Mill, where gold was once processed; a modern museum in a historic old bunkhouse; endless sightseeing. Approximately 70,000 individuals visit this park each year.

Among the many birds seen here are Mountain Chickadee, Red-breasted Nuthatch, Common Raven, Bushtit, Downy Woodpecker, Western Wood-Pewee, Golden-crowned Kinglet, Solitary Vireo, Nashville Warbler, Western Tanager, and Dark-eyed Junco.

Eureka-Plumas is off SH 89 between Quincy and Sierraville. Take County Road A14 to the west at Graeagle.

SIERRA VALLEY/YUBA PASS

The thick mixed forests, clear streams, and boggy meadows of Yuba Pass, combined with rich marshes and wetlands of Sierra Valley, afford abundant and diverse habitat in a concentrated geographic area and make this section of California one of the best in the nation for birding.

Few people reside year-round in this area, yet tourist accommodations are plentiful: motels, lodges, and bed and breakfast inns, in addition to several campgrounds in the National Forest.

Sierra City/Wild Plum Campground/Tahoe National Forest. Sierra City is a pretty little mountain town on the North Yuba River that straddles SH 49 some 12 miles below Yuba Pass. The area is graced with oak woods, conifer forests, and rushing creeks, including one named Haypress (located just before the Wild Plum Campground), which is a good place to begin a birding tour of this great Sierra hotspot.

Wild Plum Road takes off to the south just at the eastern edge of Sierra City; 1 mile of paved road and another 0.75 mile of gravel gets you to Haypress Creek. Park just before you reach the bridge and then hike the dirt road to the left. This is the Wild Plum Loop Trail, a 2.5 mile walk that crosses Haypress Creek via a footbridge further up, and offers some magnificent views of the towering Sierra Buttes.

There are several excellent trails in the area, including access to the highly scenic Pacific Crest Trail. For more information on any of these, contact Downieville Ranger District, North Yuba Ranger Station, 15924 Highway 49, Comptonville, CA 95922, or call (916) 288-3231.

Sierra City is at 4,167 feet, compared to the 6,700-ft elevation of Yuba Pass, so many birds common to lower elevations of the Sierras are readily sighted here. These include Black-headed Grosbeak, Solitary Vireo, Western Tanager, and Nashville and Black-throated Gray Warblers. But the special bird of the area is doubtless the American Dipper, which nests under the bridge over Haypress Creek.

Come in on SH 49. The easiest way is probably from the east, through Sierra Valley but another possibility is to catch 49 at Auburn from I-80, and go through Grass Valley and Nevada City.

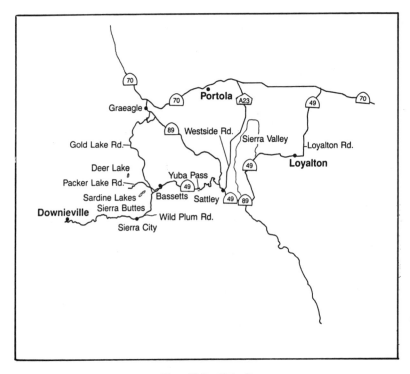

Sierra Valley/Yuba Pass

Deer Lake Trail/Downieville Ranger District. Take a short well-signed detour from Deer Lake Trail and you'll wind your way to the small and tranquil Grass Lake. Follow the route directly and you'll reach Deer Lake. Either way you'll have fine panoramic views of the massive Sierra Buttes. You'll see carpets of wildflowers, a variety of other plants, and plenty of birds. Along the way, look for Hairy and Pileated Woodpeckers, Mountain Quail, Steller's Jay, White-crowned and Golden-crowned Sparrows, Black-headed Grosbeak, Western Tanager, and Golden-crowned and Ruby-crowned Kinglets; and once you've reached the lakes, keep an eye out for Wood Duck. Osprey nest at nearby Goose Lake and are often sighted here as well.

Five miles east of Sierra City on SH 49 turn north onto Gold Lake Highway at Bassetts Station. Continue for about 1.4 miles and then turn left at the bridge across Salmon Creek. Continue on for approximately 0.3 miles up Packer Lake Road on the right. The trailhead is marked with a sign that reads "Deer Lake Trail 12 E 01."

Sardine Lake. Characterized by a peerless view of the craggy Sierra Buttes, mountains blanketed with ground-hugging manzanita, clearly reflecting lakes over which the Osprey wheel, the Sardine Lake area is lauded for its dramatic scenery, as well as for its wildlife, by a long list of Californians that includes such dedicated birders as Dave Shuford of the Point Reyes Bird Observatory. "It's truly a scenic place," Dave says. "You're looking up at these really steep cliffs, and the steepest face of all drops down right toward the lake."

The Sardine Lake area boasts a restaurant, a lodge, lakeside cabins, hiking, fishing, boating, and fine Sierra birding. Look for Green-tailed Towhee, Dusky Flycatcher, Townsend's Solitaire, Fox Sparrow, and Yellow, McGillivray's, and Orange-crowned Warblers, as well as a variety of raptors, and, in June and July, an abundance of hummingbirds. Expect a superabundance of Steller's Jays all year long.

Five miles east of Sierra City on SH 49, turn north on Gold Lake Road at Bassett's Station (where you might want to stop to fill up on gas, rent a motel room for the night, buy a snack, or sit for a while on the big front porch watching the many hummingbirds, including Calliopes, that gather around the feeders hanging there). Continue for 1.5 miles and watch for the signs. It's the same as the turn-off for Deer Lake Trail.

Sierra Nevada Field Campus. After leaving Bassett's, take SH 49 one mile east to the field campus of San Francisco State University, a mecca for birders in the summertime, a vital stop-off or staging point for many a birding tour, as well as the scene of popular ornithology classes. Stop and walk the campus for Evening Grosbeak, and Hermit and Nashville Warblers, and/or continue on to a dirt road about 100 feet further along SH 49 and look for the Pileated Woodpeckers known to nest here.

If you're interested in availing yourself of one of the wonderful summer courses offered here (Bird Identification by Song, Sierran Birds-In-The-Hand, A Bird Banding Workshop, as well as astronomy, education, and geology), a catalog is available.

But, as Jim Steele points out, it doesn't take enrollment in a college course to render a birder welcome at the Sierra Nevada Field Campus.

Steller's Jay

"People exploring the Yuba Pass and Sierra Valley area should feel free to drop in and ask questions," he states. "Often the people in our bird courses have uncovered the nests of birds that someone seeks for their life list. We will also provide a checklist of the area upon request. Simply send us a self-addressed, stamped envelope."

Those interested in the courses may obtain a catalog and/or further details, field station reservations for lodging, and carpooling information directly from Jim Steele. Before June 1st, address requests to him at the School of Science, San Francisco State University, 1600 Holloway Avenue, San Francisco, CA 94132-9087, or call (415) 338-1571 or (415) 759-0970. After June 1st, contact Jim at the Sierra Nevada Field Campus, Star Route, Sattley, CA 96124, or call (916) 862-1230.

The field station is located 1 mile above Bassett's Station and 6 miles below Yuba Pass on SH 49 in Sierra County.

Yuba Pass. Continue on up the hill to Yuba Pass, a truly spectacular area in the spring and summer, a favorite with countless birders from all over the state.

Dirt roads go both directions from the highway; there's a campground in the conifer woods on the south side that's good for birding, and a little meadow and a lot of snags on the north side that woodpeckers favor. A one-mile hike in either direction here is bound to spell fruitful birding.

Pine Grosbeak are here but hard to see. Here too are Evening Grosbeak, Dusky and Hammond's Flycatchers, Red Crossbill, Clark's Nutcracker, Townsend's Solitaire, Cassin's Finch, Pine Siskin, warblers, kinglets, vireos, chickadees, nuthatches, thrushes, and sparrows. The area is excellent for woodpeckers. Black-backed, White-headed, and Hairy Woodpeckers, and Williamson's and Red-breasted Sapsuckers are common here.

Yuba Pass is on SH 49 about 9 miles east of Sierra City.

Sierra Valley. As you come down from Yuba Pass going east, there's a vista point where the whole sweep of the Sierra Valley opens up like a great flat-bottomed bowl. A most imposing scene, and beautiful. And because it is so flat, because it doesn't drain, this high mountain valley creates the marshes and wet meadows that are vital to so many bird species, and makes it a spectacular place to bird in late spring and early summer.

County Road A23 runs north and south along the west side of the valley; about two thirds of the way up, unpaved Dyson Lane takes off to the east, through the heart of the swamp. If there's no road sign, you can recognize it by a horse corral at the southeast corner. Dyson Lane is really the key birding area of the valley. Traffic is light or nonexistent, so you can pull off the road almost anywhere.

An interesting sidelight: we discovered a hot springs about a half mile down Dyson Lane, on the north side of the road. We don't know whether or not it's visible during the wet season, but on this September day we could see the steam rising up for a hundred yards after the stream left the spring.

The area to the west of A23, as the valley starts sloping up toward the mountains, is scrubby country. A stop anywhere along here, as well as the beginning of Dyson Lane, will be good for the brush-type birds, especially Vesper Sparrow, which is fairly common here.

As you go down into the wetlands, you can do a lot of birding right from the car. A couple of particularly productive spots are the first sharp left turn in Dyson Lane, and also around the green iron bridge.

Dyson Lane runs into Road A24 after 3 miles through the main part of the marsh. You can turn north here and join SH 70 some 4 miles up the road, or continue east, which is still Dyson Lane, and hit SH 49 after 5 miles. The latter option affords more birding, through areas of ponds and fields.

In the scrub brush areas to the west, look for Brewer's Sparrow, Sage Thrasher, Horned Lark, and Common Nighthawk. As you approach the marsh you'll come across an abundance of blackbirds: Brewer's, Red-winged, and Yellow-headed. Anywhere along the way you'll see Sandhill Cranes — Sierra Valley is the southern limit of their breeding range in California. At the first sharp left turn on Dyson Lane look to the east for nesting Black Tern. Common Snipe, Wilson's Phalarope, American Bittern, rails, Black-necked Stilt, American Avocet, and a recent colony of White-faced Ibis are also here.

Further along, at the ponds, there are Cinnamon Teal, Gadwall, Northern Pintail, grebes, Redhead, and Burrowing Owl. Cliff Swallows nest at the green bridge. A goodly number of Willets are here, and sometimes Long-billed Curlews. As you get back out of the wetlands you'll run into more good habitat for Sage Thrasher, Horned Lark, and Savannah Sparrow. And the whole area is a haven for the Northern Harrier.

A Marbled Godwit was reported in July, 1988, and a Trumpeter Swan is under consideration by the Rare Bird Committee.

To reach Sierra Valley, continue on down from Yuba Pass; or come up I-80, pass the turn-off to Tahoe, go to the next exit and turn left on SH 89. Twenty-six miles later you're in Sierraville and another 4 puts you in Sattley. Turn right at the Sattley Cash Store (Westside Road), and 4 miles later you're on A23, where all this begins.

TRUCKEE

Donner Summit

Almost everyone with even the barest knowledge of California's history knows the tragic story of the Donner party, whose members were trapped here in the Sierra Nevadas in the raging winter storms of 1846-47, some to freeze to death, some to be consumed by fellow travelers maddened by starvation, others to survive with the trauma of horror etched in their minds. But there's more here than history to hold the visitor in thrall. The scenery is some of the most spectacular in California. Donner Lake is sublime, the high mountain air is bracing, the white fir and Jeffrey pines majestic, the lodgepole pines curious, the geologic features fascinating, the trails superb, and the opportunities for photography irresistible.

Species known to have nested in the vicinity include Canada Goose, Common Merganser, Goshawk, Cooper's and Sharp-shinned Hawks, Bald Eagle, Osprey, Blue Grouse, Common Poorwill, Great Horned and Northern Pygmy Owls, Calliope Hummingbird, Pileated, White-headed and Hairy Woodpeckers, Canyon Wren, Pine Grosbeak, Western Tanager, Pine Siskin, Mountain Bluebird, and Golden-crowned and Ruby-crowned Kinglets.

Common or abundant at least in the spring and summer are Eared Grebe, Canada Goose, Common Merganser, Mountain Quail, Calliope Hummingbird, White-headed Woodpecker, Clark's Nutcracker, and Dark-eyed Junco.

A checklist, *Birds of Emerald Bay, D.L Bliss, Sugar Pine Point, and Donner Memorial State Parks*, is available at any of these state parks.

Donner Memorial State Park. Because this state park was established in memoriam to the members of the Donner party, there are exhibits here in its fine Emigrant Trail Museum that focus on their tale. But here too are interpretive displays that depict other episodes in the Sierra Nevada's past — like the story of how the railroad was built over its formidable rocks and crags and chasms. And here too are exhibits pertaining to the natural history of the region, its geologic wonders, its plantlife, and its wildlife.

Activities center around the lovely Donner Lake, an undisputed beauty and a joy to water-sport enthusiasts. Its glinting waters are open to both power and sail craft. Those registered in the park campground are allowed to pull their boats up on the shore overnight. The park has no launching facilities of its own, but a public ramp is available in the northwest corner of the lake.

There are just 2.5 miles of trails in Donner Memorial State Park itself, but eager hikers are free to explore the magnificent Donner Summit Trails in the Tahoe National Forest.

This historic park has 154 campsites with tables, stoves, and parking spaces. Restrooms and hot showers are located nearby. Reservations are advisable in the summer but during the winter months, visitors in self-contained recreational vehicles can just pull up and stay overnight in the parking lot.

For further information about the state park write: Donner Memorial State Park, P.O. Box 549, Truckee, CA 95734, or call (916) 587-3789.

Donner Memorial State Park is at the east end of Donner Lake, which is visible from I-80 a couple of miles west of Truckee. Take the exit at the agricultural inspection station.

Donner Summit Trails/Tahoe National Forest. Anyone visiting this area, even if their time is limited, should take at least a short walk in this peerless Tahoe National Forest land, beginning at the trailhead of the Donner Summit Trail system. We suggest the Glacier Meadow Loop, an easy, half-mile trail at an elevation of 7,200 feet, heavily traveled from June to October.

Maps of the Glacier Meadow Loop or any of the Donner Summit Trails are available at the Donner Memorial State Park or from the National Forest.

For further information write: Tahoe National Forest, Truckee Ranger District, P.O. Box 399, Truckee, CA 95734, or call (916) 587-3558.

To reach the trailhead to the fabulous Donner Summit Trails take the Castle Peak Area/Boreal Ridge Road exit, which is located immediately west of the Donner Summit Roadside Rest Area. On the south side of the highway you'll see a sign that reads: Tahoe National Forest Trailhead, Donner Summit, Pacific Crest Trail. From this point, follow the directions on the sign. It's 0.4 mile to the trailhead, which provides access to the Pacific Crest Trail (north and south), Glacier Meadow Loop, Summit Lake, Warren Lake, and Sand Ridge Lake trails.

Martis Creek Lake

It's a sad state of affairs, but to some nature lovers, nowadays, the name "Tahoe" is more apt to call to mind slot machines and crap tables than blue waters and towering trees. It's otherwise here, for this parkland pays no jackpots. It does have all these features, however: wonderful hiking trails; good trout fishing; cross-country skiing; 25 fully developed campsites; picnic tables, tent pads, and barbecue grills; water faucets and restrooms; an amphitheater; campsites for the handicapped; a 1,050-acre wildlife management area.

Birds seen in the area include Osprey, Mountain Quail, Canada Goose, Golden Eagle, Barn Owl, Calliope Hummingbird, Red-breasted Sapsucker, Olive-sided Flycatcher, Western Wood-Pewee, Hammond's Flycatcher, Black Phoebe, and Steller's Jay.

Martis Creek Lake borders Highway 267, 6 miles southeast of Truckee off I-80.

AUBURN

Auburn State Recreation Area

There's nothing like this rugged and beautiful American River country to turn back the clock, perhaps to the years of the goldrush when prospectors' hopes ran as high as ever runs the river, or maybe back to the times when the Maidu Indians were praying to the spirits here. One way or the other, it's a timeless place, a place for dreaming. But it's also a place for recreation and leisure.

Auburn State Recreational Area, with its 30 full miles of riverfront, offers wonderful opportunities for boating, rafting, rockhounding, wildlife and landscape photography, gold panning, hiking, sunbathing, mountain biking, exploring, swimming, picnicking, camping, and birding.

A special feature of the area is the very popular Lake Clementine, well known for boating and waterskiing as well as the excellent fishing for Rainbow Trout, Small-mouth Bass, Catfish, Bluegill, Carp, and Squawfish.

There are 5 primitive campground areas here: Mineral Bar, located on the east side of the North Fork American River; Ruck-a-Chunky on the north side of the river in Placer County; Cherokee Bar on the south side of the river in El Dorado County; and 2 at Lake Clementine, which also has 25 designated boat-in campsites.

Seen at one location or another in the Auburn State Recreation Area are Wild Turkey, Black-shouldered Kite, Cooper's Hawk, Anna's Hummingbird, Golden-crowned Kinglet, Band-tailed Pigeon, Ruby-crowned Kinglet, Cedar Waxwing, Phainopepla, Rufous-sided Towhee, Steller's and Scrub Jays, Common Merganser, Mountain Chickadee, Osprey, Winter and Rock Wrens, Hutton's Vireo, Black Phoebe, Lesser and American Goldfinches, California Quail, Belted Kingfisher, Blue-gray Gnatcatcher, and Varied Thrush.

The Ranger Station is 2 miles east of Auburn, on SH 49, which goes through the southern end of the area.

Foresthill Road goes through much of the area, in a northeasterly direction, between the two forks of the American River. Catch Foresthill Road at the first exit from I-80 north of Auburn.

Lake Clementine is located off the Auburn-Foresthill Road, approximately 2 miles northeast of the historic town of Auburn.

Morning Star Lake Resort

A portion of this popular campground, which lies in the Foresthill Ranger District of the Tahoe National Forest, is owned by the Forest Service and is operated by De Anza Placer Gold Mining Company. The beach here is inviting, the lake not only lovely, but blessedly quiet.

Morning Star Lake Resort boasts 100 campsites, picnic sites with tables, fire rings, piped water, and vault toilets.

Birds seen in the Foresthill Ranger District of the Tahoe National Forest are Bald and Golden Eagles, Lazuli Bunting, Mountain Quail, Great Horned and Northern Pygmy Owls, Anna's, Calliope, and Rufous Hummingbirds, Red-breasted Sapsucker, Hairy, Pileated, and White-headed Woodpeckers, Steller's and Scrub Jays, Common Raven, Mountain Chickadee, Red-breasted Nuthatch, Bewick's and House Wrens, and Golden-crowned and Ruby-crowned Kinglets.

For more information about this fine campground write: De Anza Placer Gold Mining Company, P.O. Box 119, Foresthills, CA 95631, or call (916) 367-2129.

Morning Star Lake Resort, on Big Reservoir, is further up the same road that goes to Lake Clementine. From Auburn, take the Auburn/Forest-

Varied Thrush (immature)

hill Road through Foresthill, where the District Headquarters is located, continue about 12 miles to Elliot Ranch Road, turn left and proceed another 4 miles to the resort and campground.

LAKE TAHOE AREA

El Dorado National Forest, Pacific Ranger District

The northwest entrance to the Desolation Wilderness and the lovely Loon Lake lie in the Pacific Ranger District of the Eldorado National

Forest. This is High Sierra country (altitudes up to 7,500 feet) unsurpassed for its beauty and surprisingly accessible from both the Bay area and the Sacramento Valley.

Due to weather conditions, many of the dirt roads in the forest are closed between October and April. Major recreation areas are usually accessible by the middle of April. If you're planning to come here at that time of the year, call ahead and make sure the roads are ready.

Wildlife is abundant in the area. You're almost certain to see many deer and chipmunks. Also present, though not as frequently seen, are Badgers, Raccoons, Porcupines and the many rodents that keep the area's numerous raptors well-fed and thriving.

Some of the birds of the area are Bald and Golden Eagles, Northern Goshawk, Osprey, Sharp-shinned and Cooper's Hawks, Pileated Woodpecker, Black-headed and Evening Grosbeaks, Lazuli Bunting, Dark-eyed Junco, Common Raven, Golden-crowned and Ruby-crowned Kinglets, Blue Grouse, Mountain Quail, Rufous-sided Towhee, Pine Siskin, Purple and Cassin's Finches, vireos, and Western Tanager, as well as Black-throated Gray, Hermit, and MacGillivray's Warblers.

Wildlife Biologist Donald Yasuda is in the process of developing a wildlife atlas of the Pacific Ranger District of the Eldorado National Forest, and is asking that readers who visit the area contribute information about their sightings to him. He'd also like for any knowledgeable birders who reside in the area to contact him at their convenience. Write: Donald Yasuda, Wildlife Biologist, United States Department of Agriculture, Eldorado National Forest, Pacific Ranger Station, Pollock Pines, CA 95726, or call (916) 644-2349. Here's your chance to participate in a great project and contribute to the storehouse of knowledge about California birds.

Loon Lake. This area has a fine swimming beach with a change house located nearby; 18 inviting picnic sites; a beautifully situated campground with 34 separate units, piped water, trailer spaces, and vault toilets; a boat launching ramp; access to the Desolation Wilderness.

Birds seen in the area are the same as those listed for El Dorado National Forest, Pacific Ranger District.

The Loon Lake area is one of several staging areas for the Desolation Wilderness. Parties of more than 6 people are encouraged to enter either from here or from Meeks Bay or General Creek.

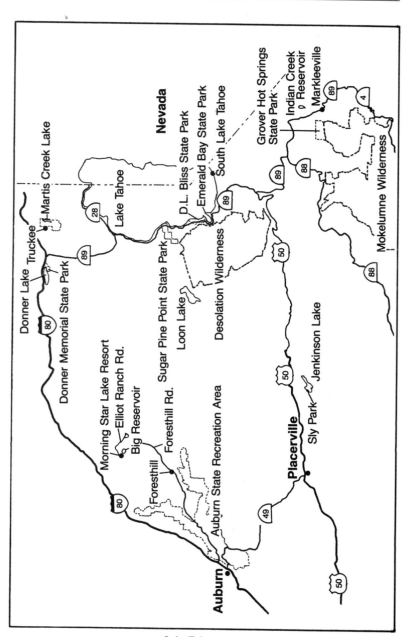

Lake Tahoe Area

Loon Lake Reservoir is located approximately 29 miles north of the town of Riverton, which is on SH 50. Take Ice House Road from the highway. There is a Forest Service Information Center located in Riverton.

Desolation Wilderness. Ironically, so many people have come to love this area for its unspoiled wilderness, peace and solitude, and rugged beauty that if there were no limits put on their number, the peace, solitude, and wilderness would be no more. In 1971, the Forest Service initiated a quota system, and permits are now required for entry. This is beautiful country, blessed with lakes full of fish, and varying habitats abounding with birds. Species seen in the area are the same as those listed for El Dorado National Forest, Pacific Ranger District.

Permits, maps, and descriptive literature can be obtained from any ranger district in the Eldorado National Forest. For further information write: Eldorado National Forest Information Center, 3070 Camino Heights Drive, Camino, CA 95709, or call (916) 644-6048.

To enter the Desolation Wilderness, see the directions for Loon Lake. For information on other entry locations, contact any ranger district of the Eldorado National Forest or write to the address given.

Sugar Pine Point State Park

Although more people visit this high, snow-belt country for the breathtaking scenery, the challenge of high mountain trails, or the joys of creek fishing than for birding, there are, nonetheless, many interesting species here including Bald Eagle, Goshawk, and Osprey.

Common or abundant in spring and summer are Calliope Hummingbird, White-headed Woodpecker, Red-breasted Sapsucker, Olive-sided Flycatcher, Steller's Jay, Clark's Nutcracker, Mountain Chickadee, White-breasted Nuthatch, Golden-crowned Kinglet, Wilson's Warbler, Red-winged Blackbird, Western Tanager, Evening Grosbeak, Dark-eyed Junco, and Fox and Song Sparrows.

Species known to have nested in the vicinity include Northern Goshawk, Cooper's Hawk, Bald Eagle, Osprey, Blue Grouse, Mountain Quail, Great Horned Owl, Belted Kingfisher, Pileated Woodpecker, and Mountain Bluebird.

Mammals in the vicinity include Mule Deer, Bobcat, Striped Skunk, Long-tailed Weasel, Chipmunk, foxes, and many other species.

Open all year despite frequent storms and deep snow packs (roads are cleared regularly), the park offers 175 family campsites and a group site for up to 400 people. Advance reservations are a must for large groups, advisable for others.

For further information write: Sugar Pine Point State Park, P.O. Box 266, Tahoma, CA 95733, or call (916) 525-7982.

Sugar Pine Point is on SH 89 on the southwest shore of Lake Tahoe, 5 miles south of Meeks Bay.

D.L. Bliss/Emerald Bay State Park

Here stands the famous Vikingsholm, constructed in 1928 by Swedish-born architect, Lennart Palme, and fashioned after an old Norse fortress built centuries ago: a fascinating building and a special feature of this state park.

Besides Vikingsholm, this recreation area boasts 6 miles of sublime Lake Tahoe shoreline; a lovely waterfall; murmuring mountain streams; a variety of trees including Sierra juniper, black cottonwood, alders, quaking aspen, and mountain dogwood; a riot of wildflowers in springtime — columbine, lupine, bleeding heart, leopard lily, mint, and nightshade; good fishing; fine hiking; panoramic views; 268 campsites with tables, cupboards, stoves, restrooms, and hot showers; a group campground for up to 50 people; 20 primitive campsites accessible only by foot or boat.

Due to the freezing winter weather here, the park is open only from May until the middle of September.

Nesting birds in the Emerald Bay area include Black-backed Woodpecker, Northern Goshawk, American Dipper, Bald Eagle, Osprey, Blue Grouse, Cooper's and Sharp-shinned Hawks, Mountain Quail, Spotted Sandpiper, California Gull, Great Horned and Northern Pygmy Owls, Common Poorwill, Calliope Hummingbird, Belted Kingfisher, Pileated Woodpecker, Olive-sided Flycatcher, Tree Swallow, Canada Goose, Common Merganser, Steller's Jay, and White-breasted Nuthatch.

Common all year long are White-headed Woodpecker, Red-breasted Nuthatch, and Mountain Chickadee.

Also seen here are Mule Deer, Striped Skunk, Raccoon, foxes, an occasional Bobcat and a wide variety of rodents.

For further information write D.L. Bliss State Park, P.O. Box 266, Tahoma, CA 95733 or call (916) 525-7277.

The park is on SH 89, on the southwest corner of the lake just 5 miles south of Sugar Pine Point State Park, and about 10 miles northwest of South Lake Tahoe.

Hangtown's Gold Mine and Stampmill

Hangtown's Gold Bug Park encompasses 61.5 acres of wooded land, located east of the Mother Lode vein. It's quiet here now, but once it was the scene of the frantic activity of the hundreds of avid gold seekers who swarmed this area, digging 250 separate mines, and netting $17 million in gold between the years of 1850 and 1880. Today, the 362-foot-long tunnel to the Gold Bug Mine, always available for tours, is well-lighted throughout, with specially-illuminated interpretive points along the way.

According to plans, the park will one day boast an amphitheater, a group picnic area, a playground, and a series of developed hiking trails. In the meantime, sightseeing and exploration pose no problem. Hiking along the creekbed is delightful.

Birds seen here include Acorn Woodpecker, Black Phoebe, Steller's Jay, chickadees, Bewick's and Winter Wrens, Hutton's Vireo, Rufous Hummingbird, Warbling Vireo, Western Wood-Pewee, Lesser Goldfinch, Fox Sparrow, Mountain Quail, and Northern Oriole, as well as Yellow, Black-throated Gray, and Nashville Warblers.

The park is open daily from 8:30 a.m. until dusk. The mine is open every day from April 1-October 1, and on weekends throughout the year.

For further information write: Placerville Recreation & Parks, 549 Main Street, Placerville, CA 95667, or phone (916) 622-4500.

Situated within the city limits of Placerville, Hangtown's Gold Bug Park is 0.9 mile north of SH 50, on Bedford Avenue.

Sly Park Recreation Area/Jenkinson Lake

Sly Park, located on land that was once the domain of Maidu and Miwok Indians, gets its name from James Calvin Sly, whose discovery of the area in 1848 led to the opening of the best possible exit route for travelers on their way eastward from California. It was a beautiful place he found, a verdant land with a fine little creek running through it, with wild berries and willow, manzanita, cedar, madrone, valley oak, and yellow pine.

Though it's referred to today as the Mormon Emigrant Trail, to wagoneers of that earlier era this well-traveled byway was simply the Mormon Wagon Road. In those days a hotel, dairy, and store stood here and the area was a wayside stop for many people, not to mention the vast numbers of cattle and sheep that were driven through on their way to pasture.

Decades rolled by; wagons rolled off into obsolescence; new roads were built; the human populace multiplied. The need for water also grew, and ultimately led to the formation of the El Dorado Irrigation District. As part of the the giant Central Valley Project, the Bureau of Reclamation constructed a dam. A lake was born and named Jenkinson, after the manager of the Irrigation District.

This popular park offers good fishing, ensured by the fish-planting program of the Department of Fish and Game; 2 concrete ramps to facilitate boat launching; a marked hiking trail that covers 8 miles of scenic shoreline; 2 self-guided nature trails; 7 family campgrounds with a total of 160 sites, all equipped with tables, fire rings, and barbecues; pit toilets and piped drinking water; youth group and regular group campgrounds; a grocery store, snack bar, and gas station. Campsite reservations are on a first-come, first-served basis.

The best birding at Sly Park is in the spring and summer months, but it should be noted that a number of especially interesting species, including White-headed Woodpecker and American Dipper, are year-round residents here. Bald Eagles, which roost on islands and around the lake, are common in the fall and winter. Black-headed Grosbeak is common in spring and fall, and truly abundant in the summer.

Common or fairly common residents include Common Merganser, Great Blue Heron, Belted Kingfisher, Northern Rough-winged Swallow, Rufous-sided Towhee, Steller's Jay, Mountain Quail, Bushtit, Ruby-crowned Kinglet, Dark-eyed Junco, Black Phoebe, and Hairy Woodpecker.

Look on the lake for Ruddy Duck, Bufflehead, Barrow's and Common Goldeneyes, Western Grebe, and other waterfowl; around the shore for Great Blue Heron; in the creek for American Dipper; around the creek inlets for swallows; and in Miwok Cove for a variety of warblers, including Black-throated Gray, Wilson's, and Orange-crowned. In various locations all over the park are Northern Orioles, and Pileated, White-headed, and Hairy Woodpeckers.

Birds of prey sighted in the area include Osprey, Northern Goshawk,

Cooper's Hawk, and the rare Spotted Owl. Roosting on the islands and around the lake, the Bald Eagle is common in the winter, and fairly common in fall.

For further information write: El Dorado Irrigation District, 2890 Mosquito Road, Placerville, CA 95667, or call (916) 644-2545 or (916) 644-2792.

From SH 50 at Pollock Pine (about 12 miles west of Placerville,) take Sly Park Road to the south and proceed 5 miles to the park.

China Flat/Placerville Ranger District, Eldorado National Forest

A good place to headquarter while scouting about this section of the Eldorado National Forest, and one that offers an excellent blend of habitats and plenty of good birding, is the China Flat Campground, which lies on the Silver Fork of the historic and handsome American River. Special birds of this section of the Eldorado National Forest are Blue Grouse, American Dipper, Western Tanager, and Golden Eagle, often seen in the vicinity of the nearby Lover's Leap.

Other birds of the Placerville Ranger District are Bald Eagle, Northern Goshawk, Osprey, Belted Kingfisher, Pileated, Hairy, and Acorn Woodpeckers, Dark-eyed Junco, Rufous-sided Towhee, Orange-crowned Warbler, Golden-crowned and Ruby-crowned Kinglets, Red-breasted Sapsucker, Great Horned and Western Screech Owls, Steller's Jay, Common Raven, Olive-sided Flycatcher, Winter Wren, and Black Phoebe.

Common mammals of the area are deer, Raccoon, and a variety of rodents. Occasionally Mountain Lion and bear are sighted.

For further information about this campground or any other locations in the Placerville Ranger District write: Eldorado National Forest Information Center, 3070 Camino Heights Drive, Camino, CA 95709, or call (916) 644-6048.

To get here, take the Silver Fork Road turnoff from SH 50 just southeast of the town of Kyburz. Follow the road for 3 miles and there you are!

Carson Pass Area /Mokelumne Wilderness

Whether your taste is for short and easy birding forays or long and challenging hikes into the spectacular 105,165-acre Mokelumne Wilderness, SH 88 over Carson Pass offers ready access to some wonderful trails you're bound to find irresistible. The deep wilderness is naturally tantaliz-ing, but there are some excellent destinations including Woodlake, Silver Lake, and Caples Lake that require little time and effort to reach and offer beautiful scenery and excellent birding. In fact, there are trailheads, rest areas, and vista points all along this designated Scenic Highway, as well as a Visitor Information Station at Carson Pass.

Permits to enter the Mokelumne Wilderness from the Carson Pass area can be obtained from the Visitor Information Station or from any office of the Eldorado National Forest.

This is a good area for raptors, including the Spotted Owl, and montane birds such as Williamson's Sapsucker, Blue Grouse, Mountain Quail, woodpeckers, Clark's Nutcracker, and White-breasted and Pygmy Nuthatches.

The Mokelumne Wilderness area, which covers parts of the Eldorado, Stanislaus, and Toiyabe National Forests, is located between SH 88 and SH 4. There are many trails entering the area. More specific directions as well as permits, maps, descriptive literature, and further information are available from any Ranger District office or from the Eldorado National Forest Information Center, at 3070 Camino Heights Drive, Camino, CA 95709, or phone (916) 644-6048.

Indian Creek Recreation Area

This parkland, set in the high Alpine County foothills, has a 160-acre reservoir; a trail that's linked to spring-fed lakes and the east fork of the Carson River; a campground with 19 drive-in sites; 10 tent campsites; hot water and showers; good fishing; and hunting in season.

The Pinyon Jay is often seen here in large flocks. Also sighted in the vicinity are Bald Eagle, Barn and Great Horned Owls, Western Wood-Pewee, Hammond's Flycatcher, Black Phoebe, Steller's Jay, Lewis' Wood-pecker, Gray Flycatcher, Black-billed Magpie, Pygmy Nuthatch, and Green-tailed Towhee.

The Indian Creek campground is open from mid-April until late Sep-tember, depending, of course, upon the weather. For further information write United States Department of the Interior, Bureau of Land Manage-ment, Carson City District Office, 1535 Hot Springs Road, Suite 300, Carson City, Nevada, 89706, or call (702) 882-1631.

From SH 89 north of Markleeville, turn east on Airport Road, pass

Alpine County Airport and proceed to the park entrance. It's about 4 miles from SH 89. Markleeville is approximately 30 miles southeast of South Lake Tahoe.

Grover Hot Springs State Park

Activities such as birding, hiking, and botanizing have always taken a back seat to bathing in the steaming waters of these famous old, high valley hot springs where the ailing, the troubled and weary have been coming with hope for so many decades. But the park has more to offer than its reputedly healing waters: a picturesque, high valley setting at an altitude of 6,000 feet; a fine view of the 10,023-foot Hawkins Peak; winter sports like skiing and snowshoeing; good trout fishing in season; an opportunity to sight some very special birds.

The 2 campgrounds at Grover Hot Springs boast 76 sites in all, with stoves, cupboards, picnic tables, piped water, and restrooms with showers. Although the campgrounds are closed from early October until May, camping is still allowed in the picnic area adjacent to the park entrance.

Birds commonly sighted at Grover Hot Springs State Park are American Dipper, Steller's Jay, Mountain Bluebird, chickadees, Warbling Vireo, Pine Siskin, and other birds tolerant of high altitudes. Less common are Great Gray Owl, Merlin, Northern Goshawk, and Spotted Owl. A free bird list is available at the park.

Mammals seen in the area are Pika, Marmot, Porcupine, skunks, Badger, a variety of rodents, and an occasional bear or fox.

For information, write Grover Hot Springs State Park, P.O. Box 188, Markleeville, CA 96120, or call (916) 694-2248.

From Markleeville, turn west on Hot Springs Road and proceed 3.5 miles to the park.

Indian Grinding Rock State Historic Park

History, in the form of 1,185 Indian mortar cups (more than at any other site in California), is etched in the limestone outcropping of this High Sierra meadow where once the Miwok Indians ground acorns into flour. From group tours, slide shows, and fascinating displays, you can learn about the mortar cups and other artifacts, as well as about the people who created them, at the park's Museum Cultural Center.

The park has 21 campsites, picnic tables and stoves, piped water and restrooms, and a day-use picnic area. There is also a unique environmental campground, *U'ma-cha'tam'a*, where visitors may sleep in bark dwellings constructed in the Miwok fashion.

Appropriately enough, the Acorn Woodpecker is one of the most common birds of Indian Grinding Rock State Historic Park. Other regular residents are California Quail, Red-breasted Sapsucker, Hairy Woodpecker, Black Phoebe, Scrub and Steller's Jays, Wrentit, Plain Titmouse, Bushtit, White-breasted Nuthatch, House, Bewick's and Winter Wrens, Golden-crowned and Ruby-crowned Kinglets, California Thrasher, Hutton's Vireo, Rufous-sided Towhee, American and Lesser Goldfinches, and Purple and House Finches, as well as Vesper, Song, White-crowned, Golden-crowned, Fox, Lincoln, and Lark Sparrows.

Some less common year-round residents are Northern Goshawk, Nuttall's and Downy Woodpeckers, Rufous-crowned Sparrow, Red-breasted Nuthatch, and Barn, Short-eared, Long-eared, Spotted, Great Horned, Western Screech, and Northern Pygmy Owls.

Common in spring and summer are Western Kingbird, Black-headed Grosbeak, Northern Oriole, Western Tanager, and Ash-throated, Olive-sided, Dusky, and Pacific Slope Flycatchers.

Seen occasionally are Red-shouldered Hawk, Mountain Quail, Band-tailed Pigeon, and Lazuli Bunting.

For further information about the park, write Indian Grinding Rock State Historic Park, 14881 Pine Grove-Volcano Road, Pine Grove, CA 95665, or call (209) 296-7488.

To get here, go east from Jackson on SH 88 to Pine Grove, turn left on Pine Grove/Volcano Road and proceed about 1 mile to the park.

CALAVERAS BIG TREES STATE PARK

Woh-woh-nau. This is the name that the Indians gave to the Big Trees like these at Calaveras, the greatest of them all. Although, to the Indian's way of thinking, it was the owls who dwelt in the branches who first named these towering giants. And to those early Californians — both the Indians and the owls — the Woh-woh-nau were sacred.

In the words of the nineteenth-century, self-styled anthropologist Stephen Powers, "It is productive of bad luck to fell this tree, or to mock or shoot the owl, or even to shoot in his presence." Apparently, according to Powers'

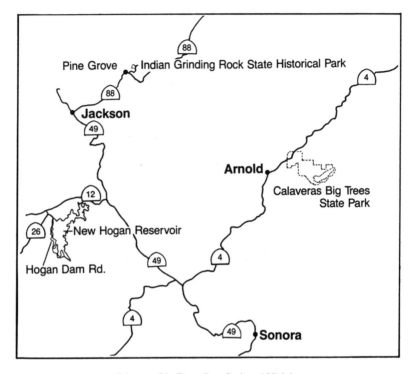

Calaveras Big Trees State Park and Vicinity

sources, the Indians tried their best to warn the white man. "When they
see a teamster going along the road with a wagon-load of lumber made
from these trees, they will cry out after him, and tell him the owl will
visit him with evil luck."

But the white men felled the sacred giants nonetheless. In 1853, the
famous "Discovery Tree" was cut down by a group of opportunists who
sought to create a travelling exhibit, and thereby fatten their wallets. Not
long afterward, the North Grove's finest specimen, the so-called "Mother
of the Forest," was felled for yet another travelling exhibit. And despite
the hoot of the owls, the desecration continued. Another early observer
who came here in 1863 noted in his journal, "A tree was felled a few years
ago. It took four men twenty-seven days to get it down. It was cut off by
boring into it with long augers. This tree lies here still."

Today the trees are protected at Calaveras. And so, for that matter, are the owls, who can still be heard uttering the ancient name Woh-woh-nau into the hush of the night. No augers here. No saws. But what is to be found, besides the two famous groves of spectacular Sequoias, is all of the following: 6,000 acres of pine forest on both sides of the Stanislaus River; excellent campgrounds; environmental campsites for backpackers; swimming and wading in the distinctly chilly, unquestionably invigorating river water; good fishing; prime picnic areas; self-guiding trails; challenging hikes for those who like to rough it; an interpretive center near the North Grove; brochures, maps, and trail guides; a printed checklist of area birds.

There's much to enjoy here, as eleven-year-old birder Tyler Gannon attests: "Calaveras Big Trees State Park is a beautiful vacation getaway where you can go to relax in the peace of the California Sierras. There is a rushing river which you can reach just a few miles from the campground. There is also a stream called Beaver Creek which is a longer way away but is a beautiful drive. There are wasps, bears, raccoons, and other pesky animals, so you have to watch it. But all in all, the park is a beautiful and exciting place to be."

Calaveras offers a good representation of the animals and plants that thrive in a middle elevation location in that type of environment previously known as the Yellow Pine belt. There's fine riparian habitat, ridge tops, and wonderful meadows. Birding and wildlife observation is best on the North Grove, South Grove, and river trails, and in the natural preserve which lies in the South Grove.

Visitors who want to camp in a secluded area should try for a site in the beautiful Oak Hollow. Those who favor the "beaten track," prefer being close to planned park activities, and are willing to trade the highway sounds for the convenience of easy access to other locations within the county may choose the North Grove campsites. Winter temperatures are comparatively mild at this elevation, so portions of the North Grove campground are generally open all year long. Advance reservations are advisable.

Bird species sighted at Calaveras Big Tree State Park include American Dipper, Blue Grouse, Mountain Quail, Band-tailed Pigeon, Western Tanager, Western Screech, Great Horned, and Northern Pygmy Owls, Belted Kingfisher, Pileated, Hairy, and White-headed Woodpeckers, Redbreasted, White-breasted, and Pygmy Nuthatches, Clark's Nutcracker, House, Bewick's and Winter Wrens, Hermit and Swainson's Thrushes, Black-headed Grosbeak, Lazuli Bunting, Green-tailed Towhee, Purple

Finch, Pine Grosbeak, and Pine Siskin, as well as Nashville, Yellow, Black-throated Gray, Hermit, MacGillivray's and Wilson's Warblers.

Commonly sighted animals include Raccoon, fox, Porcupine, deer, Chipmunk, and Gray and California Ground Squirrels. Less often seen, but dwelling in the park as well are Black Bear, Bobcat, and Coyote.

For more information, write: Calaveras Big Trees State Park, P.O. Box 120, Arnold, CA 95223, or call (209) 765-2334.

SH 4 runs through a corner of the park, and right past park headquarters. It's about 20 miles north of Sonora.

NEW HOGAN LAKE

This park lies so close to certain prime historic sites such as the town of Angel's Camp (famous for its jumping frogs) that proximity alone would ensure its appeal. But, aside from location, New Hogan Lake has all these attractions: 50 miles of enticing shoreline, year-round fishing, a nature trail, camping and picnicking on the scenic north shore, an equestrian trail that leads toward Whiskey Creek, a fine swimming area at Wrinkle Cove, a marina in the Fiddleneck Day Use area, slip rentals and boat storage, fishing supplies, and boat-in camping.

Common year-round birds are Great Blue Heron, Belted Kingfisher, California Quail, Acorn Woodpecker, Scrub Jay, Ring-billed Gull, Yellow-billed Magpie, White-breasted Nuthatch, and Rufous-sided and California Towhees.

Common at least half the year are Say's Phoebe, Western Grebe, Plain Titmouse, Black Phoebe, Bushtit, House Finch, Lesser Goldfinch, Lark Sparrow, Dark-eyed Junco, and White-crowned and Golden-crowned Sparrows. In spring look for Western Kingbird, Wood Duck, and a variety of swallows.

Less commonly sighted are Horned Lark, Pied-billed Grebe, Canada Goose (fall and winter), Cooper's Hawk, Sandhill Crane (spring and winter), California Gull, Lewis' Woodpecker (fall and winter), Greater Roadrunner, Great Horned Owl, Anna's Hummingbird, Forster's Tern (spring and fall), Band-tailed Pigeon, Bewick's and Rock Wrens, and Phainopepla. A bird list is available at the office.

Also seen here are Mule Deer, Striped Skunk, Raccoon, foxes, an occasional Bobcat, and a wide variety of rodents.

For other information about New Hogan Lake, write to Corps of Engineers, New Hogan Lake, P.O. Box 128, Valley Springs, CA 95252, or call (209) 772-1343.

From SH 26, just 0.5 mile south of its junction with SH 12 in lower Calaveras County, take Hogan Dam Road to the east. The road splits on entering the recreation area. Take the right hand fork to the dam and park headquarters.

YOSEMITE NATIONAL PARK

Except for the teeming crowds that come to eye them, the wonders of Yosemite National Park appear now much as they did when Professor William H. Brewer toured the area in the 1800's and penned his impressions of Tutucanula, the giant bluff known today as El Capitan.

"Now the valley begins to assume its characteristic and grand features," Brewer wrote, after describing his first view of the Bridal Veil Fall, which in those days was called Po-hono. "By the Ponono Fall rises the Cathedral Rock, a huge mass of granite nearly 4,000 feet high; while opposite is Tutucanula, a bluff of granite, rising from this plain perpendicularly 3,600 feet . . . It rises from the green valley to this enormous height without any talus at the foot. You cannot conceive the true sublimity of such a cliff . . ."

Now, as surely as in the days of Brewer, this area boasts some of the nation's lushest meadows, biggest trees, most spectacular geologic wonders, and stunning variations in habitat.

Elevations at Yosemite range from 2,000 feet above sea level to more than 13,000 feet. The three features for which it is best known (or perhaps we should call them complexes of features, since each one is so extensively represented) are its alpine wilderness, its groves of Giant Sequoias, and the beautiful Yosemite Valley. The 200 miles of roads within the parkland give access to all of these features and their separate wonders by auto or shuttle bus.

Special points of interest in Yosemite include Tuolumne Meadows and the High Country, Glacier Point, the Giant Sequoia Groves, the famous old Wawona Hotel built way back in 1875 and still in operation today, the excellent Valley Visitor Center, the Indian Cultural Museum and Indian Village, the Happy Isles Nature Center, self-guided tours, and wonderful trails.

The Valley Visitor Center offers an orientation slide program, a vast

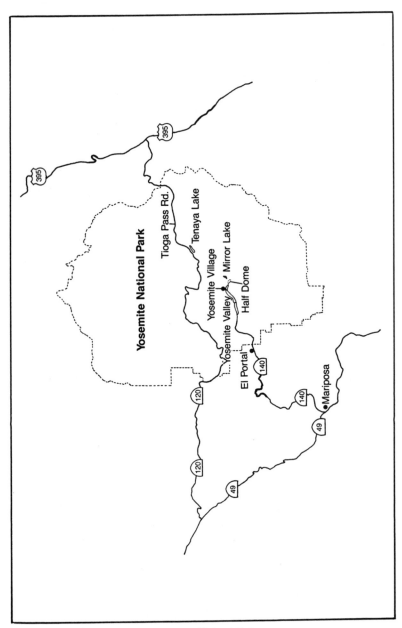

Yosemite National Park

assortment of publications; interpretive displays; descriptive brochures with good park maps; and a bird list, *Field Checklist of the Birds of Yosemite National Park.*

The park boasts several campgrounds (often good birding locales in their own right) at various locations throughout, one in the valley, and others at Wawona and Hodgdon Mead. All campgrounds have restrooms and toilets. Restaurants, stores, and lodging are available in Yosemite Valley, Wawona, El Portal, Tuolumne Meadows, and White Wolf. Reservations are highly recommended, and should be made well in advance.

Special birds of Yosemite National Park include the Great Gray Owl, Spotted Owl, Bald Eagle, Northern Goshawk, Western Tanager, and the Black-backed Woodpecker.

Many raptors are known breeders in the area. Here are Flammulated, Western Screech, Great Horned, Northern Pygmy, Spotted, Great Gray, Long-eared and Northern Saw-whet Owls, as well as Sharp-shinned and Cooper's Hawks, Northern Goshawk, Golden Eagle, and Peregrine and Prairie Falcons. Many woodpeckers nest here too: Acorn, Nuttall's, Downy, Hairy, White-headed, Black-backed, and Pileated. Other breeding species include Harlequin Duck, Common Merganser, Blue Grouse, Mountain Quail, Band-tailed Pigeon, Black and White-throated Swifts, Belted Kingfisher, American Dipper, Clark's Nutcracker, Hermit and Swainson's Thrushes, Black-headed Grosbeak, Lazuli Bunting, Green-tailed Towhee, House, Canyon, Bewick's, Rock and Winter Wrens, and Nashville, Yellow, Black-throated Gray, Hermit, MacGillivray's, and Wilson's Warblers.

Wildlife seen at Yosemite include bear, deer, Coyote, Golden Marmot, Porcupine, Raccoon, and a variety of rodents.

To reserve a campsite, write to Yosemite Park and Curry Company Reservations, 5410 East Home, Fresno, CA 93727, or call (209) 252-4848.

A major route to Yosemite is SH 140 from Mariposa. Check into the entrance station and plan your trip from there. This same road continues into Yosemite Valley with access to all the campgrounds, tourist facilities, and views of El Capitan, Half Dome, and the waterfalls.

Tenaya Creek and Mirror Lake. In the conifers that surround the beautifully reflecting Mirror Lake, or along the nearby Tenaya Creek, look for Pileated Woodpecker, Black Swift, Winter Wren, MacGillivray's Warbler, and American Dipper.

To reach this area, simply follow the general directions to Yosemite and continue to the very end of the road.

The Groves of Sequoias. Besides the usual forest birds like Brown Creeper and Golden-crowned Kinglet, look for Pileated and White-headed Woodpeckers while birding the cathedral-like depths of these famous groves.

SH 41 comes up from the south, through the town of Oakhurst, and provides direct access to the Mariposa Grove. SH 120 goes by the Tuolumne and Merced Groves.

The High Meadows. In the conifer-rimmed high meadows, which are scattered here and there in the Canadian Zone forests (reached via Glacier Point Road) keep an eye out for Calliope Hummingbird, Evening Grosbeak, Pine Siskin, Lincoln's Sparrow, Pine Grosbeak, Red Crossbill, Blue Grouse, and Hermit Warbler. Scour the borders of the meadows for the Great Gray Owl.

Take SH 120, pass the Tuolumne and Merced Groves, and proceed upward to Tuolumne Meadows.

Lake Tenaya. "We came on to Lake Tenaya," wrote that prodigious journal keeper, Professor Brewer, one day in June of 1850, "a most picturesque alpine lake, about a mile long and a half mile wide, of clear, cold, ice water, lying 8,250 feet above the sea. Its clear waters are very blue and very deep . . . Scattered pines are around the lake, or grow in the crevices of the granite. Above rise domes of granite, many of them naked, while patches of snow lie around on every side. Of course it freezes every night."

The fine stands of lodgepole pines that grow near the lake, as well as the white-bark pines yet higher up in the Hudsonian Zone forests serve almost as well as a printed checklist when it comes to revealing the birds you can expect to find in the Yosemite high country. These are all the mountain-dwelling species who feed on the needles and/or seeds of the pines. Here you're apt to sight Blue Grouse, Band-tailed Pigeon, White-headed and Black-backed Woodpeckers, Red-breasted Sapsucker, Mountain Chickadee, Red Crossbill, Rosy Finch, Northern Flicker, Evening and Pine Grosbeaks, Steller's Jay, Hermit Warbler, and Pygmy, Red-breasted, and White-breasted Nuthatches.

To reach Lake Tenaya, take SH 120 by the Tuolumne and Merced Groves and continue up the hill.

MARIPOSA

At an elevation of 2,000 feet, Mariposa is blessed with a climate that appeals to a large variety of Sierran birds, those who love the high country, those who hover in the foothills, those who favor creekside habitat, and those who roam back and forth. Birding is excellent right in town and also at the county fairgrounds just outside the city limits.

Species readily sighted on a short walk through the back streets or around the fairgrounds include Lazuli Bunting, Yellow-breasted Chat, Black Phoebe, Wrentit, Plain Titmouse, Bushtit, White-breasted Nuthatch, Bewick's Wren, and Western Bluebird.

Mariposa is at the junction of SH 140 and SH 49.

Ben Hur/White Rock Road Loop and Eastman Lake. If a longer outing is to your liking, consider this day trip. Drive down Old Highway to White Rock Road, turn on West Westfall and continue to Preston Road, then turn left on Ben Hur Road, and loop back to Mariposa. Or, instead of looping back directly, turn right on Ben Hur from Preston Road to the historic railroad town of Raymond and continue on to Eastman Lake.

Whether you take the short loop or go on to the lake, expect to see Phainopepla, Western Tanager, Greater Roadrunner, Wild Turkey, Anna's and Rufous Hummingbirds, Belted Kingfisher, Western Kingbird, Ash-throated Flycatcher, Black Phoebe, Horned Lark, Scrub Jay, Wrentit, Black-headed Grosbeak, California and Rufous-sided Towhees, Northern Oriole, and 5 species of swallow, as well as Lawrence, American, and Lesser Goldfinches. Here too are Red-breasted Sapsucker, Acorn, Lewis', and Downy Woodpeckers, and Chipping, Lark, Golden-crowned, White-crowned, and Savannah Sparrows.

Eastman Lake sightings include Bald and Golden Eagles, Greater Roadrunner, Great Blue Heron, Great and Snowy Egrets, Western and Pied-billed Grebes, Cinnamon Teal, Ruddy Duck, Great Horned Owl, American Wigeon, and Say's Phoebe.

For more information about Eastman Lake, write: Senior Park Ranger Perry R. Crowley, P.O. Box 67, Raymond, CA 93653.

THE MONO BASIN

"A country of wonderful contrasts, hot deserts bordered by snow-laden mountains, cinders and ashes scattered on glacier-polished pavement, frost and fire working together in the making of beauty." This is how John Muir depicted this unique land, which to modern-day cowboy/poet, Ted Ellico, is "a place where the visitor leaves a small piece of his very soul." Any way it's described, this unusual country, cradled in its volcanic basin at the base of the towering High Sierra, is a wonderland.

This vicinity has several worthwhile birding locales, among them Lundy Lake, Lee Vining Canyon, Mono Lake County Park, and, most importantly, of course, that most extraordinary body of water, Mono Lake.

Mono is an Indian word meaning flies. This is a most fitting name, for it's the brine flies, together with the brine shrimp, here in such incredible numbers (4,000 flies in a square foot, 55,000 shrimp in a cubic yard!) that attract the millions of migrating birds for which the area is known. Because the lake is far too saline and alkaline to support fish life, the birds have this cornucopia all to themselves.

Within the area, 295 species of birds have been identified. To five of these Mono Lake plays a particularly critical role. Each spring as many as 50,000 California Gulls come here to breed on the lake's islands. Small numbers of Wilson's Phalaropes breed and raise their young here, but this is a staging area for migration and in midsummer up to 90,000 have been counted at one time. Red-necked Phalaropes join the Wilson's a little later on, so that by late July these two species can total 150,000. In the early autumn, staggering numbers of Eared Grebes (as many as 800,000) use Mono Lake as a staging area for their migration; and finally, the tiny Snowy Plover breeds on the glaring alkaline flats.

But Mono Lake is in trouble, and has been for several years, because of the diversion of water from its tributary streams to the City of Los Angeles. To quote from *Mono Lake, Endangered Oasis*, a position paper of the Mono Lake Committee: "Between 1941 and 1981, the lake dropped 45 vertical feet. Its volume decreased by half and its salinity doubled. At least 16,000 acres of alkali-crusted lake bottom were laid bare to the sun and the wind." The Mono Lake Committee heads up the efforts to save the lake. (If you'd like to help, write Mono Lake Committee, P.O. Box 29, Lee Vining, CA 93541.) The committee also runs the Mono Lake Visitor Center in Lee Vining, which has an excellent book store, a "rare bird alert" chalkboard, and a knowledgeable staff. The center is open 9 a.m. to 5 p.m. during the off season, and 9 a.m. to 9 p.m. during the summer.

Red-necked Phalarope (winter plumage)

In addition to those already mentioned, the migrating birds sighted at Mono Lake include Common Loon, Pied-billed Grebe, Canada Goose, Green-winged and Cinnamon Teal, Mallard, Northern Pintail, Northern Shoveler, Gadwall, Ring-necked Duck, Bufflehead, Common Merganser, and Ruddy Duck. Shorebirds commonly seen are Semipalmated Plover, American Avocet, Common Snipe, 3 species of sandpiper, and Short-billed and Long-billed Dowitchers.

Besides this extraordinary lake, the Mono Basin area has much to offer the birder.

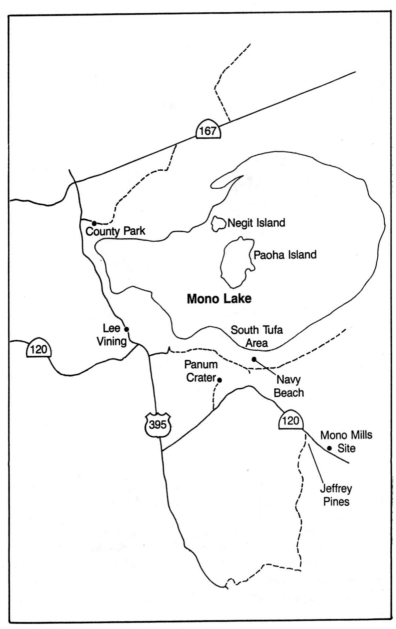

Mono Lake

Mono Lake is at the eastern base of the Sierra, directly east from Yosemite National Park, over Tioga Pass. Lee Vining, the nearest town, is on US 395, some 140 miles south of Reno, Nevada, and 95 miles east of Stockton.

South Tufa Area. The South Tufa Area, off SH 120 on the south shore of Mono Lake, is recognized as the best place around the entire lake to see the strange and spectacular formations known as tufa. These tufa towers are formed when deposits of white limestone build up around a fresh water spring welling up from the bottom of the lake, and become exposed as the water level of the lake drops.

As interesting to see as the tufa are the many birds for which this area is known: species that run the gamut from a pair of nesting Osprey, here in 1988, to the thousands upon thousands of gulls that breed here.

South Tufa and nearby Navy Beach are also excellent places to observe water birds and shorebirds, as well as birds of the surrounding scrubland. There are separate parking areas. After you've turned off SH 120, the road to the left leads to South Tufa, the one to the right to Navy Beach, but a short walk along the shore between the two yields some good views, and some excellent birding. Simons Springs, five miles further to the east, is also a prime spot. It's an easy but long walk along the shore, with good birding all the way.

Facilities at South Tufa include a self-guided nature trail, interpretive exhibits, toilets, and picnic tables. Back a bit to the west, with a separate entrance from the highway, is Panum Crater, which also has hiking trails and interpretive exhibits.

In the scrubland of the area you'll find Green-tailed Towhee, Brewer's and Sage Sparrows, Sage Thrasher, Black-billed Magpie, Violet-green Swallow, Rock Wren, Say's Phoebe, and Loggerhead Shrike.

There are usually some ponds just behind the shoreline that offer good sightings of Marbled Godwit, Western and Spotted Sandpipers, Willet, American Avocet, Black-necked Stilt, and Wilson's Phalarope.

From US 395 south of Lee Vining, take SH 120 to the east about 5 miles to the South Tufa Area entrance.

Jeffrey Pines/SH 120. As you come back out to SH 120 from the South Tufa Area, you're facing the Mono Craters, a series of volcanic craters that constitute the youngest mountain range in North America. Panum Crater, the northernmost of these, erupted only 600 years ago. It's across the highway from the main range and has its own self-guided tour and hiking trails.

At the base of these craters you'll find forests of Jeffrey Pine that offer excellent birding. As these forests extend lakeward they interface with the sagebrush and bitterbrush scrub habitat of the valley floor to produce another entirely different environment.

Heading east from the Tufa Reserve, the first place where the Jeffrey pines come down to the highway is a "must stop" area for anyone birding the south end of Mono. Just pull off alongside the road and walk uphill on a little dirt road. Here Lewis' Woodpeckers breed and Pinyon Jays are often sighted. Then continue east on SH 120 for 1.5 miles to the site of Mono Mills. There's a historical marker there, so you can't miss it. Walk 0.25 mile to the left and you'll see a water trough that a lot of birds visit. The particular appeal here is the Red Crossbill, plentiful some years, absent in others, depending on the seed crop.

Other birds seen in the vicinity are Western Tanager, Hairy Woodpecker, Townsend's Solitaire, Mountain Chickadee, and Western Wood-Pewee, as well as Pygmy, White-breasted and Red-breasted Nuthatches. In the scrub you may find nesting Blue-gray Gnatcatcher, Green-tailed Towhee, and Gray Flycatcher. And up above, you'll frequently see Golden Eagles soaring around the edge of the cliffs. Bald Eagles have been sighted here too.

Mono Lake County Park/Cemetery Road. About 5 miles north of Lee Vining on US 395, is Mono Lake County Park, a fine recreation area with restroom, playground, and picnic tables. Here too is a boardwalk that will lead you out among the tufa towers, and provide excellent views of the lake and shoreline. There's also grassland, scrub, and some excellent riparian habitat — willows, thickets, marshes, and wet meadows attractive to vagrants.

After birding the area around the park, you can continue on Cemetery Road through a lot of brush and across a couple of creeks to DeChambeau Ponds. Don't take the turn-off to Black Point, but continue on the main road until it makes a sharp left turn just past an abandoned ranch (on the left side) with some tall trees. Instead of making the sharp left, go straight and then bear right. You'll see a little shack and the ponds. There's plenty of good birding here, but the main attraction is a large colony of Yellow-headed Blackbirds. This is also a good vantage point for scoping the nesting island.

This is an excellent place to observe the special birds of Mono: California Gulls, and Wilson's and Red-necked Phalaropes will all be here in July; the Eared Grebes in the fall.

The riparian habitat may produce Red-winged Blackbird, Common Yellowthroat, Snowy Egret, and Green-backed Heron, and be sure to scan the willow groves for MacGillivray's Warbler. DeChambeau Ponds are a good place to see Yellow-headed Blackbird, Gadwall, Cinnamon Teal, Green-winged Teal, Northern Shoveler, Solitary Sandpiper, herons, egrets, rails, and — with great luck — perhaps a White-faced Ibis.

Lundy Lake/Lee Vining Canyon. The Sierras rise up quickly and dramatically from Mono Basin into a world of steep canyons, tumbling creeks, high meadows, and alpine lakes. Mount Warren, with an elevation of 12,327 feet, is only 4 miles in a straight line from Mono Lake, which is at about 6,400 feet, depending on how much water the city of Los Angeles is drawing at any given time.

There's a series of National Forest Service campgrounds in Lee Vining Canyon off Tioga Pass Road (SH 120) and a Ranger Station about a mile from US 395. About 2.5 miles further up there's a sign pointing left to Big Bend Campground. The four camps — Lower Lee Vining, Upper Lee Vining, Aspen, and Big Bend — are all on Lee Vining Creek, and all offer excellent montane birding. Before you reach Aspen Campground, you'll find a big meadow with willows in the middle which may be the only spot in the Mono Basin area where Willow Flycatchers are seen.

Lundy Lake is about 5 miles up Lundy Canyon from US 395, and is fairly heavily used in the summertime. You can bird the lower canyon, and scan the lake on the way by, but the most exciting birding is generally higher up. You can park at the resort on the west end of the lake, and then walk up the dirt road from that point until you reach a beaver pond (the first open pond you'll see), a flooded-out area where the birding is sometimes excellent.

Be sure to check all area ponds and streams for American Dipper and Belted Kingfisher as well as breeding Green-winged Teal. Look for Dusky Flycatcher, Rosy and Cassin's Finches, Western Wood-Pewee, Townsend's Solitaire, Clark's Nutcracker, Blue Grouse, Mountain Quail, and, in season, nesting Mountain Bluebird. Scan the chaparral for Green-tailed Towhee, Fox Sparrow, and Hermit Thrush. You may sight Great Horned, Flammulated, and Northern Pygmy Owls, and Yellow, Yellow-rumped, and Mac-

Northern Flickers nest in the abandoned buildings in the ghost town of Bodie.

Gillivray's Warblers.

To get to Lundy Lake, go north on US 395 from Lee Vining for 7 miles, and turn left on Lundy Lake Road.

Bodie

Today, in the historic old ghost town of Bodie, Sage Grouse strut the streets where once gunfighters strode. No longer a haven for rascals and scamps, this is still a most unusual town, a great place for hunting ghosts as well as for birding.

Besides the Sage Grouse, which is seen and heard readily in July, the most interesting species of Bodie are Golden Eagle, Common Nighthawk, Common Poorwill, Loggerhead Shrike, Mountain Bluebird, and Black-billed Magpie, as well as Great Horned and Burrowing Owls. Some very common species, which wouldn't rate mention otherwise, offer such fine opportunities for close up viewing and behavior observation that they can't be ignored. These include the Northern Flickers nesting in holes under the eaves of a ramshackle hotel, and the many swallows whose domiciles plaster the walls (both inside and out) of so many of Bodie's deserted houses.

From US 395, 7 miles south of Bridgeport, turn east on Bodie Road. This is a paved road, and it's 13 miles to the town.

From Highway 167 north of Mono Lake, take unpaved Cottonwood Canyon Road north 11 miles to Bodie.

Appendix 1
A Check List of Northern California Birds

 This appendix contains information about species sighted in northern California rather than the entire state and has been drawn from many sources, both written and verbal. These include local check lists, ornithological field lists, and Christmas bird counts, as well as the reports of area biologists, park rangers, and Audubon Society members from literally every nook and cranny in northern California.

This list names 517 species sighted in northern California, one of which is extirpated, plus four species under review by the Western Field Ornithologists California Bird Records Committee, for a total of 521 species.

To clarify the status of birds sighted in northern California, the following symbols are used:

(C)	Common to abundant in appropriate habitat, at appropriate season
(En)	Endangered species in California. Status determined by State of California Resources Agency, Department of Fish and Game
(E)	Extirpated
(X)	Extinct
(FC)	Fairly Common
(I)	Introduced species
(IR)	Irregular
(L)	Local, or very local in distribution
(LC)	Locally common
(OC)	Occasionally seen in large numbers, as during migration, etc.
(RR)	Rare

(Th)   Threatened species in California. Status determined by the State
         of Resources Agency, Department of Fish and Game
(Un)   Uncommon to rare
(V)   Stragglers, vagrants, casual visitors
(VV)   Rarest of vagrants. Very few verified sightings over a period of years
(S)   Sensitive species. Status determined by the U.S. Fish and Wildlife
         Service, Portland, Oregon
*   Known to nest in northern California. Includes species nesting off-
         shore, sometimes only very locally.

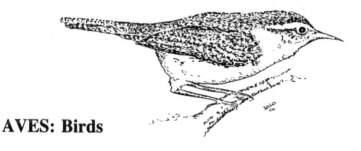

AVES: Birds

GAVIIFORMES: Loons
GAVIIDAE: Loons
   Red-throated Loon (C)
      Gavia stellata
   Arctic/Pacific Loon (C)
      G. arctica/pacifica
   Common Loon* (C, S)
      G. immer
   Yellow-billed Loon (V)
      G. adamsii

PODICIPEDIFORMES: Grebes
PODICIPEDIDAE: Grebes
   Pied-billed Grebe* (FC)
      Podilymbus podiceps
   Horned Grebe (C)
      Podiceps auritus

   Eared Grebe* (C)
      P. nigricollis
   Red-necked Grebe (Un)
      P. grisegena
   Western Grebe* (LC)
      Aechmophorus occidentalis
   Clark's Grebe
      A. clarkii

PROCELLARIIFORMES: Tube-nosed Swimmers
DIOMEDEIDAE: Albatrosses
   Black-footed Albatross
      Diomedea nigripes
   Laysan Albatross (Un)
      D. immutabilis

Short-tailed Albatross (VV)
  D. albatrus
PROCELLARIDAE:
Shearwaters, Petrels
  Northern Fulmar (OC)
    Fulmarus glacialis
  Streaked Shearwater (VV)
    Calonectris leucomelas
  Sooty Shearwater (C)
    Puffinus griseus
  Short-tailed Shearwater (OC)
    P. tenuirostris
  Flesh-footed Shearwater (Un)
    P. carneipes
  Pink-footed Shearwater (C)
    P. creatopus
  Buller's Shearwater (L)
    P. bulleri
  Greater Shearwater (VV)
    P. gravis
  Black-vented Shearwater (OC)
    P. opisthomelas
  Solander's Petrel (VV)
    Pterodroma solandri
  Mottled Petrel (VV)
    P. inexpectata
  Cook's Petrel (VV)
    P. cookii
HYDROBATIDAE:
Storm-Petrels
  Leach's Storm-Petrel* (Un, LC)
    Oceanodroma leucorhoa
  Black Storm-Petrel (Un)
    O. melania
  Fork-tailed Storm-Petrel* (Un)
    O. furcata
  Least Storm-Petrel (OC, L)
    O. microsoma

Ashy Storm-Petrel* (L)
  O. homochroa
Wedge-rumped Storm-Petrel (VV)
  O. tethys
Wilson's Storm-Petrel (Un)
  O. oceanicus

PELECANIFORMES:
Totipalmate Swimmers
PHAETHONTIDAE:
Tropicbirds
  Red-tailed Tropicbird (VV)
    Phaethon rubricauda
  Red-billed Tropicbird (V)
    P. aethereus
SULIDAE: Boobies and Gannets
  Blue-footed Booby (V)
    Sula nebouxii
  Red-footed Booby (V)
    S. sula
  Brown Booby (VV)
    S. leucogaster
PELECANIDAE: Pelicans
  American White Pelican* (LC)
    Pelecanus erythrorhynchos
  Brown Pelican* (LC, En)
    P. occidentalis
PHALACROCORACIDAE:
Cormorants
  Double-crested Cormorant* (C)
    Phalacrocorax auritus
  Brandt's Cormorant* (Un)
    P. penicillatus
  Pelagic Cormorant* (L)
    P. pelagicus
FREGATIDAE: Frigatebirds
  Magnificent Frigatebird (IR, Un)
    Fregata magnificens

CICONIIFORMES:
Herons, Ibises, and Storks
ARDEIDAE: Bitterns and Herons
American Bittern*
Botaurus lentiginosus
Least Bittern* (Un)
Ixobrychus exilis
Great Blue Heron* (C)
Ardea herodias
Great Egret* (C)
Casmerodius albus
Snowy Egret* (C)
Egretta thula
Little Blue Heron (Un)
E. caerulea
Tricolored Heron (VV)
E. tricolor
Reddish Egret (VV)
E. rufescens
Cattle Egret*
Bubulcus ibis
Green-backed Heron*
Butorides striatus
Black-crowned Night-Heron*
Nycticorax nycticorax
Yellow-crowned
Night-Heron (VV)
N. violaceus

THRESKIORNITHIDAE:
Ibises and Spoonbills
White Ibis (VV)
Eudocimus albus
White-faced Ibis* (Un)
Plegadis chihi

CICONIIDAE: Storks
Wood Stork (V)
Mycteria americana

ANSERIFORMES:
Swans, Geese, and Ducks
ANATIDAE: Swans, Geese, and
Ducks
Fulvous Whistling-Duck (RR)
Dendrocygna bicolor
Trumpeter Swan (IR, R)
Cygnus buccinator
Tundra Swan (L)
C. columbianus
Greater White-fronted Goose
Anser albifrons
Snow Goose* (IR)
Chen caerulescens
Ross' Goose (IR)
C. rossii
Emperor Goose (V)
C. canagica
Brant
Branta bernicla
Canada Goose*
B. canadensis
Wood Duck* (Un)
Aix sponsa
Green-winged Teal* (FC)
Anas crecca
Mallard* (FC)
A. platyrhynchos
American Black Duck (VV)
A. rubripes
Northern Pintail* (C)
A. acuta
Blue-winged Teal* (Un)
A. discors
Baikal Teal (V)
A. formosa
Garganey (VV)
A. querquedula

Cinnamon Teal* (C)
  A. cyanoptera
Northern Shoveler* (C)
  A. clypeata
Gadwall* (FC)
  A. strepera
Eurasian Wigeon (Un)
  A. penelope
American Wigeon* (C)
  A. americana
Canvasback* (C)
  Aythya valisineria
Redhead* (Un, LC)
  A. americana
Ring-necked Duck* (FC)
  A. collaris
Tufted Duck (V)
  A. fuligula
Greater Scaup (C)
  A. marila
Lesser Scaup* (C)
  A. affinis
King Eider (V)
  Somateria spectabilis
Steller's Eider (V)
  Polysticta stelleri
Harlequin Duck* (Un)
  Histrionicus histrionicus
Oldsquaw (Un)
  Clangula hyemalis
Black Scoter (Un)
  Melanitta nigra
Surf Scoter (C)
  M. perspicillata
White-winged Scoter* (LC)
  M. fusca
Common Goldeneye (FC)
  Bucephala clangula

Barrow's Goldeneye* (Un, L)
  B. islandica
Bufflehead* (C)
  B. albeola
Hooded Merganser* (Un)
  Lophodytes cucullatus
Common Merganser* (C)
  Mergus merganser
Red-breasted Merganser (C)
  M. serrator
Ruddy Duck* (C)
  Oxyura jamaicensis
Smew (VV)
  Mergellus albellus

FALCONIFORMES:
Diurnal Birds of Prey
CATHARTIDAE:
American Vultures
  Turkey Vulture* (C)
    Cathartes aura
  California Condor* (E)
    Gymnogyps californianus
ACCIPITRIDAE:
Kites, Hawks, and Eagles
  Black-shouldered Kite* (C)
    Elanus caeruleus
  Mississippi Kite (V)
    Ictinia mississippiensis
  Bald Eagle* (Un)
    Haliaeetus leucocephalus
  Northern Harrier* (C)
    Circus cyaneus
  Cooper's Hawk*
    Accipiter cooperii
  Northern Goshawk* (Un)
    A. gentilis

Sharp-shinned Hawk* (FC)
  A. striatus
Red-shouldered Hawk* (FC)
  Buteo lineatus
Rough-legged hawk (UN)
  B. lagopus
Broad-winged Hawk (IR)
  B. platypterus
Swainson's Hawk* (OC)
  B. swainsoni
Red-tailed Hawk* (C)
  B. jamaicensis
Ferruginous Hawk* (Un)
  B. regalis
Golden Eagle*
  Aquila chrysaetos
Osprey*
  Pandion haliaetus
FALCONIDAE:
Caracaras and Falcons
  Crested Caracara (VV,
  Under review)
    Polyborus plancus
  American Kestrel* (C)
    Falco sparverius
  Merlin* (Un)
    F. columbarius
  Peregrine Falcon* (LC, En)
    F. peregrinus
  Prairie Falcon* (Un)
    F. mexicanus
  Gyrfalcon (VV)
    F. rusticolus

GALLIFORMES:
Gallinaceous Birds
PHASIANIDAE:
Grouse, Turkeys, and Quail

Blue Grouse* (L)
  Dendragapus obscurus
Ruffed Grouse* (Un)
  Bonasa umbellus
Sharp-tailed Grouse (X)
  Tympanuchus phasianellus
Sage Grouse* (Un)
  Centrocercus urophasianus
California Quail* (C)
  Callipepla californica
Mountain Quail*
  Oreortyx pictus
Ring-necked Pheasant* (I, C)
  Phasianus colchicus
Wild Turkey* (I, L)
  Meleagris gallopavo
Chukar* (I, Un, L)
  Alectoris chukar
White-tailed Ptarmigan* (I, L)
  Lagopus leucurus

GRUIFORMES:
Cranes and Rails
RALLIDAE:
Rails, Gallinules, and Coots
  Yellow Rail* (RR)
    Coturnicops noveboracensis
  Black Rail* (Un, Th)
    Laterallus jamaicensis
  Clapper Rail* (L)
    Rallus longirostris
  Virginia Rail* (FC)
    R. limicola
  Sora* (FC)
    Porzana carolina
  Common Moorhen* (Un)
    Gallinula chloropus

American Coot* (C)
Fulica americana
Purple Gallinule (VV)
Porphyrula martinica
GRUIDAE: Cranes
Sandhill Crane
Grus canadensis

CHARADRIIFORMES:
Shorebirds, Gulls, and Alcids
HAEMATOPODIDAE:
Oystercatchers
Black Oystercatcher* (FC)
Haematopus bachmani
RECURVIROSTRIDAE:
Stilts and Avocets
Black-necked Stilt* (C)
Himantopus mexicanus
American Avocet* (C)
Recurvirostra americana
CHARADRIIDAE: Plovers
Black-bellied Plover (C)
Pluvialis squatarola
Lesser Golden-Plover (Un)
P. dominica
Snowy Plover* (Un)
Charadrius alexandrinus
Semipalmated Plover (C)
C. semipalmatus
Killdeer* (C)
C. vociferus
Mountain Plover (Un)
C. montanus
Eurasian Dotterel (VV)
C. morinellus
Mongolian Plover (VV) (No
recent sightings)
C. mongolus

SCOLOPACIDAE:
Sandpipers and Phalaropes
Greater Yellowlegs (FC)
Tringa melanoleuca
Lesser Yellowlegs (Un, L)
T. flavipes
Spotted Redshank (VV)
T. erythropus
Solitary Sandpiper* (Un)
T. solitaria
Willet* (C)
Catoptrophorus semipalmatus
Spotted Sandpiper* (FC)
Actitis macularia
Wandering Tattler (Un)
Heteroscelus incanus
Whimbrel (FC)
Numenius phaeopus
Long-billed Curlew* (FC)
N. americanus
Hudsonian Godwit (VV)
Limosa haemastica
Bar-tailed Godwit (VV)
L. lapponica
Marbled Godwit (LC)
L. fedoa
Ruddy Turnstone (FC)
Arenaria interpres
Black Turnstone (LC)
A. melanocephala
Surfbird (C)
Aphriza virgata
Red Knot (Un)
Calidris canutus
Sanderling (C)
C. alba
Semipalmated Sandpiper (IR)
C. pusilla

Western Sandpiper (C)
C. mauri
Least Sandpiper (C)
C. minutilla
Rock Sandpiper (Un)
C. ptilocnemis
Sharp-tailed Sandpiper (IR)
C. acuminata
White-rumped Sandpiper (VV)
C. fuscicollis
Baird's Sandpiper (VV)
C. bairdii
Rufous-necked Stint (VV)
C. ruficollis
Little Stint (VV)
C. minuta
Pectoral Sandpiper (Un)
C. melanotos
Dunlin (C)
C. alpina
Curlew Sandpiper (VV)
C. ferruginea
Stilt Sandpiper (IR)
C. himantopus
Upland Sandpiper (VV)
Bartramia longicauda
Buff-breasted Sandpiper (V)
Tryngites subruficollis
Ruff (Un)
Philomachus pugnax
Short-billed Dowitcher (C)
Limnodromus griseus
Long-billed Dowitcher(C)
L. scolopaceus
Common Snipe* (FC)
Gallinago gallinago
European Jacksnipe (VV)
Lymnocryptes minimus

Wilson's Phalarope* (C)
Phalaropus tricolor
Red Phalarope (OC)
P. fulicaria
Red-necked Phalarope (C)
P. lobatus

LARIDAE: Skuas, Jaegers, Gulls, Terns, and Skimmers
South Polar Skua (IR)
Catharacta maccormicki
Pomarine Jaeger (V)
Stercorarius pomarinus
Parasitic Jaeger (Un)
S. parasiticus
Long-tailed Jaeger (V, IR)
S. longicaudus
Laughing Gull (V)
Larus atricilla
Franklin's Gull (Un)
L. pipixcan
Little Gull (VV)
L. minutus
Bonaparte's Gull (LC)
L. philadelphia
Heermann's Gull (C)
L. heermanni
Iceland Gull (VV)
L. glaucoides
Swallow-tailed Gull (Under Review)
Leucophaeus furcatus
Mew Gull (C)
Larus canus
Common Black-headed Gull (V)
L. ridibundus
Lesser Black-backed Gull (VV)
L. fuscus

Ring-billed Gull* (C)
  L. delawarensis
California Gull* (C)
  L. californicus
Herring Gull (FC)
  L. argentatus
Thayer's Gull
  L. thayeri
Western Gull* (C)
  L. occidentalis
Glaucous Gull (Un)
  L. hyperboreus
Glaucous-winged Gull (C)
  L. glaucescens
Black-legged Kittiwake (FC)
  Rissa tridactyla
Sabine's Gull (Un, IR)
  Xema sabini
Black Tern* (RR)
  Chlidonias niger
Arctic Tern (IR)
  Sterna paradisaea
Caspian Tern* (LC)
  S. caspia
Royal Tern (Un, IR)
  S. maxima
Elegant Tern (IR)
  S. elegans
Common Tern (IR)
  S. hirundo
Forster's Tern* (C)
  S. forsteri
Least Tern* (RR)
  S. antillarum
Black Skimmer (V)
  Rynchops niger
ALCIDAE: Auks and Relatives
  Common Murre* (C)
    Uria aalge

Thick-billed Murre (V, IR)
  U. lomvia
Pigeon Guillemot* (L)
  Cepphus columba
Marbled Murrelet* (L)
  Brachyramphus marmoratus
Xantus' Murrelet (RR, IR)
  Synthliboramphus hypoleucus
Craveri's Murrelet (Un, VL)
  S. craveri
Ancient Murrelet (OC, L)
  S. antiquus
Least Auklet (VV)
  Aethia pusilla
Crested Auklet (VV)
  A. cristatella
Cassin's Auklet* (L)
  Ptychoramphus aleuticus
Parakeet Auklet (VV)
  Cyclorrhynchus psittacula
Rhinoceros Auklet* (C)
  Cerorhinca monocerata
Tufted Puffin* (Un)
  Fratercula cirrhata
Horned Puffin (RR, IR)
  F. corniculata

COLUMBIFORMES:
Pigeons and Doves
COLUMBIDAE: Pigeons and Doves
  Band-tailed Pigeon* (IR)
    Columba fasciata
  Rock Dove* (I, C)
    C. livia
  White-winged Dove (Un)
    Zenaida asiatica
  Mourning Dove* (C)
    Z. macroura

Common Ground-Dove (V)
Columbina passerina

CUCULIFORMES:
Cuckoos and Anis
CUCULIDAE: Cuckoos and Anis
  Black-billed Cuckoo (VV)
    Coccyzus erythropthalmus
  Yellow-billed Cuckoo*
  (Un, L, En)
    C. americanus
  Greater Roadrunner (L)
    Geococcyx californianus

STRIGIFORMES: Owls
TYTONIDAE: Barn Owls
  Barn Owl* (C)
    Tyto alba
STRIGIDAE: Typical Owls
  Flammulated Owl* (L)
    Otus flammeolus
  Western Screech-Owl* (FC)
    O. kennicottii
  Great Horned Owl* (C)
    Bubo virginianus
  Snowy Owl (V)
    Nyctea scandiaca
  Northern Pygmy-Owl* (FC)
    Glaucidium gnoma
  Elf Owl (Un, VL, En)
    Micrathene whitneyi
  Burrowing Owl* (FC)
    Athene cunicularia
  Spotted Owl* (Un, S)
    Strix occidentalis
  Great Gray Owl* (RR, L, En)
    S. nebulosa
  Barred Owl (RR)
    S. varia

Long-eared Owl* (Un, IR)
    Asio otus
  Short-eared Owl* (IR)
    A. flammeus
  Northern Saw-whet Owl* (OC)
    Aegolius acadicus

CAPRIMULGIFORMES:
Goatsuckers
CAPRIMULGIDAE:
Goatsuckers
  Lesser Nighthawk* (Un)
    Chordeiles acutipennis
  Common Nighthawk* (C)
    C. minor
  Whip-poor-will (VV)
    Caprimulgus vociferus
  Chuck-will's-widow (RR)
    C. carolipensis
  Common Poorwill* (C)
    Phalaenoptilus nuttallii

APODIFORMES:
Swifts and Hummingbirds
APODIDAE: Swifts
  Black Swift* (Un)
    Cypseloides niger
  Chimney Swift* (Un)
    Chaetura pelagica
  Vaux's Swift* (FC)
    C. vauxi
  White-throated Swift* (C)
    Aeronautes saxatalis
  White-collared Swift (VV)
    Streptoprocne zonaris
TROCHILIDAE: Hummingbirds
  Broad-billed Hummingbird (V)
    Cynanthus latirostris

Black-chinned
Hummingbird* (Un)
 Archilochis alexandri
Anna's Hummingbird* (C)
 Calypte anna
Costa's Hummingbird* (Un)
 C. costae
Calliope Hummingbird* (Un)
 Stellula calliope
Broad-tailed Hummingbird (V)
 Selasphorus platycercus
Rufous Hummingbird* (FC)
 S. rufus
Allen's Hummingbird* (C)
 S. sasin

CORACIIFORMES: Kingfishers
ALCEDINIDAE: Kingfishers
Belted Kingfisher* (C)
 Ceryle alcyon

PICIFORMES: Woodpeckers
PICIDAE: Woodpeckers
Lewis' Woodpecker* (L)
 Melanerpes lewis
Red-headed Woodpecker (VV)
 M. erythrocephalus
Acorn Woodpecker* (C)
 M. formicivorus
Yellow-bellied Sapsucker*
(Un, IR)
 Sphyrapicus varius
Red-breasted Sapsucker*
 S. ruber
Red-naped Sapsucker (Un)
 S. nuchalis
Williamson's Sapsucker*
 S. thyroideus

Three-toed Woodpecker (RR)
 Picoides tridctylus
Black-backed Woodpecker*
(Un, L)
 P. arcticus
Nuttall's Woodpecker* (C)
 P. nuttallii
Downy Woodpecker* (C)
 P. pubescens
White-headed Woodpecker*
 P. albolarvatus
Hairy Woodpecker* (C)
 P. villosus
Northern Flicker* (C)
 Colaptes auratus
Pileated Woodpecker* (Un)
 Dryocopus pileatus

PASSERIFORMES:
Passerine Birds
TYRANNIDAE: Tyrant Flycatchers
Olive-sided Flycatcher* (FC)
 Contopus borealis
Greater Pewee (VV)
 C. pertinax
Eastern Wood-Pewee (VV)
 C. virens
Western Wood-Pewee* (C, L)
 C. sordidulus
Brown-crested Flycatcher (VV)
 Myiarchus tyrannulus
Ash-throated Flycatcher* (LC)
 M. cinerascens
Dusky-capped Flycatcher (VV)
 M. tuberculifer
Great Crested Flycatcher (VV)
 M. crinitus

Yellow-bellied Flycatcher (VV)
  Empidonax flaviventris
Hammond's Flycatcher* (LC)
  E. hammondii
Dusky Flycatcher* (Un)
  E. oberholseri
Gray Flycatcher* (IR)
  E. wrightii
Pacific Slope Flycatcher* (C)
  E. difficilis
Willow Flycatcher* (Un)
  E. traillii
Least Flycatcher (IR, L)
  E. minimus
Black Phoebe* (C)
  Sayornis nigricans
Eastern Phoebe (Un)
  S. phoebe
Say's Phoebe* (FC)
  S. saya
Vermilion Flycatcher (V)
  Pyrocephalus rubinus
Tropical Kingbird (V, IR)
  Tyrannus melancholicus
Cassin's Kingbird* (IR, Un)
  T. vociferans
Thick-billed Kingbird (VV)
  T. crassirostris
Western Kingbird* (C)
  T. verticalis
Eastern Kingbird (Un)
  T. tyrannus
Scissor-tailed Flycatcher (VV)
  T. forficatus
ALAUDIDAE: Larks
Horned Lark* (C)
  Eremophila alpestris
Eurasian Skylark (VV)
  Alauda arvensis

HIRUNDINIDAE: Swallows
Purple Martin* (Un)
  Progne subis
Tree Swallow* (C)
  Tachycineta bicolor
Violet-green Swallow* (C)
  T. thalassina
Northern Rough-winged
Swallow* (L)
  Stelgidopteryx serripennis
Bank Swallow* (L, Th)
  Riparia riparia
Cliff Swallow* (C)
  Hirundo pyrrhonota
Barn Swallow* (C)
  H. rustica

CORVIDAE: Jays, Crows, and
Magpies
Gray Jay* (L)
  Perisoreus canadensis
Steller's Jay* (C)
  Cyanocitta stelleri
Blue Jay (VV)
  C. cristata
Scrub Jay* (C)
  Aphelocoma coerulescens
Pinyon Jay* (L)
  Gymnorhinus cyanocephalus
Clark's Nutcracker* (L)
  Nucifraga columbiana
Black-billed Magpie* (C)
  Pica pica
Yellow-billed Magpie* (C, L)
  P. nuttallii
American Crow (C)
  Corvus brachyrhynchos
Common Raven* (FC)
  C. corax

PARIDAE: Titmice and Chickadees
   Black-capped Chickadee*
   (FC, L)
      Parus atricapillus
   Mountain Chickadee* (C)
      P. gambeli
   Chestnut-backed Chickadee* (C)
      P. rufescens
   Plain Titmouse* (C)
      P. inornatus
AEGITHALIDAE: Bushtits
   Bushtit* (C)
      Psaltriparus minimus
SITTIDAE: Nuthatches
   Red-breasted Nuthatch* (IR)
      Sitta canadensis
   White-breasted Nuthatch* (C)
      S. carolinensis
   Pygmy Nuthatch* (FC)
      S. pygmaea
CERTHIIDAE: Creepers
   Brown Creeper* (LC)
      Certhia americana
CINCLIDAE: Dippers
   American Dipper* (FC)
      Cinclus mexicanus
TROGLODYTIDAE: Wrens
   Cactus Wren (VV)
      Campylorhynchus
      brunneicapillus
   Rock Wren* (FC)
      Salpinctes obsoletus
   Canyon Wren* (L)
      Catherpes mexicanus
   Bewick's Wren* (C)
      Thryomanes bewickii

House Wren* (C)
   Troglodytes aedon
Winter Wren* (FC)
   T. troglodytes
Marsh Wren* (C)
   Cistothorus palustris
Sedge Wren (VV)
   C. platensis
MUSCICAPIDAE: Muscicapids
   Wrentit* (C)
      Chamaea fasciata
   Dusky Warbler (VV)
      Phylloscopus fuscatus
   Golden-crowned Kinglet* (C)
      Regulus satrapa
   Ruby-crowned Kinglet* (C)
      R. calendula
   Blue-gray Gnatcatcher* (Un)
      Polioptila caerulea
   Western Bluebird* (C)
      Sialia mexicana
   Mountain Bluebird* (LC)
      S. currucoides
   Townsend's Solitaire* (OC, L)
      Myadestes townsendi
   Veery (VV)
      Catharus fuscescens
   Gray-cheeked Thrush (VV)
      C. minimus
   Swainson's Thrush* (C)
      C. ustulatus
   Hermit Thrush* (C)
      C. guttatus
   Wood Thrush (V)
      Hylocichla mustelina
   American Robin* (C)
      T. migratorius

Varied Thrush* (C, IR)
Ixoreus naevius
Northern Wheatear (VV)
Oenanthe oenanthe
LANIIDAE: Shrikes
Northern Shrike (Un)
Lanius excubitor
Loggerhead Shrike* (C, S)
L. ludovicianus
Brown Shrike (VV)
L. cristatus
MIMIDAE:
Mockingbirds and Thrashers
Gray Catbird (V)
Dumetella carolinensis
Northern Mockingbird* (C)
Mimus polyglottos
Sage Thrasher* (IR)
Oreoscoptes montanus
Brown Thrasher (V)
Toxostoma rufum
Bendire's Thrasher (V)
T. bendirei
California Thrasher* (C)
T. redivivum
Le Conte's Thrasher (RR)
T. lecontei
MOTACILLIDAE:
Pipits and Wagtails
Water Pipit* (C)
Anthus spinoletta
Sprague's Pipit (VV)
A. spragueii
Red-throated Pipit (V)
A. cervinus
Yellow Wagtail (VV)
Motacilla flava

Black-backed Wagtail (VV)
M. lugens
White Wagtail (V)
M. alba
BOMBYCILLIDAE: Waxwings
Bohemian Waxwing (IR, OC)
Bombycilla garrulus
Cedar Waxwing* (C)
B. cedrorum
PTILOGONATIDAE:
Silky Flycatchers
Phainopepla* (V)
Phainopepla nitens
STURNIDAE: Starlings
European Starling* (I, C)
Sturnus vulgaris
VIREONIDAE: Vireos
White-eyed Vireo (V)
Vireo griseus
Bell's Vireo* (V)
V. bellii
Solitary Vireo* (FC, IR)
V. solitarius
Hutton's Vireo* (FC)
V. huttoni
Warbling Vireo* (C)
V. gilvus
Philadelphia Vireo (V)
V. philadelphicus
Red-eyed Vireo (Un)
V. olivaceus
Yellow-throated Vireo (V)
V. flavifrons
EMBERIZIDAE: Emberizids
Blue-winged Warbler (VV)
Vermivora pinus

Golden-winged Warbler (V)
V. chrysoptera
Tennessee Warbler (Un)
V. peregrina
Orange-crowned Warbler* (C)
V. celata
Nashville Warbler* (Un)
V. ruficapilla
Virginia's Warbler* (V)
V. virginiae
Lucy's Warbler (VV)
V. luciae
Northern Parula* (IR, Un)
Parula americana
Yellow Warbler* (C)
Dendroica petechia
Chestnut-sided Warbler (IR)
D. pensylvanica
Magnolia Warbler (VV)
D. magnolia
Cape May Warbler (VV)
D. tigrina
Black-throated Blue
Warbler (VV)
D. caerulescens
Black-throated Green
Warbler (VV)
D. virens
Yellow-rumped Warbler* (C)
D. coronata
Black-throated Gray
Warbler* (LC)
D. nigrescens
Townsend's Warbler* (LC)
D. townsendi
Hermit Warbler* (LC)
D. occidentalis
Golden-cheeked Warbler (VV)
D. chrysoparia

Blackburnian Warbler (V)
D. fusca
Yellow-throated Warbler (V)
D. dominica
Pine Warbler (VV)
D. pinus
Prairie Warbler (VV)
D. discolor
Palm Warbler (Un)
D. palmarum
Bay-breasted Warbler (VV))
D. castanea
Blackpoll Warbler (VV)
D. striata
Cerulean Warbler (V)
D. cerulea
Black-and-white Warbler (Un)
Mniotilta varia
American Redstart* (Un)
Setophaga ruticilla
Prothonotary Warbler (V)
Protonotaria citrea
Painted Redstart (V)
Myioborus pictus
Worm-eating Warbler (VV)
Helmitheros vermivorus
Ovenbird (Un)
Seiurus aurocapillus
Northern Waterthrush (Un, IR)
S. noveboracensis
Kentucky Warbler (VV)
Oporornis formosus
Connecticut Warbler (V)
O. agilis
Mourning Warbler (V)
O. philadelphia
MacGillivray's Warbler* (C)
O. tolmiei

Common Yellowthroat* (C)
Geothlypis trichas
Yellow-breasted Chat* (L)
Icteria virens
Hooded Warbler (Un)
Wilsonia citrina
Wilson's Warbler* (C)
W. pusilla
Canada Warbler (V)
W. canadensis
Northern Cardinal (V)
Cardinalis cardinalis
Rose-breasted Grosbeak (Un)
Pheucticus ludovicianus
Black-headed Grosbeak* (C)
P. melanocephalus
Blue Grosbeak* (Un)
Guiraca caerulea
Lazuli Bunting* (LC)
Passerina amoena
Indigo Bunting* (Un)
P. cyanea
Painted Bunting (V)
P. ciris
Dickcissel (V)
Spiza americana
Lark Bunting (V, IR)
Calamospiza melanocorys
Green-tailed Towhee* (IR)
Pipilo chlorurus
Rufous-sided Towhee* (C)
P. erythrophthalmus
California Towhee* (C)
P. fuscus
Cassin's Sparrow (V)
Aimophila cassinii
Rufous-crowned Sparrow* (FC)
A. ruficeps

American Tree Sparrow (Un)
Spizella arborea
Chipping Sparrow (C)
S. passerina
Clay-colored Sparrow (Un)
S. pallida
Brewer's Sparrow* (IR)
S. breweri
Field Sparrow (V)
S. pusilla
Black-chinned Sparrow* (Un)
S. atrogularis
Vesper Sparrow* (Un)
Pooecetes gramineus
Lark Sparrow* (C)
Chondestes grammacus
Black-throated Sparrow* (Un)
Amphispiza bilineata
Sage Sparrow* (FC)
A. belli
Savannah Sparrow* (C)
Passerculus sandwichensis
Grasshopper Sparrow* (Un)
Ammodramus savannarum
Baird's Sparrow (VV)
A. bairdii
LeConte's Sparrow (V)
A. leconteii
Sharp-tailed Sparrow (L)
A. caudacutus
Fox Sparrow* (C)
Passerella iliaca
Song Sparrow* (C)
Melospiza melodia
Lincoln's Sparrow*
M. lincolnii
Swamp Sparrow (Un)
M. georgiana

White-throated Sparrow (Un)
  Zonotrichia albicollis
Golden-crowned Sparrow* (C)
  Z. atricapilla
White-crowned Sparrow* (C)
  Z. leucophrys
Harris' Sparrow (Un)
  Z. querula
Dark-eyed Junco* (C)
  Junco hyemalis
McCown's Longspur (Un)
  Calcarius mccownii
Lapland Longspur (Un)
  C. lapponicus
Chestnut-collared Longspur (Un)
  C. ornatus
Snow Bunting (V)
  Plectrophenax nivalis
Rustic Bunting (VV)
  Emberiza rustica
Bobolink (Un)
  Dolichonyx oryzivorus
Red-winged Blackbird* (C)
  Agelaius phoeniceus
Tricolored Blackbird* (LC)
  A. tricolor
Western Meadowlark* (C)
  Sturnella neglecta
Yellow-headed Blackbird* (LC)
  *Xanthocephalus
  xanthocephalus*
Rusty Blackbird (Un)
  Euphagus carolinus
Brewer's Blackbird* (C)
  E. cyanocephalus
Common Grackle (V)
  Quiscalus quiscula

Great-tailed Grackle (V, L)
  Q. mexicanus
Brown-headed Cowbird* (C)
  Molothrus ater
Orchard Oriole (Un)
  Icterus spurius
Hooded Oriole* (Un)
  I. cucullatus
Northern Oriole* (C)
  I. galbula
Scott's Oriole (V)
  I. parisorum
Scarlet Tanager (V)
  Piranga olivacea
Western Tanager* (C)
  P. ludoviciana
Summer Tanager (Un)
  P. rubra
Hepatic Tanager (V)
  P. flava
PASSERIDAE: Weavers
  House Sparrow* (I, C)
    Passer domesticus
FRINGILLIDAE: Finches
  Pine Grosbeak* (LC)
    Pinicola enucleator
  Purple Finch* (C)
    Carpodacus purpureus
  Cassin's Finch* (V)
    C. cassinii
  House Finch* (C)
    C. mexicanus
  Rosy Finch* (Un)
    Leucosticte arctoa
  Red Crossbill* (IR)
    Loxia curvirostra

Common Redpoll (V)
  Carduelis flammea
Pine Siskin* (C)
  C. pinus
Lesser Goldfinch* (C)
  C. psaltria
Lawrence's Goldfinch* (Un)
  C. lawrencei
American Goldfinch* (C)
  C. tristis

Evening Grosbeak* (L)
  Coccothraustes vespertinus
Oriental Greenfinch (VV) (Under Review)
  Carduelis sinica
Brambling (VV)
  Fringilla montifringilla

Appendix 2
Contacts for Birders

To Report Rare Bird Sightings

 To report rare or unusual species sighted while birding in the Modesto area, call (209) 571-0246; in the Monterey area, call (408) 449-6100; in the Sacramento area, call (916) 481-0118; in the San Francisco Bay area, call (415) 528-0288; in or near the Klamath Basin National Wildlife Refuges, call (916) 667-2231 or contact Ralph or Charlotte Opp at (503) 882-8488; in the Mono Basin area, call Melanie Findling of the Mono Lake Committee at (619) 647-6595.

For unusual sightings to be reported for consideration in the updating of local check lists or for other records: in Stanislaus County contact Harold M. Reeve, 1404 Bandera Lane, Modesto, CA 95355; in the Sacramento area, contact the Records Committee, C/O Dr. Jeri Langham, Department of Biological Sciences, California State University, Sacramento, CA; in the Lake Tahoe Basin, contact Lake Tahoe Audubon Society, P.O. Box 1105, South Lake Tahoe, CA 95705; in Del Norte, Humboldt, northern Mendocino, western Trinity, and western Siskiyou counties, contact Stanley W. Harris, Humboldt State University, Arcata, CA 95521; in Siskiyou County (overall), contact Mike Robbins, 308 Hillcrest Drive, Yreka, CA 96097, or call (916) 842-2801; in the Klamath Basin National Wildlife Refuges, call (916) 667-2231.

To gain or share pertinent information about birds and birding in the Yuba Pass and Sierra Valley area in the spring and summer months, serious birders may contact Jim Steele at the Sierra Nevada Field Campus, Star Route, Sattley, CA 96124, or call (916) 862-1230. In fall or winter months, call Jim at (415) 338-1571 or (415) 759-0970.

To report rare birds or other unusual wildlife sighted in the Eldorado National Forest (and in so doing contribute to the compilation of a wildlife atlas of the area), write Donald Yasuda, Wildlife Biologist, United States Department of Agriculture, Eldorado National Forest, Pacific Ranger Station, Pollock Pines, CA 95726, or call (916) 644-2349.

To gain or share pertinent information about hawk watching in the San Francisco Bay region, call Allen Fish, of the Golden Gate Raptor Observatory, at (415) 331-0730.

Details of rare bird sightings (preferably documented, as with photographs) *anywhere* within the state of California may be sent to: Don Roberson, Secretary, California Bird Records Committee, 282 Grove Acre, Pacific Grove, CA 93950.

National Audubon Society

Many birders are already members of the National Audubon Society, but those who aren't and would like to be, or those who wish to contact and/or join a new chapter, in northern California or elsewhere, may write for free explanatory literature from:

National Audubon Society
Chapter Membership Data Center
P.O. Box 266
Boulder, CO 80321

For correspondence in reference to specific Audubon Society programs, please address inquiries to the appropriate addresses below:

Audubon Activist
950 Third Avenue
New York, NY 10022
(212) 546-9196

Audubon Wildlife Report
950 Third Avenue
New York, NY 10022
(212) 546-9183

Camps and Workshops
National Environmental Education Center
613 Riversville Road
Greenwich, CT 06831
(203) 869-2017

Citizens Acid Rain Monitoring Network
950 Third Avenue
New York, NY 10022
(212) 832-3200

Education Program:
Audubon Adventures
National Education Office
R.R. 1, Box 171
Sharon, CT 06069
(203) 364-0520

Government Affairs
801 Pennsylvania Avenue, S.E.
Suite 301
Washington, D.C. 20003
(202) 546-9009

Information Services
950 Third Avenue
New York, NY 10022
(212) 546-9119

Sanctuaries
93 West Cornwall Road
Sharon, CT 06069
(203) 364-0048

Television Programs
801 Pennsylvania Avenue, S.E.
Suite 301
Washington, D.C. 20003
(202) 547-9009

Travel and Tours
950 Third Avenue
New York, NY 10022
(212) 546-9140

The California Nature Conservancy

Anyone interested in learning about the California Nature Conservancy, its purposes, its projects, and/or the location of its preserves, write:

The California Nature Conservancy
785 Market Street
San Francisco, CA 94103
(415) 777-0487

The Central Valley Habitat Joint Venture

Birders interested in helping to preserve and restore wetlands for the thousands upon thousands of birds who depend upon the Central Valley for sustenance may wish to band together with other concerned individuals and become a part of The Central Valley Habitat Joint Venture. For a explanatory brochure and other information:

California Department of Fish and Game
1416 9th Street
Sacramento, CA 95814
(916) 445-5250

The Save-the-Redwoods League

For information about the Save-the-Redwoods League and what it does to help preserve the habitat of redwood wildlife:

Save-the-Redwoods League
114 Sansome Street, Room 605
San Francisco, CA 94104
(415) 362-2352

Outdoor Recreation Guide

For an attractively illustrated brochure, the *Outdoor Recreation Guide,* which contains a useful map and descriptions of all California recreational facilities that lie under the aegis of the U.S. Army Corps of Engineers:

Sacramento District
U.S. Army Corps of Engineers
650 Capitol Mall
Sacramento, CA 95814
(916) 440-2183

The Californias

A free 196-page travel guide, *The Californias,* is a book that's chock full of beautiful photographs and valuable information for anyone touring northern California. To get your copy, write:

California Office of Tourism
P.O. Box 9278
Department T107
Van Nuys, CA 91409
1-800-TO-CALIF, extension T107

Wildlife and Fish Challenge Grant Program

Anyone interested in joining with the USDA Forest Service as a partner in the Wildlife and Fish Challenge Grant Program or in learning precisely what this program is and how it helps manage our priceless wildlife and fishery resources may contact the National Forest Service in the district or ranger station closest to you. Consult your telephone directory and call the information number listed under United States Government — Agriculture, Department of — Forest Service, or call:

The Pacific Northwest Region
San Francisco, CA
(415) 556-5666

Free Brochure about the California Park System

For a free general brochure about the California Park System, write:

Department of Parks and Recreation
State of California-the Resources Agency
P.O. Box 2390
Sacramento, CA 95811

Information Regarding National Forests

For a guide to the national forests, complete with a good readable map, write:

Pacific Southwest Region
630 Sansome Street
San Francisco, CA 94111

The North American Waterfowl Management Plan

To obtain the informative and attractively illustrated booklet, *Waterfowl for the Future*; to learn about the management of waterfowl; and/or to contribute your support to help fulfill the needs of the North American Waterfowl Management Plan, write:

The National Fish and Wildlife Foundation
Room 2626
Department of the Interior
18th and C Streets NW
Washington, DC 20240

National Wildlife Refuge System

For a free brochure about the National Wildlife Refuge System, write:

U.S. Fish and Wildlife Service
(Attn: National Wildlife Refuges)
Department of the Interior
18th and C Streets, NW
Washington, DC 20240

Visitor Directory for the Pacific Region, U.S. Fish and Wildlife

For a free directory to the Pacific region of the U.S. Fish and Wildlife Service, containing addresses, and introductions to National Wildlife Refuges, National Fish Hatcheries, and other offices throughout the region, write:

Rolf Wallenstrom
Regional Director
U.S. Fish and Wildlife Service
500 NE Multomah St., Suite 1692
Portland, OR 97232
(503) 231-6828

Nature Guide

For information on how to purchase a copy of *Nature Guide, A Directory for World-Traveling Nature Lovers,* replete with valuable information for birding in northern California, write:

Clara Strode
Nature Guide
5535 Francis Ave.
Tacoma, WA 98422
(206) 952-4640

Help Save Mono Lake

Anyone wishing to learn more about Mono Lake, the vital role it plays in the lives of so many thousands of birds, the threats to its future, and what can be done to ensure its preservation, write:

The Mono Lake Committee
P.O. Box 29
Lee Vining, CA 93541

Free Catalogs of Useful Publications

For a free catalog of a wide variety of nature study courses offered by

San Francisco State University's Sierra Nevada Field Campus, write:

Jim Steele, Director
Sierra Nevada Field Campus
School of Science
San Francisco State University
1600 Holloway Avenue
San Francisco, CA 94132-9987

For a newsletter/brochure describing the programs, tours, and special events at the spectacular Sutter Buttes, write or call:

Ira Heinrich
The Middle Mountain Foundation
P.O. Box 576
Forest Ranch, CA 95942
(916) 343-6614

For a free catalog listing many excellent and reasonably priced publications about places to go and things to do in California, including teachers' guides, archeological reports, and descriptions of particular state parks in the system, write:

Publication Section
California Department of Parks and Recreation
P.O. Box 942896
Sacramento, CA 94296-0001
(916) 322-7000

To obtain a catalog of gifts, books, posters, and conservation kits that pertain to the plants, animals, history, and geology — as well as the plight — of the Mono Basin region, write:

Matthew Graves
The Mono Lake Committee
P.O. Box 29
Lee Vining, CA 93541

To obtain a catalog that lists a wide variety of field guides, check lists, and regional books for birders, write:

The Book Nest
Richardson Bay Audubon Center
376 Greenwood Beach Road
Tiburon, CA 95920
(415) 388-2524

Other Important Resources

Sierra Club
730 Polk St.
San Francisco, CA 94109
(415) 776-2211

National Wildlife Federation
1412 16th St. NW
Washington, DC 20036

Defenders of Wildlife
1244 19th St. NW
Washington, DC 20036

ElderHostel
800 Boylston St., Suite 400
Boston, MA 02116
(617) 426-7788

American Youth Hostels
P.O. Box 37613
Washington, DC 20013-7613
(212) 783-6161

American Birding Association
Box 4335
Austin, TX 78765

Friends of the Earth
530 7th St. SE
Washington, DC 20003
(202) 543-4312

Audubon Canyon Ranch
P.O. Box 577
4900 Highway One
Stinson Beach, CA 94970
(415) 868-9244

Camping and Outdoor Information

Available free of charge from the California State Park System is a comprehensive free list of family camping facilities. In addition to a handy family camping reservation application, this brochure describes all state parks, gives directions to reach them, and contains information on how and when to make and/or cancel reservations, how to obtain refunds, the availability of special programs, disabled veteran and senior citizen discounts, etc. To obtain this brochure and the family camping reservation application, or simply to make reservations or ask for other information, call 1-800 444-PARK.

For other information about camping in northern California, contact:

Department of Parks and Recreation
P.O. Box 942896
Sacramento, CA 94296-0838

National Parks and Forests
U.S. Forest Service
Appraiser's Building
630 Sansome Street
San Francisco, CA 94111
(415) 556-0122

Western Regional Information Office
National Park Service
Fort Mason, Building 201
San Francisco, CA 94123
(415) 556-0412 or (415) 556-0560

Appendix 3
Selected References

Audubon, John Woodhouse, *Audubon's Western Journal 1849 - 1850,* Tucson: The University of Arizona Press, 1984.

Bakker, Elna, *An Island Called California, an Ecological Introduction to its Natural Communities,* University of California Press, 1972.

Benyus, Janine M., *The Field Guide to Wildlife Habitats of the Western United States,* New York: A Fireside Book, 1989.

Bolander, Gordon L. and Parmeter, Benjamin D., *Birds of Sonoma County, California,* Benjamin D. Parmeter, Publisher, 1978.

Bontadelli, Pete (Director and Editor), *Outdoor California,* California: Department of Fish and Game, 1989.

Brewer, William H., *Up and Down California in 1860 - 1864,* Los Angeles: University of California Press, 1974.

Brown, Vinson et al., *Handbook of California Birds,* Healdsburg, California: Naturegraph Publishers, 1973.

Bryant, Edwin, *What I Saw in California,* Palo Alto: Lewis Osborne, 1967.

Caras, Roger A., *North American Mammals,* New York: Galahad Books, 1967.

Collins, Henry Hill Jr. et al., *Familiar Garden Birds of America,* New York: Harper & Row, 1965.

Cruickshank, Allan D. and Cruickshank, Helen G., *1001 Questions Answered About Birds,* New York: Dodd, Mead & Company, 1958.

Dewitt, John B., *California Redwood Parks and Preserves,* San Francisco: Save-the-Redwoods League, 1985.

Ehrlich, Paul R. et al., *The Birder's Handbook,* New York: A Fireside Book, Simon & Schuster Inc., 1988.

Evens, Jules, *Natural History of Point Reyes Peninsula,* California: Point Reyes National Seashore Association, 1988.

Evers, Anne (Executive Editor), *Discover the Californias,* Pasadena, California: California Tourism Corporation, 1989.

Fuller, David L., *California Patterns, a Geographical and Historical Atlas,* Northeridge, California: California State University, 1983.

Grinnell, Joseph and Miller, Alden H., *The Distribution of the Birds of California,* Lee Vining, California: Artemisia Press, reprinted 1986.

Gross, Marguerite B. (Editor), *Best Birding in Napa and Solano Counties,* Suisun City, California: Napa-Solano Audubon Society, 1989.

Holing, Dwight, *California Wild Land, a Guide to The Nature Conservancy Preserves,* San Francisco: Chronicle Books, 1988.

Jackson, Ruth A., *Combing the Coast,* San Francisco: Chronicle Books, 1985.

Kozlik, Frank M. et al., *Waterfowl of California,* California: Department of Fish and Game.

Kroeber, A. L., *Handbook of the Indians of California,* New York: Dover Publications, Inc., 1976.

Lentz, Joan Easton, *Great Birding Trips of the West,* Santa Barbara: Capra Press, 1989.

Martin, Alexander C. et al., *American Wildlife & Plants, a Guide to Wildlife Food Habits,* New York: Dover Publications, 1951.

McCaskie, Guy (compiler), *Field List of the Birds of California,* San Diego: San Diego Field Ornithologists, 1986.

McCaskie, Guy et. al., *Birds of Northern California,* Berkeley, California: Golden Gate Audubon Society, Inc., 1979.

National Geographic Society, *Field Guide to the Birds of North America,* second edition, Washington: National Geographic Society, 1987.

Olympus Press (Editors of), *California State Parks Guide,* Santa Barbara, California: Olympus Press, 1988.

Peterson, Roger Tory, *A Field Guide to the Birds,* Fourth Edition, Boston: Houghton Mifflin Co., 1980.

Pettingill, Olin Sewall Jr. (Editor), *The Bird Watcher's America,* New York: Thomas Y. Crowell Company, 1974.

Powers, Stephen, *Tribes of California,* Berkeley: University of California Press, 1976.

Reedy, Edward C. and Stephen L. Granholm, *Discovering Sierra Birds,* California: Yosemite Natural History Association, 1985.

Robbins, C. S., Bruun, B., and Zim, H. S., *Birds of North America*. Racine, Wisconsin: Western Publishing Company, 1983.

Russo, Ron and Olhausen, Pam, *Mammal Finder*, Nature Study Guild, 1987.

Scanlan-Rohrer, Anne (Editor), *San Francisco Peninsula Birdwatching*, Belmont, California: Sequoia Audubon Society, 1985.

Scott, Virgil E. et al., *Cavity-Nesting Birds of North American Forests*, Agriculture Handbook 511. Washington, DC: Forest Service, U.S. Department of Agriculture, 1977.

Small, Arnold, *The Birds of California*, New York: Collier Books, Macmillan Publishing Co., 1974.

State of California, The Resources Agency, Department of Fish and Game, *1988 Annual Report on the Status of California's State Listed Threatened and Endangered Plants and Animals*, Department of Fish and Game, 1989.

Strode, Clara N. (Editor), *Nature Guide*, Tacoma: Tacoma Audubon Society, 1989.

Taber, Tom, *Where to See Wildlife in California*, San Mateo, California: The Oak Valley Press, 1983.

Udvardy, Miklos D. F., *The Audubon Society Field Guide to North American Birds, Western Region*, New York: Alfred A. Knopf, Inc., 1977.

U.S. Fish and Wildlife Service, *Sensitive Bird Species*, Portland: U.S. Fish and Wildlife Service, 1985.

Westrich, LoLo, *California Herbal Remedies*, Houston, Texas: Gulf Publishing Co., 1989.

Index of Birds

This index is of English names only. The last page for each species refers to the page in Appendix 1, *A Check List of Northern California Birds,* where scientific order, family, genus, and species names are listed.

Index of Locations

Notes

Notes